APPS FOR AUTISM

Revised and Expanded

More than 200 Effective Apps for Behavioral, Social, Creative, Communication, and Cognitive Development

LOIS JEAN BRADY, M.A., CCC-SLP

FUTURE HORIZONS INC.

Arlington, Texas

APPS FOR AUTISM, Revised and Expanded

More than 200 Effective Apps for Behavioral, Social, Creative, Communication, and Cognitive Development

All marketing and publishing rights guaranteed to and reserved by:

FUTURE HORIZONS INC.

721 W. Abram Street

Arlington, TX 76013

Toll-free: 800.489.0727

Phone: 817•277•0727

Fax: 817•277•2270

Website: www.FHautism.com

Email: info@FHautism.com

The information provided in this book is educational and is not meant to be used, nor should it be used, to diagnose or treat any medical condition. If professional guidance or assistance is needed, the services of an autism professional should be sought. Readers should be aware that the information provided in this book is subject to change.

Publisher's Cataloging-In-Publication Data

(Prepared by The Donohue Group, Inc.)

ISBN: 9781941765005

Dedication _____

To D'Artagnan, an amazing young man whose abilities have surpassed all expectations. I have learned much of what I know while "following" him down the technology trail. His resilience inspires me to keep moving forward, and he reminds me to never put limits on what a child is capable of achieving.

Acknowledgments

Once again, I owe a huge thank you to over 300 people around the globe who have had a part in bringing this book and the ideas herein to life. You will find the contributions of each and every one of them (therapists, developers, moms, dads, writers, bloggers and educators) within the pages of this book.

A big hug and thank you to my family who, once again, did their best to support me with attempts to "help out"; thanks for trying! And of course, thank you, Mom, my biggest cheerleader.

Big thanks to my fellow professionals who unselfishly gave their time and expertise to fill these pages with leading-edge information so that *Apps for Autism* will be an indispensable resource for the autism community. To Matthew Guggemos, my good friend, business partner, and editing genius who painstakingly went through the entire book to make sure every predicate had a subject, amend comma misuse and run-on sentences, and eradicate all punctuation errors—thank you!

One final heartfelt thank you goes to Wayne Gilpin, Jennifer Gilpin, and all of the folks at Future Horizons, once again, for giving me the chance to share this information with you, the mindful reader.

Contents

Part IV: Pragmatics and Social Skills

Chapter 12: Video Modeling

Chapter 13: Social Skills Group Activities

Chapter 27: Math 261

Chapter 28: Preschool 271

Foreword

With such high levels of interest in this topic, it is crucial for books like this one to be written. I was honored and excited when Lois asked me to contribute the Foreword. Let me share with you a bit about how I became involved with this tremendous movement towards ubiquitous educational technology for people with autism.

Being the co-creator of the original *Proloquo2Go* augmentative and alternative communication (AAC) App for the iOS, I have learned about the sheer strength of people coming together with a goal of making a difference. I had a vision and I acted on it, collaborating along the way in order to try to make a difference. With the success of *Proloquo2Go* and my credentials as an AAC specialist and an assistive technology specialist, I have been fortunate to have great opportunities to present and teach both in the U.S. and internationally on the topic of new mobile technologies for individuals with disabilities. It has been a phenomenal experience teaching and connecting with parents and teachers who seem so excited that they could burst.

I will always remember the intense feelings I had when I first started pitching my idea to build an AAC application for the iPhone and iPod touch (the iPad did not yet exist as a product). The setting was a national conference, and I met with a few "large" companies and a few independent software developers who all said "no" or that it couldn't be done (including some with whom I would later collaborate). One conversation in particular will always stick with me. In a meeting focused on pitching my idea to one of those larger companies, I was posed the question, "But what's so special about the iPhone, why is it any different than the PDA-based communication devices out there now?" Being a bit sheepish about the question, as it was one of my first big meetings in the field, I hesitantly said something about how it was Apple and was cool. Little did I know that, less than a year later, I would come back to one of those developers with a proposition to collaborate, and then less than a year after that, the vision would become a reality.

David Niemeijer of Assistiveware and I built what would become *Proloquo2Go*, and it was officially released to the public in April 2009 (Sennott and Bowker, 2009). It came about because the community believed in it and because David and I were able to come together with complementary skills at the right place and the right time.

The first major story about *Proloquo2Go* (and about the iPhone and autism, for that matter) was published in *USA Today*. It was about a young boy with autism who was able to tell his mom for the first time that he loved Chinese food. My fiancée would later remind me about how clearly this showed how simple, random things one would be hard-pressed to know about someone are revealed when there is a communication system that works.

From there, our initiative really took off, with features being conducted by *ABC News*, IEEE, and *Good Morning America* about the users of *Proloquo2Go*. Then the dam broke. A mom with ALS and her young son with Down syndrome, both *Proloquo2Go* users, were featured on the front page of the *New York Times* in a full-color photograph. There was public outrage that the Centers for Medicare and Medicaid Services (CMS) would readily purchase devices and equipment at the near $7,000 funding level (each) but not provide these two individuals with iPod touch devices for a few hundred dollars. The world was talking about Augmentative and Alternative Communication.

I started to feel like a bit of a revolution was happening. We were getting streams of emails from people saying that, for the first time, their son or daughter was communicating. At the peak of this growth, *Proloquo2Go* hit number four in the top-grossing section of the Apple iTunes Store. Thousands of people were gaining access to communication tools.

Sometimes I would be moved to tears upon hearing these stories or seeing the analytics of the numbers of people served. At one point, my father shared with me a quote by Buckminster Fuller about how to create change: "You never change things by fighting the existing reality. To change something, build a new model that makes the existing model obsolete." That being said, educational software was not created through the Apple iPhone, iPod touch, and iPad. In fact, there has already been a rich tradition of high-quality educational software. Yet what the iOS devices and platform have done is make educational software more personal. It is exciting to be a part of this shift.

At this moment in time, we can see that technology is changing our lives and that change is exponential (Kurzweil, 1999, Moore, 1998). New mobile technologies for people with autism are creating new opportunities at an exponential rate. The message is that we can create tools that can make profound differences in the trajectory of people's lives and in education in general. If we try, we can harness that exponential innovation. However, the diffusion of innovation must proceed successfully: early adopters are charged with sharing the good news. We must share our current knowledge about what is available, along with the benefits and limitations of these new tools. That is why this book is so important.

The first time I saw Lois Jean Brady was in a photograph of her, Temple Grandin, and Buttercup, Lois's pot-bellied therapy pig. Yes, Lois has a therapy pig, as well as a dog, and a horse too! I proceeded to read about how she thoughtfully used animal-assisted therapy as a way to make speech pathology sessions motivating and dynamic. She certainly seemed to work outside of the box in a refreshing and very relevant way! I looked forward to meeting her in person.

When we first met at the ASHA Convention, we spoke about this book and its importance. We shared our enthusiasm for the newest Apple technologies and for what they were doing to help the individuals with disabilities whom we serve. We spoke about the need for basic information and for the knowledge of a select group of early adopters to be communicated to a broader audience. Clearly, Lois was driven to educate parents and teachers about this topic, which she herself was so passionate about. What a gift.

Lois has taken an important leap in writing this book, providing a much-needed primer for considering the newest, mobile educational technologies from Apple.

> 'Zach's a Mac' poignantly reveals the experience of one family's search for a way to communicate with each - other; something that neurotypical families take for granted. Lois' focus on individual student needs is a particularly relevant message and is essential to the responsible introduction of educational technologies. She says, 'Have a clear focus on the individual's needs. Educators and caregivers should clearly understand and commit to common goals based on the individual's unique needs and abilities.'

With all of the enthusiasm about new mobile technologies, there is danger that we can lose sight of the need to custom tailor educational solutions for each individual. The knowledge shared in this book can help combat the temptation to disregard thoughtful, individualized solutions by providing information about features, benefits, and limitations.

For parents, teachers, and therapists, it is important to understand what the individual apps can and cannot do and to carefully consider features relevant to individual needs. From communication to literacy, recreation, and accessories, *Apps for Autism* provides a wealth of useful information to read and reference.

In March 2011, Steve Jobs' announced at a company event the release of the iPad 2. A video was shown featuring the myriad ways in which the iPad was helping individuals with autism and demonstrated just how big this technological innovation had become. Now in 2015, we all are aware of the various benefits these tools offer. We all can learn from Lois' insight and generous sharing of this much-needed knowledge.

Samuel Sennott

Assistant Professor of Special Education at Portland State University

www.alltogetherwecan.com

References

Kurzweil, R. *The Age of Spiritual Machines: When Computers Exceed Human Intelligence.* New York, New York: Penguin Books, 1999.

Moore, G. "Cramming More Components onto Integrated Circuits." *Proceedings of the IEEE.* 1998; 8:82-85.

Sennott, S., & Bowker, A. "Autism *Proloquo2Go.*" *Perspectives on Augmentative and Alternative Communication.* 2009; 18:137-145.

Introduction

"What we're finding is that a lot of these [non-verbal] people have a good brain hidden inside, and technology allows them to express themselves, and I think that's wonderful."

—Temple Grandin, PhD

Since its release in April 2010, the iPad has quickly become one of the most effective, motivating, indispensable learning tools ever for those on the autism spectrum – and just about everyone else! In the past few years, we have seen an explosion in what mobile technology has to offer for the special needs population. Apple has incorporated terrific new accessibility features, developers have created fantastic apps, and companies are producing accessories to meet the needs of every user. But the most impressive of all is the way this technology is opening new possibilities for the special needs population: many users are showing capabilities that defy our expectations. Non-verbal individuals are communicating; some are writing blogs and even books! Students who would not touch a pencil have begun tracing letters on apps and can now write not only letters and words but also sentences! Others are developing speech, becoming literate, acquiring social skills, and getting just plain excited to learn. As a matter of fact, many are using educational apps as reinforces: they are essentially working to "work." The iPad is so appealing that I have not had to open a bag of Skittles or chips in months – these are boring compared to a new app. It has truly been an exciting few years.

Thank you, Apple, for continuing to provide excellent devices, features, and settings that support communication, scheduling, academics, social interactions, video modeling, and leisure time wrapped up in handheld super-cool packages. Individuals who cannot use a mouse or keyboard can use the iPad, iPhone, and iPod touch because there is no disconnect between the screen and the keyboard/mouse. Parents are thrilled, and therapists are seeing goals met and exceeded. iPhones, iPod touches, and iPads are used to entertain, communicate, and educate students and learners of all ages and abilities. "There is no flicker or high-pitched noise. Some kids are sensitive to the flicker of traditional screens and do much better with laptops and tablets because the flat panel displays don't flicker," according to Temple Grandin

I am a speech-language pathologist and have worked in the field for 25+ years. I have spent years trying to make traditional devices fit into the world of autism. Ultimately, they end up as very expensive doorstops. *USA Today*'s Greg Toppo wrote, "text-to-speech machines are huge, heavy, and expensive. . . "

Alas, there is one negative aspect of owning these exciting and valuable devices: theft. A colleague once mentioned, "A clunky ol' Augmentative Communication device is not something the neighborhood thugs are going to pinch, but the temptation changes when it's an iPhone hooked onto a shoulder strap or wheelchair." Ironically, a thief would have to steal 16 iPads, 35 iPod touches, or 24 iPhones to equal the cost of one Dynavox, Springboard, or Say-it-Sam (approx $8,000). Given the cost and awkwardness of the old devices, I'll take my chances with an iPad.

I wrote this book to help parents, educators, therapists, and individuals with disabilities navigate through the mountain of apps and gadgets available. In this revised edition of *Apps for Autism*, you will see considerable emphasis on how to use the iPad with your child or student from leading experts in their field. I encourage everyone to explore the apps and features to see what these "magical" devices can do. I have been using the iPad for over four years; my students have not only made tremendous success, but have also mastered operating systems, navigated apps, and developed an interest in technology. Students carry their devices with pride, not protest.

Apps come and go, prices change, and features are upgraded (for updates, go to my website, *www.iTherapyLLC.com*), but the core fundamental knowledge of how/why to use an app with an iPad stays the same. So I urge everyone to use *Apps for Autism*, explore the apps, discover a new feature, communicate, calculate, read, write, socialize, have fun, and enjoy life!

About Apps for Autism

How to Use This Book

Definition

What is an app? The term *app* is an abbreviation for computer application. Simply put, a computer application, or app, refers to a program that allows the user to accomplish a task. There are more than a million apps available from the iTunes store. Thousands are added each week. I have made my best effort to search through and find the apps that would be most beneficial to individuals with special needs. It would be impossible for *Apps for Autism* to include every app available; however, a sample of several especially awesome apps that represent categories, characteristics, and skills sets are included so that you will be better informed of the choices available and better equipped to match individual needs to specific apps using Feature Matching.

Structure

I have spent over three years using, testing, taking notes, combing through research, and collecting opinions from colleagues, parents, and users to present the most useful, up-to-date information possible. *Apps for Autism* is divided into chapters that focus on a specific area of need; it was very difficult to decide the appropriate chapter for each app! The *Toca Boca Doctor*, for example, would be equally at home in the Occupational Therapy section or could fit into the Creative Learning or Activities of Daily Living sections. In the end, I just went with how my students use it best. I felt strongly enough about several apps to include them in more than one section so that they would not be overlooked; for example, the *VAST Keywords* app is in the Apraxia chapter. However, it is also an excellent app for articulation, so you will find it in both sections. I have added success stories, articles, insights, and testimonials from colleagues and parents as well as my own to demonstrate the endless possibilities. Please remember that everyone on the autism spectrum is an individual with diverse interests and abilities. Individuals will have a unique combination of apps that will fit their needs and expand as they grow. Our job is to guide and reinforce, not dictate and insist.

Content

Prices are listed for each app and were accurate at the time I bought the app. Developers may change prices and upgrade frequently. Upgrades are free and usually make the app better and/or easier to use. The information listed is correct at this moment; however, it may change tomorrow.

Throughout *Apps for Autism*, I may refer to an iPhone, iPod touch, or iPad; however, they are interchangeable, and in most cases, I really mean all three. Almost all apps can run on iPhone, iPod touch, iPad mini, and iPad. Many times I will simply use the word iDevice. Also note that the terms iPod touch and iTouch have been used interchangeably throughout the book by parents and professionals alike.

I have formatted the pages with screen shots, logos, websites, prices, reviews, and some information from the developers themselves. The first paragraph is the developer's information, or what he/she wants you to know about the app. The second paragraph is a review. Reviews are collected from personal experience, colleagues, teachers, parents, and users themselves.

Last but not least, some apps are available in a Lite or Freemium version. *Freemium* is a new term that popped up in the iTunes store a few months back. It is the equivalent of a free trial and an excellent way to determine if the app is right for you. I wholeheartedly recommend trying the Lite, Free, or Freemium version first. If you like the app, buy it; if you do not like it, delete it—no money frittered.

Icons

There are three features that have become very important when using an app in the educational setting. I have given each of these features an icon. The icon will appear under the title of the app if the feature is included in that app. The exclamation point lets the reader know an important piece of information that was not given in the description or emphasizes an important feature of an app.

NEW: Apps for Autism will have a Google Play icon that will let Android users know if a favorite app is available in an Android version.

REPORTS: The email envelope icon lets you know that the end product, data, or message can be emailed directly from the iDevice to parents, teachers, or you for review, record keeping, or generalization. This feature also allows educators to keep in touch with families, friends, or caregivers to share accomplishments.

 DATA: The pencil icon represents data collection. Educators can spend much of their time collecting and analyzing data. If an app can do that, great – more time can be spent working with the students.

 CUSTOMIZATION: The tools icon lets you know that an app can be personalized for images, voice output, and/or graphics. Having the ability to tailor just the right image or words to represent a concept, person, place, or thing is highly motivating to both students and educators.

 ANDROID: Android users will be delighted to know at a glance if their desired app is available on Google Play.

What is iTherapy?

Technology, for the most part, serves for the betterment of society. In the realm of education, technology has become an integral part of the system. Educators from all over the nation are using technology in their repertoire to enhance classroom learning. Among the many benefits is greater access to education for everyone, but in particular, technological advancements have opened education more than ever to learners with disabilities like autism spectrum disorders. *iTherapy* capitalizes on the latest technologies available from Apple like the iPad, iPad mini, iPod touch, and the iPhone. At its core, *iTherapy* refers to the use of an Apple product in combination with an app (computer application) in a therapy environment as a modality to meet goals implemented by a team of professionals.

Software (apps) for any of the Apple products is readily available from the app store, which is located within the iTunes website. As I mentioned previously, there are about one million apps, with more added on a daily basis. You can use these apps individually or combine them to achieve or set goals. Whether you are using voice output, building vocabulary, correcting articulation, or strengthening muscle coordination, iDevices make learning easier, more fun, and reinforcing.

In addition, learning on an iDevice can still occur long after the therapy session has ended. Unlike other computer-based therapies, students can take their iDevice wherever they go, which allows them to engage in learning whenever the opportunity presents itself.

In short, when you combine Apple's hardware with innovative software like *InnerVoice* or *Proloquo2Go*, the result is powerful, portable, desirable, yet affordable Augmentative and Alternative Communication (ACC). Set this combination into a therapy environment with a focus on predetermined Individualized Educational Plan (IEP) goals, and, with little effort, you can achieve school-based *iTherapy*.

Best Practices and Educational Guidelines

In this section, I will review the strategies, techniques, and guidelines that have been successful in a variety of settings. The term "best practices" is used to describe the techniques and strategies that work well in a particular situation or environment. Grover J. Whitehurst refers to best practices as the integration of the professional wisdom of educators and family members with research-based practice. With that in mind, here are a variety of best practices and teaching strategies that are relevant for using technology in education.

- *Have a clear focus on the individual's needs.* Educators and caregivers should clearly understand and commit to common goals based on the individual's unique needs and abilities.

- *Model, model, model*—Individuals on the spectrum have strong visual skills and learn from seeing and observing. It is not enough to explain or verbally give instructions; it is essential that we also provide visual models more than once. Verbal instructions and explanations may be unclear due to auditory processing and/or attentional challenges, so once again – model, model, model.

- *The iPad supports, not replaces, the educator.* The iPad is only a tool for education or communication. We as parents, therapists, and educators must continue to teach, guide, and instruct as we use this powerful tool to support our goals.

- *Be flexible.* Assistive technology is a process that changes continually with the needs of the individual.

- *Maintain high standards and expectations for all individuals to succeed.* Assume that each individual can learn how to use technology in a capacity that is relevant to them. Most people can achieve great success when standards of performance are clear, consistent, and achievable.

- *Consider the individual's environments and the skills needed to function in those environments.* Home, school, and community, for example, present various challenges. We need to consider what set of skills an individual needs in order to participate and to be productive in each environment. In essence, we should draw upon the entire community to foster student achievement.

- *Take care when choosing the tools, gadgets, devices, apps, programs, and accessories that can be effectively accessed by an individual.* Consideration must be given to the individual's vision, motor planning, attention, sensory processing, memory, and cognitive ability to provide the most effective tools for success. If possible, consult with an assistive technology professional, speech therapist, occupational therapist, and/or educator.

- *Use prompting and reinforcement, as necessary, to establish a skill, then decrease prompting and reinforcement systematically to the natural environment.* This approach helps a person generalize newly learned behaviors and skills.

- *Most individuals take to the iDevice like a fish takes to water.* However, there is the occasional student who needs a bit of encouragement. Not to worry—find something that appeals to the individual and use that to build interest in an iDevice: play a favorite song, show a movie, or display a favorite character. Once "hooked," special needs' users will likely be more receptive to learning challenges and structured activities if they are introduced slowly.

- *For individuals on the autism spectrum, high-quality voice output is extremely important!* Many people with autism have additional challenges with auditory processing, making it difficult to understand spoken language. A high-quality text-to-speech voice literally improves understanding and encourages vocalizations. Text-to-speech delivers the spoken message consistently, with no change in tone or inflection. And text-to-speech messages can be repeated as many times as needed by the user in order to process the information.

- *Finally, and perhaps most importantly, teach turn-taking, or you may not get your iDevice back!*
I have heard one common gripe amongst parents and colleagues: "I can't get my device back." Instilling the "My turn, your turn" approach works extremely well in teaching children to share and give up the iDevice when their turn is over. And always take your turn first, to set a good example. Even the most challenging students will hand over the device when I announce, "My turn." Time limits, timer apps, and short task-orientated activities also work well in establishing good turn-taking habits. Good luck and rest assured: you will eventually get your device back.

In The Spotlight:
AAC Boot Camp—Getting AAC Users Communicating

The AAC Boot Camp is a downloadable, reproducible poster created by Lauren Enders, Pat Mervine, Melissa Skocypec, & Cathie VanAlstine, February 2013, to provide reminders on how to best support AAC users. The tips on this poster are meant to support communication regardless of the system or app used and can be used by family members as well as educators and therapists. Make several copies to keep handy for use at home and/or school.

https://www.dropbox.com/s/2mi4c2mzdiqk0pt/AAC%20BOOT%20CAMP%20SHEET%204a.pdf

AAC BOOT CAMP
Getting AAC Users COMMUNICATING
regardless of AAC system used (no tech, low tech, high tech) or skill level...

🚫 DON'T do this......	🙊 DO this......
DON'T expect a user to know how to communicate w/o direct models & instruction	✓ MODEL MODEL MODEL *model expected communication behaviors BEFORE expecting to see those behaviors from the user*
DON'T do ALL the talking	✓ PRESUME COMPETENCE
DON'T overprompt	✓ FOLLOW prompt hierarchy
DON'T teach ONLY requesting	✓ TEACH language functions *including directing, commenting, requesting assistance, etc...*
DON'T re-prompt too quickly	✓ WAIT 10-20 sec. (w/an expectant look) before re-prompting!! *Count in your head!!* 123
DON'T provide ONLY nouns	
DON'T focus on vocabulary that won't be functional/used tomorrow	✓ PROVIDE CORE WORDS *including verbs & describing words (in addition to nouns)*
	✓ COLOR CODE parts of speech
DON'T remove the device	✓ KEEP icon placement constant *keep repeated icons in the same location on each page/screen*
DON'T move symbols	
DON'T stop all "babbling" *(exploring, button pressing)*	✓ ALLOW user time to explore and learn the system
DON'T keep the AAC system in their desk, cubbie, or backpack	✓ MAKE AAC available at all times
	✓ PROVIDE Aided Language Input
DON'T expect sentences right away	✓ ASK open-ended questions

Created by Lauren Enders with content by Lauren Enders, Pat Mervine, Melissa Skocypec, & Cathie VanAlstine - February 2013

Getting Started

Choosing an iDevice

Size & Portability vs. Eyesight & Motor Capabilities

Size is an aspect of the iDevice we should consider before making a purchase. What size is right for me, my child, and/or my student? The iPod touch and iPad Mini are more portable; however, the iPad is easier to see and control. In general, if your students have vision or motor challenges or will be using the iDevice primarily on a desktop, then the iPad may be the right device for them. If your students have adequate vision and motor control and will be carrying their devices for communication, reference, location, or leisure, then the smaller iPod touch or iPad mini may be the right choice for a device. Most of my students use iPads because they are in a classroom or therapy setting, using their devices for academics and communication. Students who primarily use the device for communication have iPods and/or iPad minis that are easily stuffed into pockets and backpacks.

Use this table to help determine the best size iDevice for your individual needs. Use the blank boxes to check off the important features and/or take notes. If convenient, arrange to take your student/child to an electronics store for a hands-on trial of the devices and their various sizes.

Ability/ Feature	iPad (large)	iPad mini (medium)	iPod touch (small)
Eyesight			
Motor Control			
Portability			
Size (inches)	9.5 x 7.31	7.87 x 5.3	4.86 x 2.31

1. **Motor control:** Do individuals have adequate motor control to activate a single button without touching others? The iPod touch and iPhone require more precise fine motor control than the iPad. Consequently, if motor control is an issue, consider the iPad.

2. **Vision:** Both the iPhone and iPod touch have smaller screens than the iPad. Individuals who have challenges with visual acuity and perception may favor the iPad

3. **Portability:** The iPad is much larger than the iPhone and iPod touch; this makes it difficult to drop it into your pocket. Therefore, if the student will be using her iDevice on the go, a smaller device may be the best choice.

Basic iDevice Operations

At a Glance

The basic buttons and controls are the same on the iPad, iPad mini, and iPod touch. The iPhone has a few more external (phone-related) controls. Quite frankly, I have never used more than the basics on any of my devices, but there is so much to explore!

Indispensable iOS Features & Settings

Over the past few years, the iPad has become an invaluable tool for those of us working and living with individuals on the spectrum. Developers have created thousands of innovative apps for everything from communication and literacy to fine motor and daily living skills, giving educators/therapists a fresh approach and renewed enthusiasm for teaching. But did you know that there are many great features and settings built into your iPad right out of the box?

Apple enhances every iPad with more than 200 features and settings that make working with these cool devices even cooler, more accessible, and convenient. It's a huge set of options, but don't worry: the features and settings are your allies. They can help keep you and your student on track while maximizing the benefits of mobile technology. Let's take a look at a few of the features that have proven to be instrumental when working with students on the spectrum.

iPad User Guide

Apple has two incredibly easy ways to access the User Guide built into every iDevice. This handy User Guide is easy to read with clear pictures and graphics. A search bar makes it easy to pinpoint only the information you want.

1. Access User Guide from Safari.
   a. Open Safari.
   b. Tap on Bookmark.
   c. Tap Favorites.
   d. Scroll to Bottom & Tap on iPad User Guide.
2. Access the Guide from the free iPad User Guide App.
   a. Download the iPad User Guide App from the iBooks Store.
   b. To read the iPad User Guide, open it in iBooks.

Guided Access

Guided Access was originally introduced in iOS 6 to help parents and educators keep the device operating a specific app so a child can have an uninterrupted learning experience. With iOS 8, Apple will add Guided Access Time Limits, which helps a child with transitions and allows a caretaker to assign a specific amount of time the child should use the app. Basically, the child receives a warning, helping him to prepare for the next activity. Users will also be able to access Touch ID to exit from Guided Access — perfect for busy educators and parents who want to regulate iPad use at home or in the classroom.

Starting Guided Access

1. Turn on Guided Access from your Settings and set a passcode.
2. Open an app that you would like your child to focus on.
3. Triple-click the Home button.
4. Circle any part of the screen you would like to disable.
5. Set time limits.
6. Touch "Start" in the upper right corner.

Ending Guided Access

1. Triple click the Home button.
2. Enter the passcode for Guided Access.
3. Touch "End" in the upper left corner.

Speak Selection & Speak Screen

Speak Selection is a terrific feature that I use on *all* of my iPads. Speak Selection will read your highlighted text from email, apps, websites, messages, etc., and highlight words as the text is read. Speak Selection is an excellent feature to support literacy and auditory comprehension. To turn on Speak Selection (I recommend every iDevice has this feature turned on.)

1. Turn on Speak Selection in Accessibility Settings.

2. Turn on Highlighted Words (optional).

3. Double tap text to be spoken and highlight.

4. Choose "Speak" from the formatting bar options.

Speak Screen is great for anyone who might have trouble reading the screen; you can make a simple gesture or ask Siri to speak the screen to you, and the device will start reading whatever's on the screen.

Subtitles and Captioning

Turning on Subtitles & Captioning will automatically opt you into using closed captioning and subtitles when they are available. This feature is meant for individuals who are deaf and hard of hearing; however, it is effective in supporting literacy and understanding spoken language for those with auditory processing challenges.

1. From the accessibility settings, choose Subtitles & Captioning.

2. Turn on Subtitles & Captioning.

3. Customize size and font by choosing "Style."

Creating Folders

Is your iPad desktop getting crowded? Are you having trouble finding the app you want? Your iPad can display 20 apps per page and has 11-15 pages. In order to avoid constant swiping from page to page, try creating folders. Folders allow you to organize, store, and categorize your apps to fit your needs. For example, you may want the folders you use throughout the day—such as expressive language, visual supports, fine motor and literacy—to appear on your Home screen, ready to go. So, let's clean up that desktop, get organized, and keep those apps at our fingertips.

1. Touch and hold any app icon until is wiggles (edit mode) and an X appears in the upper left corner.

2. While the icons are wiggling, they can be moved to other locations and pages or grouped to create folders.

3. To create a folder, drag and drop an icon on top of another icon you would like in the same folder and release.

4. Name the folder and press the Home button when you are finished.

5. To access apps in the folder, simply tap the folder and choose an app.

6. More apps can be added by simply dragging the "wiggling" icons on top of the folder.

7. To remove apps from folders, open the folder, touch and hold the app to be removed until it wiggles, and drag it out of the folder.

8. Tap the Home button again to exit the editing mode.

Screenshots

Capture student work or any interesting, compelling images by taking screenshots. There are times when a student has created a magnificent piece of art, has excelled on a task, or just found the perfect visual support for a project; screenshots will allow you to capture those moments so that you can save and/or share them with others.

Sleep/wake

Home

1. To capture any screen, press Home button and the Sleep/Wake button at the same time.

2. Screenshots will be saved in the Camera Roll.

3. From Camera Roll, you can integrate the image into apps, books, and projects or send it to family/friends.

Capture Images from the Web

Images from the web or Google Images can be captured, stored on the Camera Roll, and used to create any visual support. Capturing images is a great way to get content for eBooks, story boards, communication apps, or social stories.

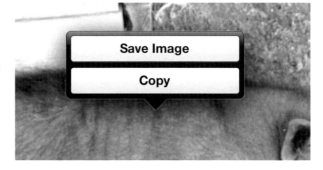

1. Touch an image you want to save until the Save Image/Copy prompt appears.

2. Touch Save Image, and it will be stored in your Camera Roll to use or share.

Invert Colors

If you prefer higher contrast, you can change the display on your iPad to white on black. Inverting colors may help the brain accurately process visual information and improve reading, comprehension, and attention. The Invert Colors option is definitely worth a try if you or your student has visual processing challenges; this feature can be readily turned on/off in the Accessibility section of the settings.

iOS8 Word Prediction

Word Prediction is one of the cool new features that came with the iOS8 update. Now you can communicate entire thoughts with just a few taps. As you type, choices of words or phrases you'd probably type next will appear in

the text bar just above the keyboard. One tap places the entire word or phrase into your message significantly reducing the time it takes to type the entire message yourself. iOS 8 will also take into account your communications style whether it be a casual style you might use in messages with a family member or a more formal language style you probably use in mail to your boss. Your conversation data is kept only on your device, so it's always private.

Updates

Keep your iDevices updated to get most advanced accessibility features!

Apple and app developers will periodically update their products. These updates make the iPad and the apps better, easier, and faster with more powerful features. Make updating a part of your maintenance routine to get the most from your iDevice.

Update notices appear in the upper right-hand corner of the app icon. An iOS system update will appear on the settings icon.

Volume Purchase Program
Step-by-Step Instructions

In August 2010, Apple launched its Volume Purchase Program (VPP) for iTunes and the App Store. The program allows qualified educational institutions to purchase iOS Apps in volume at a discounted price and distribute those apps to end users. The VPP allows app developers to offer a discount of 50% for the purchase of 20 apps or more. Follow this link to search educational apps that are available for a discount:

http://volume.itunes.apple.com/us/store

There are four main characters in the VPP program:

1. Authorized Purchaser: The Authorized Purchaser is often the purchasing agent at an institution. This person provides vouchers to the Program Facilitator(s) in denominations of $100, $500, $1,000, $5,000, and $10,000 to match, as closely as possible, the value of the requested apps.

Volume Voucher(s) take about three to five business days to be received via US mail. Once received, the Program Purchaser forwards the vouchers to the Program Facilitator.

2. Program Manager: This person is responsible for managing Program Facilitator accounts. The Program Manager will provide the necessary information related to the accounts or Apple IDs that will be designated to the Program Facilitator. Once these accounts are provided to Apple via the Program Manager portal, the Program Facilitator will be able to access the volume purchase site, redeem vouchers, and purchase application redemption codes.

3. Program Facilitator: The Program Facilitator can be a principal, a professor, a school teacher, a therapist, etc. The Program Facilitator determines what apps and what quantities to purchase and then calculates the cash value of the needed applications to submit to the Authorized Purchaser. The Program Facilitator is also the person who redeems the vouchers in the App Store Volume Purchase Program and distributes the app-specific codes as necessary to the end users. In addition, the Program Facilitator is responsible for keeping records of activation codes for each device, onto which an app will be installed. *Be Aware: Apple reserves the right to audit purchases to make sure that institutions are following usage rules, terms, and conditions.

4. End User(s): Apple divides end users into three different categories:

    a. Single user (school account) – codes are distributed and redeemed by single users on a school-managed iTunes account.

    b. Classroom or multiple users – (Assume a classroom of 30) 30 codes are purchased for a classroom. One code is redeemed to a single iTunes account. That account can be authorized on up to five computers. The teacher can then sync all 30 devices using one code. The remaining 29 codes are kept on file in the event of an audit.

    c. Single user (personal account) – The school purchases vouchers and distributes codes to individuals. Users redeem codes using their own personal iTunes account and install the app onto their personal devices. That app becomes the property of the student.

Part I

Apps to Get the Word(s) Out:
Expressive Language

"The hardest part of autism is the communication challenge. I feel depressed often by my inability to speak. I talk in my mind, but my mind doesn't talk to my mouth. It's frustrating even though I can communicate by pointing now. Before I could, it was like a solitary confinement. It was terrible having experts talk to each other about me, and to hear them be wrong in their observations and interpretations, but to not be capable of telling them."

— *Ido Kedar,* Ido in Autismland: Climbing Out of Autism's Silent Prison

Who would have thought that Apple would be the company to design sleek and stylish communication devices that not only entertain—via books, movies, magazines, music, and videos—but also have the muscle to become serious communication and educational devices? Whether you are using voice output, building vocabulary, correcting articulation, or strengthening muscle coordination, your iDevice makes it easier, more fun, and reinforcing. My students will sit quietly or wait in line for a chance to use these "magical" devices, even if just for just a few minutes.

This section presents applications that will turn your iDevice into a voice output, sign language, sentence generating, articulating paragon of communication. Individuals will be able to communicate and share thoughts and feelings in lieu of frustration and behavior challenges.

According to the Centers for Disease Control, it is estimated that one out of 68 children will be diagnosed with an autism spectrum disorder. Studies indicate that up to 60% of these children will be unable to communicate their wants, needs, and thoughts verbally. This means that up to 17,000 children are born each year who will be diagnosed with autism and remain functionally non-verbal.

So let's get down to the business of communication. Let's give individuals who have difficulty communicating the ability to say what they want to say, when they want to say it, through access to a multitude of words, signs, gestures, and vocalizations. A new way to communicate lies ahead!

Chapter 1: Voice Output

Augmentative Alternative Communication (AAC)

Voice Output applications are speech-generating apps that support individuals who are unable to use natural speech to meet all of their communication needs. This category of app has seen tremendous growth in the past few years. In fact, there are now sub-categories of AAC apps (traditional grid, visual screen display & video based) and a couple of very unique hybrids. Since we are familiar with the traditional Grid-style AAC app, I will start with some fresh, unique communication apps, or "hybrids."

New and Innovative AAC

Fabulous new AAC apps from pioneers in the industry offer exciting, never-before-seen features, while costing thousands of dollars less than traditional speech-generating devices. Older AAC systems used picture grids, which were first developed in the '60s, but since then, little has changed. With new advances in technology, developers are able to build original augmentative communication systems that challenge the status quo and create new avenues for research.

INNERVOICE: AUGMENTATIVE ALTERNATIVE COMMUNICATION *by iTherapy / MotionPortrait, Inc.*

www.innervoiceapp.com

$9.99

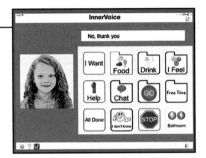

FROM THE DEVELOPER

InnerVoice is the next generation of Augmentative & Alternative Communication (AAC) apps. Designed specifically for individuals with strong visual skills such as autism, *InnerVoice* provides a voice for individuals who have challenges speaking and teaches them how to speak for themselves. *InnerVoice* will immerse you into a total communication environment in which you not only hear the desired message, but also see it being produced. This award-winning, patented, and affordable app takes full advantage of all the iPad has to offer.

iREVIEW

A talking avatar delivers the message! Not only do the students love having their message produced by a 3D animated avatar, but it also makes the communication environment fun for the listener too. Communication should be enjoyable and not a chore. A child can choose his or her favorite avatar from any photo of him- or herself, mom, friend, teacher, etc. *InnerVoice* also incorporates a new prompting level—Remote Prompting (RP). In a nutshell, RP provides the student prompts via his avatar that guides him to the correct response. This is a great example of innovation in AAC developed by speech pathologists who work hands-on with students on a daily basis. Apparently Mensa thought so too; *InnerVoice* won the 2013 Mensa Education & Research Foundation Intellectual Benefit to Society Award.

"Kudos to you for InnerVoice and [for introducing] a different paradigm for AAC apps! About time someone 'broke the mold."

> —*RJ Cooper, developer of software and hardware products for persons with special needs.*

InnerVoice is available for a free trial! You can also visit the developer's website for a demo of how this new design in AAC works: *www.innervoiceapp.com*

Success Story: Arthur

Arthur is a young man who is non-verbal and has abandoned every AAC device he has been given. He has learned to ask for food but appears to have little interest in communicating more than requests. Arthur's grandmother gave an expensive AAC app to Arthur for Christmas, but that was abandoned also.

Knowing that Arthur loves his big brother Mark, using *InnerVoice*, I animated a photo of Mark to encourage communication. It worked; Arthur spent the next 45 minutes having his brother say silly stuff and exploring the app. We found out that day that Arthur enjoys being funny—he is a comedian. Arthur now has 3D avatars of his entire family along with a couple Star Trek characters, and, interestingly enough, his neighbor. He is making more attempts to communicate and has an outlet for his humor.

AACORN AAC *by aacorn*
http://aacornapp.com
$189.99

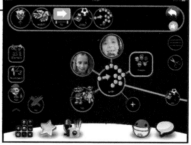

FROM THE DEVELOPER

aacorn introduces the unique "word tree" in which words present themselves automatically when your child needs them. No more "hunting and pecking" for words hidden in grids or folders! No need to be able to use a keyboard, no requirement to have an exceptional memory to find words, and no more grids or robotic voices. Truly an app of the next generation!

iREVIEW

aacorn may have given us a better way to communicate! By making it easier to access personal vocabulary sets, less time is spent searching through folders for word(s). My students really like its friendly interface and the "pop" sounds when a choice is made. It is not the traditional grid; rather, a "Smart Tree" that adapts and grows with the user. This is truly a remarkable app; the more I use it, the more I like it.

 aacorn comes equipped with real child voices only. If your child has auditory processing challenges, this may not be the best fit.

Visual Scene Display (VSD) AAC

VSD are basically interactive photos that are programmed to say a message when a designated area is activated. VSD are great for beginners, users with cognitive challenges, and/or limited language. VSD may be helpful to people with complex communication needs because of the high degree of contextual support they provide. Therefore, if you are struggling with your current AAC system, try a Visual Scene Display.

TINYTAP *by TinyTap Ltd.*
www.tinytap.it
FREE

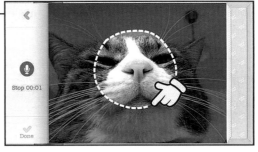

FROM THE DEVELOPER

On *TinyTap*, you can easily create your own educational games and play thousands of games created by teachers, authors, and kids worldwide. To create your own personalized games, just add photos or images, record questions, trace the answers, and you're ready to play!

iREVIEW

TinyTap is the easiest visual scene display ever! I love this app and use it almost every day. I can create a sound board, puzzle, or language activity in under one minute. Better yet, I can save and share my activity with other educators or family members, and vice versa. If you are not sure that your child would benefit from a visual screen display, then give *TinyTap* a try (for free!).

 TinyTap, like all visual screen displays, is open-ended, allowing you to create any activity for any age and ability. That being said, *TinyTap* does have a very preschool look and sound.

SCENE&HEARD *by Therapy Box Limited*

www.therapy-box.com

$49.99

FROM THE DEVELOPER

Scene&Heard is an interactive context-based communication aid and learning tool. Parents, teachers, therapists, and helpers can import photos and allocate actions including audio messages, short videos, Widget symbols, and scene links to transition to a new scene. This makes the scene interactive!

iREVIEW

Scene&Heard is a visual scene display that offers tons of features and is easy to operate. This VSD is flexible and can be used as simple communication, complex concepts, visual task analysis, or just about any visual support needed. Import photos, take photos, or use videos to create communication scenes as simple or as intricate as desired.

 The Lite version has some good examples and lets you create one free scene for yourself.

SCENE SPEAK *by Good Karma Applications, Inc.*

www.goodkarmaapplications.com

$9.99

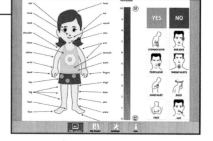

FROM THE DEVELOPER

Scene Speak is a versatile, customizable app that provides a framework on the iPad to create interactive visual scene displays and social stories. *Scene Speak* allows an image to be edited with active "hotspots." A hotspot is an area of the screen that can activate selectable "sound areas," which can be used as a means of communication. An image can have multiple hotspots that can be edited to add sound, text labels, or link to another visual scene. In addition, images with text can be then can be added into "books" by theme or area of interest.

iREVIEW

Scene Speak is a visual scene display that lets you import images, add text, and record your voice to create personal visual supports for communication and social stories. This app has a bit of a learning curve, but, once mastered, it can be a valuable and flexible tool. Luckily, a 31-page user manual is available on the Good Karma website.

Video-Based AAC

Video-Based AAC takes traditional Grid-style AAC to a new level. When a cell is activated, the user will see a short video describing the word or delivering the message. This is awesome for concepts, verbs, and emotions that cannot be described easily with a photo.

WORDTOOB: LANGUAGE LEARNING WITH VIDEO MODELING

by John Halloran
http://wordtoob.com
$5.99

FROM THE DEVELOPER

Language learning, whether just beginning to learn one's native language or learning a second language, requires combined information from the senses. *WordToob* makes this fun and easy by pairing words with illustrative videos. The learner benefits not only from playing *WordToob* but also through engaging in creating personalized videos. Personalized videos can be easily created with the iPad camera and attached to words within the app to maintain novelty and increase motivation.

WordToob is another of those great apps that has a variety of uses. Cells/buttons can be programmed to communicate one word or a complete thought/idea coupled with a short video(s). What makes *Word-Toob* really unique is the ability to add more than one example (video) to a cell. According to Dr. Temple Grandin, "Individuals on the autism spectrum learn to form concepts by putting many specific examples of a particular concept into a 'folder' in their brain labeled with that concept." Dr. Grandin refers to this concept as "bottom-up learning." *WordToob* also has a terrific speech recognition feature that lets the user activate cells saying the words, thus allowing the user to practice articulation and clear speech. With so many great features that let you learn word meanings while communicating and support literacy, *WordToob* is well worth the price.

FUNCTIONAL COMMUNICATION SYSTEM
by The Conover Company
www.conovercompany.com
$19.99

FROM THE DEVELOPER

The *Functional Communication System* app does not use symbols, but rather real images (and videos) from our Functional Skills System software. The video functionality allows you to use the *Functional Communication System* app as more than just a communication tool. The built-in videos also make it a great literacy & learning tool, and you can shoot your own videos right in the application.

iREVIEW

The *Functional Communication System* is one of those apps that have multiple uses. It is picture/word based, making it a good choice for beginning AAC users. This app goes further by combining video/video modeling with voice output to teach both communication and language skills. One of my students uses this app to make short videos of his vocabulary/spelling words. It is so easy to program that I have my older students create custom boards and videos for concepts such as verbs or emotions for my younger students.

Additional voices and text-to-speech keyboard functions can be acquired via in-app purchase. Try the free version, and then decide if the *Functional Communication System* is right for you.

GOTALK NOW *by Attainment Company*

www.attainmentcompany.com

$79.99

FROM THE DEVELOPER

The new *GoTalk Now* offers three styles of communication pages: Standard, Express, and Scenes. In Standard pages, the action occurs when the location is pressed. In Express pages, recorded or text-to-speech messages build in a speech bar and play in sequence when the bar is pressed. Scene pages are built around a single photo or image. When you arrange invisible hotspots over people or objects in the photo, the hotspots play speech, music, or videos! Feel free to mix and match pages within a communication book.

iREVIEW

I added *GoTalk Now* to the video-based AAC category, because that is the feature my students most commonly use with *GoTalk Now*. Moderately priced, this app lets the user mix and match communication styles. Start with a blank sheet and create the communication boards that are just right with videos, pictures, or icons. The customization features are endless, with infinite ways to share and save. Tons of in-app purchases let you further customize and expand as your students grow. I like the idea of buying only what you need or want. Like any great app with seemingly limitless features, there will be a learning curve. GoTalk Now has webinars, video tutorials, manuals, and friendly phone support.

 A free version of *GoTalk Now* is available for a test drive.

Traditional Grid-style Communication

Grid-style AAC is the arrangement of pictures, icons, or symbols into columns and rows. The user taps a symbol to deliver a message, build a sentence, or open a folder that reveals additional choices. Displays are arranged by the user by categories, topics, events, and/or parts of speech to fit the needs of the individual user. We have seen tremendous growth in Grid-based communication with the introduction of mobile technology into the field of assisted technology. Let's take a look at a few of these powerful communication tools.

PROLOQUO2GO *by AssistiveWare*
www.assistiveware.com
$219.99

FROM THE DEVELOPER

First released in 2009, *Proloquo2Go*'s research-based vocabularies, highly customizable features, natural-sounding voices, and unique innovations make it the premier Augmentative and Alternative Communication (AAC) solution for children and adults with autism, cerebral palsy, Down syndrome, developmental disabilities, apraxia, stroke, or traumatic brain injury.

iREVIEW

Thank you, *Proloquo2Go*! Not only is this a fabulous app with high-quality voice output system, *Proloquo2Go* has also opened doors for new technology to be taken seriously. Since its release in 2009, *Proloquo2Go* has remained at the forefront of AAC apps and continues to offer great features, such as multi-student capability, choice of two vocabularies, high-quality voices, switch accessibility, color, and size and grid selection, that make this app highly customizable.

Success Story: Igor

My colleague and friend, Harumi Kato, a Speech-Language Pathologist, has an amazing success story using the iPod touch in conjunction with the *Proloquo2Go*: "Igor began therapy with Harumi when he was 13 years old. He had no verbal language and was able to identify three pictures (goldfish, book, and bathroom). She started using the Tech Talk 32 with Igor and taught him colors, shapes, and requesting. It was soon obvious that the Tech Talk was limiting and bulky and that Igor was becoming averse to using it. Harumi began using her iPod touch with *Proloquo2Go* to support Igor's communication. Igor loved it! To make a long story short, Igor now has a 300+ word vocabulary, and his average sentence is four to six words. And the most amazing thing is that, at 13 years of age, Igor gained enough confidence to attempt verbal communication and can communicate with three-word utterances. Way to go, Harumi!

 ## AVAZ PRO - AAC APP FOR AUTISM (AUGMENTATIVE PICTURE COMMUNICATION SOFTWARE FOR CHILDREN WITH SPECIAL NEEDS)

by Invention Labs
www.avazapp.com
$99.99

FROM THE DEVELOPER

Avaz uses picture symbols and high-quality voice synthesis to help users create messages. The program comes with three research-based picture vocabularies and a Core Words set that will help a child begin to communicate. These vocabularies have been designed to facilitate spontaneous novel utterance generation, encouraging a child to use language in a variety of settings —school, home, or the community. While *Avaz* helps a child get started quickly with pictures, it's also greatly suited for facilitating easy transition into text. *Avaz*'s keyboard has support for saving and loading text, a quick response bar for frequently used messages, and a picture-assisted text prediction capability for sight readers.

Avaz tracks my data for me during a therapy session! Tracking data during a therapy session can interfere with the quality of the services I deliver, so if an app can track my data and let me focus on my student(s), I want it. Other fantastic, unique features of *Avaz* include integrated text with keyboard, word prediction with picture support, and reinforcement through animation. This is a great communication app for under $100.

 Try out the Lite version and check out their website to see video clips of all the exceptional features *Avaz* has to offer.

 **QUICK TALK AAC** *by Digital Scribbler, Inc.*
http://digitalscribbler.com
$24.99

FROM THE DEVELOPER

Our goal is to make it as quick and easy as possible for you to talk. We made this app as mobile, simple, and flexible as possible, so for one small fee you can have everything you need to communicate. Don't spend your time setting up; spend your time talking! There is a huge need for assistive technology that can equip those who are non-verbal with the ability to communicate. We developed *Quick Talk* with the advice and guidance from experts in speech therapy, educators, and individuals who use AAC devices to pack it full of features, while keeping simplicity and cost in mind. The outcome is a one-of-a-kind app that we believe will change many lives.

iREVIEW

Load and go with *Quick Talk AAC*. This is a new design in AAC apps that offers you three easy-use and navigation options, text-to-speech, sentence generation, and single-button communication.

 Multiple user set-up and customization makes *Quick Talk AAC* a super affordable app that can be utilized by a classroom teacher, therapist, or parent.

TOUCHCHAT HD - AAC WITH WORDPOWER

by Silver Kite

http://touchchatapp.com

$299.99

FROM THE DEVELOPER

TouchChat fits into the category of assistive technology known as Augmentative and Alternative Communication (AAC) and includes features that were previously only available in much more expensive dedicated devices. Words, phrases, and messages are spoken with a built-in voice synthesizer or through playback of recorded messages. Five US English and two British English synthesized voices are available, allowing the user to choose a voice that fits his or her own personality. *TouchChat* also has a unique feature with which one can simply tilt the device to make the message expand to fill the screen in large letters. This feature allows a person to communicate silently or in a noisy environment. *TouchChat* gives an individual the ability to navigate through page sets and speak messages. Page sets are linked pages, each of which is divided into a number of buttons. The buttons are programmed to perform specific actions. For example, buttons may be programmed to speak a message, navigate to a different page, change the volume, or clear the display. Four page sets are included with the *TouchChat*: VocabPC, MultiChat-15, Primary, and Spelling. Each page set targets individuals with different communication needs. Additional page sets, including Essence, are available as in-app purchases.

iREVIEW

Start communicating immediately using *TouchChat with WordPower*. *TouchChat* developed by Nancy Inman, combines the features of core vocabulary, spelling, and word prediction to offer easy, intuitive language generation. This super-powerful, customizable app stands up to the dedicated devices that cost thousands of dollars. The features are truly impressive and seemingly endless. For me, it feels a little like the toothpaste aisle at the grocery store—so many choices make using this app a bit overwhelming. *TouchChat with WordPower* is an outstanding app for any individual who has communication challenges. The TouchChat website offers a multitude of avenues of support, such as a reference guide, webinars, articles, tutorials, trainings, Facebook groups, and certified trainers.

Be sure to allocate plenty of extra time to become familiar with this app. There are 12 vocabulary sets to choose from, and that is just the beginning.

MYTALK MOBILE *by 2nd Half Enterprises LLC*
www.mytalktools.com
$99.99

FROM THE DEVELOPER

MyTalkTools Mobile for the iPhone, iPod touch, and iPad enables people with communication difficulties to express their needs and desires to those around them. Your purchase provides permanent access to *MyTalkTools Mobile* (completely stand-alone software) and a 30-day trial of optional *MyTalk Workspace.* Together they represent a major breakthrough in augmentative, alternative communications (AAC) by making it easy to customize how you communicate through a variety of images, pictures, symbols, and video and audio files, including the human voice. Within five minutes, you can create your very own content and communicate in a way that YOU choose. You also won't have to worry about losing your information if you lose or break your device; all information is backed up on *MyTalk Workspace. MyTalk* offers ease of use and time savings in a portable, effective, and cool communication tool. *MyTalk* helps people communicate in a whole new way.

iREVIEW

I was surprised that the set-up was not as complicated as it seemed initially. *MyTalkTools Mobile* was easy to customize. *MyTalk* has an optional companion web application/sync that allows the user to personalize voice, visual language sets, social stories, story boards, or just about anything. The text-to-speech feature allows the user more flexibility during conversations and naturally occurring situations. Technical support was friendly and helpful. Users will want to customize this app to fit their individual needs; it is not a load-and-go communication app.

 Try the free version and view the demo! www.mytalktools.com/dnn/Support/Demos.aspx

Success Story: Heidi

Kari Valentine, an Occupational Therapist with Wholistic Therapy Services in Nebraska has this to say about *MyTalk* and Heidi: "I am currently using *MyTalk* with a five-year-old non-verbal female. She knows immediately when she sees the iPad that she uses it to communicate. She takes it and holds it and presses up to nine buttons to ask for what she wants. She has

Heidi uses MyTalk to make a presentation to her classmates.

even figured out how to press the cancel button to navigate back to the last page. She is in kindergarten, and there was some question about whether she could attach meaning to pictures, so her teachers basically used sign language. She knows all of her colors, a majority of her letters, and now, using *MyTalk*, she is able to tell people what she knows so there is no denying that she is smart. She is also able to sign about 50 different signs. The only thing we have not figured out with our student is how to calm her down when we have to take the iPad away; she throws a huge fit because she wants it with her all the time."

Chapter 2: Sign Language

Sign language is a visual-gestural system of communication. Sign language was originally developed as a means of communication for the deaf and hard-of-hearing community. Likewise, it is a viable mode of communication for non-verbal individuals and those with emerging speech.

In The News:

The Power of Sign Language Helps Children with Autism Create Meaning in Language

By Michele Ricamato, MA, CCC-SLP (West Chicago, IL)

As a practicing speech and language pathologist working primarily with children diagnosed with autistic spectrum disorders, I have witnessed firsthand the benefits of sign language as a means for augmenting communication.

My therapeutic work with children who have disorders relating to communication has been influenced heavily by Drs. Stanley Greenspan and Serena Wieder's Developmental Individual/Difference Relationship Based Therapy (DIR) and by developmental language acquisition models (Bloom and Lahey, Bloom and Tinker). As a result of these influences, my understanding of how a linguistic system develops has taken on a much broader and more holistic conceptualization.

In order to fully appreciate the benefits of sign language for children with limited ability to express themselves, it is important to understand language in a more comprehensive way. In my research, I found that language comprises far more than the sounds or sentence structures that make up the utterances we make. In fact, sounds and words without meaning are devoid of substance. It is the arbitrary meaning that each culture assigns words and word combinations that supports true communication.

Research proves that language has critical beginnings within the first three months of life. Early precursors include the ability to reference another (using eye gaze for communicative purposes), sharing attention with a caregiver and, later, using gestures and facial expressions during communicative exchanges. These non-verbal capacities build solid and critical foundations that support language levels later.

Typically developing children develop and expand their language by experiencing their world and environment in multi-sensory contexts. Their meanings of concepts and events and the relations between people, actions, and objects become gradually expanded as they encounter the world through relationships with their primary caregivers. Language gives children the ability to express ideas, communicate novel thoughts, and represent themselves to others. As a result, relationships flourish through a mutually agreed upon way of communication.

Children diagnosed with Autistic Spectrum Disorder often have challenges developing robust gestural and non-verbal communication. Due to very complex challenges in visual, auditory, spatial, and tactile sensory systems, children with relating and communicative disorders often experience difficulty comprehending a broad range of meanings for the concepts and relations expressed through words. Their ability to become intentional communicators can be limited by the above deficits. I find that sign language often provides a bridge to support a child's ability to gesture more frequently and with greater complexity and provides more information about the meanings of words, events, concepts, and relations.

Children with motor deficits may find it challenging to use sign language accurately, but because of their exposure to sign language, they have the ability to express novel ideas through gestures that can be interpreted by primary communicative partners, which supports a child's intentionality. The child is able to see that they are, in fact, a communicator and that her message is received and acted upon within her environment. She is also able to share experiences, which leads to a more powerful desire to communicate further. The power to be understood and to send messages that are received readily fosters more intentionality and the desire to make more meaning within one's world; they become more empowered, the more they feel understood by others.

Using sign language specifically as an alternative communication form has often raised fears for families that, if this method is employed for children who have not yet developed verbal expression, verbal expressive language may never develop. However, research within the field of speech and language pathology as well as alternative and augmentative communication has conclusively proven otherwise. I have found that language and communication is less about the production of sounds and words and more about the expression of shared meanings within primary relationships. It stands to reason that the creative process is critical to language development and is more acutely demonstrated in the sharing of experiences and ideas than of the actual verbal production of words. Again, words without meaning lack the hallmarks of communication. Therefore, children who use sign language as a means to communicate have the ability to express their inner ideas and other cognitive processes with another.

Within my own clinical work, I have witnessed the power of sign language. Families have often related stories of meeting with professionals who have indicated that the severity of the motor deficits impacting speech production for their child indicates that they will never verbally produce words. Explaining the process of typical language acquisition and the importance of laying foundations rooted in later language development is often comforting as we begin our work together. We focus on building meaning and comprehension for the child while using a wide range of non-verbal modalities and a variety of means of expression.

It is always miraculous to see a child share experience and meaning with their caregiver through signs and more conventional gestures, demonstrating sheer joy at the power of communicating. It is even more miraculous to see many children who, when well supported in this manner, begin to verbally communicate in combination with gestures and signs. Verbal production that is meaningful builds from these very interactions where meaning has already been shared in many other ways, much like the foundations that babies share by pointing and commenting with early gestures before verbally expressing the words for which they have already "made meaning."

The *Signing Time* video series in particular has had an impact on many of the clients and families that I support. *Signing Time* offers a unique sign language experience for children. Rachel's songs are captivating and provide a multi-sensory platform for learning signs that go beyond needs and wants or labels of objects. Children are exposed to a variety of signs in a multitude of contexts in which the relations between the sign, the child, and the word's meaning are effortlessly combined and reinforced. Repetition of signs demonstrated is offered with many children in many different environments. Songs support interest, attention, and engagement so that learning is easily accessible. I recently had a child sign "happy" to me during a fun interaction on the trampoline. I looked inquisitively at his mother who indicated that he had learned that while watching the Signing Time series. It was beautiful to see him so easily and meaningfully use the sign to share his state of feeling within our interaction. What power to be able to communicate such a complex emotional idea when he verbally cannot express this yet!

Sign language offers the power to share meaning with another and build further connections in relationships in which a mutual understanding of each other is enhanced by that sharing. For children diagnosed with Autistic Spectrum Disorders, this is a primary goal that we strive for and can certainly achieve when we are open to the many modalities and possibilities of communication.

SIGNED STORIES *by ITV Broadcasting Limited*
www.signedstories.com/apps
FREE (new books every month)

FROM THE DEVELOPER

READ – WATCH – LISTEN – SIGN – PLAY – LEARN

We all rely on good educational resources to learn how to read and write. But deaf children and those with special needs have been starved of what they require to develop good literacy. Parents have struggled to find quality accessible storybooks which their children can share. Teachers are all too aware of the shortage of good classroom teaching materials. We have created *Signed Stories* to fill that void. We believe passionately in the right of every child to have access to books in whatever format suits them best. Working with some of the best international publishers, we will continue to produce a wide range of animated picture books with optional ASL, captions, and narration. It is our hope that Signed Stories will make a real and lasting difference within the standards of literacy by enriching the lives of all children as they find their place in the world.

iREVIEW

Brilliant, just brilliant! Finally, there are literacy materials that appeal to every learner and learning style. *Signed Stories* can be used for whole-class (including staff) instruction via Apple TV or individual sessions. The ASL storytellers are actually performers who bring the story to life with expression and feeling. Once a week, I have a language group during which we use Signed Stories and follow-up with the interactive language games that accompany each book. Everyone learns and everyone has fun, and the best part is that no one is left out.

 The first story, *Three Billy Goats Gruff*, along with a Sign Dictionary, is free to try. Additional books range from $0.99 to $5.99.

SIGN 4 ME *by Vcom3D*

http://signingapp.com/sign4me_desktop.html
(demo available)
$9.99

FROM THE DEVELOPER

Vcom3D, the original developer of sign language software using SigningAvatar® characters, wants you to be able to learn sign language the way you need to communicate. If you have friends or co-workers who are deaf or hard-of-hearing, now you can learn signs to communicate with them. The playback is in Signed English for the hearing person who wants to learn basic sign.

iREVIEW

Sign 4 Me was designed to be the ultimate tool for learning sign language. For my student who is deaf and has autism, *Sign 4 Me* is his only means of communication. There are many people in his environment who do not know sign language; therefore, Sign 4 Me bridges the gap between him and us. To use *Sign 4 Me*, simply type in a word, phrase, or sentence, and the avatar will sign it for you (Your entries will be saved alphabetically into the history for easy reference). An indispensable feature of this app is that the user can adjust signing speeds and rotate the avatar for the best view of hand shapes and movements. If you are interested in learning the alphabet, type in ABCDE, etc. with no space in between each letter. The character will show you what each letter sign looks like.

Sign 4 Me uses Signed Exact English (SEE), not ASL. Dynamic translation from English to true ASL is a complex problem, just as translation from any language into another would be. We are currently researching this technology.

Success Story: Omar

New to our school, Omar struggled to transition to his classroom. He was a severely hard-of-hearing, cognitively challenged, non-verbal young adult with autism. To make the situation even more challenging, Omar's classroom staff did not know sign language. When Omar felt disoriented, frustrated, or confused, he attempted to escape the situation and isolate himself. He at times attempted to hit or push if a staff member tried to intervene, and Omar misinterpreted others' messages.

The third day at Omar's new school was a minimum day, when all students leave at 12:00. This new schedule and unfamiliar environment were tough for Omar. At 12:10, I heard loud yelling from the office area and looked to see Omar surrounded by the staff. He was crying, hollering, and swinging. I overheard staff whispering, "Looks like a 5150.*"

My sign language skills are fair, so I grabbed my iPad with *Sign 4 Me* and went to talk with Omar. I found out that, Omar simply misunderstood the scheduling of the minimum day and mistakenly thought we were trying to kick him out of school. When I was able to communicate to Omar that it was a half day of school and all students go home at lunchtime, he instantly sat down, took a deep breath, and, in a few minutes, gathered his backpack and got on the bus. *Sign 4 Me* quite literally saved this young man from going through the trauma of a 5150 situation.

*   5150 is a police code for people who present a danger to themselves, property, or others. As a result of a 5150, a person is taken for psychiatric evaluation and intervention for up to 72 hrs.

   **ASL BABY SIGN** *by Software Studios LLC*
www.asl-dictionary.com
FREE

FROM THE DEVELOPER

This fun *ASL Baby Sign* app offers over 170 ASL videos plus an interactive A-Z Picture Dictionary that's completely customizable. Add your own pictures, video, voice, and words.

The customization features set *ASL Baby Sign* apart from the pack! You can create a personalized sign language dictionary for your child or student including audio, video, text, and pictures. *ASL Baby Sign* is also a perfect way to show others what a personal interpretation or approximation of a sign may look like. Because *ASL Baby Sign* was meant for a very young audience, the images and graphics are designed for that population; however, it can be used with any learner due to the customization features.

MY SMART HANDS BABY SIGN LANGUAGE DICTIONARY *by My Smart Hands*
http://mysmarthands.com
$4.99

FROM THE DEVELOPER

Try the condensed version to test out all the cool features of our dictionary app for free before upgrading to the full version, or try our finger-spelling game for tons of fun wherever you are – fun for kids and adults! There are also flash card apps to make everyday learning that much easier. Have fun watching Fireese teach you and your child how the signs are made!

iREVIEW

My Smart Hands Baby Sign Language Dictionary is the app my co-workers use when they want to learn a new sign. Not only do you see the sign

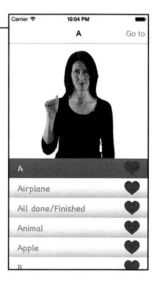

clearly, but there are also verbal instructions for making the correct hand shapes. *My Smart Hands* is available in beginner and intermediate versions as well as in flash cards and finger-spelling apps. *My Smart Hands* is easy to navigate, offers clear video, and includes good audio with quiz and favorites features. I would recommend this app to anyone learning ASL vocabulary, especially babies.

Chapter 3: One-Touch Message

Now you can convey, declare, inform, answer, and be heard with a touch of the finger. One-touch switches allow users to communicate whole messages with one easy tap. I have assembled an array of serious and fun switches to choose from. Choose the best one for your needs or choose them all.

In The News:

iPod Touch helps autistic kids learn to speak, communicate

By Alana Greenfogel

Parents and teachers of children with autism and other verbal disabilities know how challenging it can be at times to communicate with their kids. That's changing at schools in Plymouth with the help of the iPod touch.

Paulina is a kindergartener. She sits at a table with other students, coloring her assignment, but she needs the help of an aide because she can't speak—well, she *couldn't* speak until a few weeks ago, when she started using the iPod touch.

Paulina can answer her aides' and teachers' questions or indicate how she's feeling by pushing the buttons on the iPod. She can indicate that she's "hungry" or "has to go to the bathroom" or something as simple as she "wants to use the green crayon."

This is a tangible, hands-on learning tool that connects with the kids more than other types of therapy. The schools' aides and speech pathologist say they've never seen progress quite like this before. Hearing the voice from the iPod encourages the kids to repeat the words on their own.

"Just in these couple of weeks, she's had great progress with the words that she can use and the phrases she can say," says Michelle Richter, Paulina's aide.

"They are frustrated. They know what they want to say but they're just not able to express themselves," says Rita Large, the district's speech pathologist. "I love technology, because it's so exciting and it lets us do so much more."

TAPSPEAK BUTTON *by Ted Conley*
http://tapspeak.com/drupal
$14.99

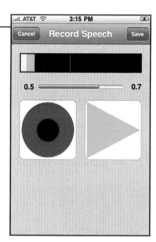

FROM THE DEVELOPER

TapSpeak Button modernizes the idea of a mechanical switch that records and plays messages. We have taken the idea and extended it to provide a portable, convenient, and stigma-free tool to use for basic teaching and communication tasks. *TapSpeak Button* is especially useful for teaching cause and effect relationships.

iREVIEW

If you use a switch or single message AAC communicator, you will love *TapSpeak Button*. It is an easy-to-use program and can save favorite words or phrases for quick playback. The graphics are bright, clear, and appealing. *TapSpeak Button* is essentially a digital Big Mac.

TAPSPEAK SEQUENCE FORK iPAD
by Ted Conley

http://tapspeak.com/drupal/sequence

$29.99

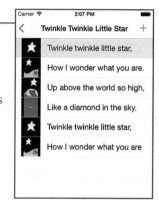

FROM THE DEVELOPER

TapSpeak Sequence for iPad revolutionizes how parents, speech therapists, vision therapists, schools, and institutions create and use message sequences to help disabled children learn to communicate. Use *TapSpeak Sequence* instead of sequential message switches to record and customize messages without losing any previously recorded sequences.

iREVIEW

Sequence a social scenario, song, circle time, task analysis, and story book so that everyone can participate. *TapSpeak Sequence* for iPad gives unlimited sequencing abilities for optimal customization and picture support for the phrase/sentence. *TapSpeak* apps have switch support courtesy of RJ Cooper.

ANSWERS:YESNO HD *by SimplifiedTouch*

www.simplifiedtouch.com/SimplifiedTouch/Welcome.html

$3.99

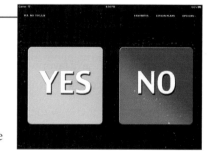

FROM THE DEVELOPER

Answers:YesNo HD was designed with one purpose in mind: provide an easy-to-use, affordable way for a non-verbal young person with autism and motor planning issues to communicate with those around him. The application is straightforward. It has two, large, color-coordinated buttons; one for yes, and one for no. Press either, and you will hear a voice read your selection. New in *Answers:YesNo HD* is the ability to create custom button pages which will allow the user to place custom text and pictures on buttons, record custom audio to play when the custom buttons are selected, and save up to 30 custom button pairs.

iREVIEW

Making choices is not easy, but now you can have up to 30 pre-programmed choices at your fingertips with five voices and record your own voice/language option. My students love the cartoon voice, and this motivates them to communicate more.

CLICK N' TALK *by von Intermediate District 287*

http://asoft11122.accrisoft.com/district287/index.php?src=gendocs&ref=Click_n_Talk

$2.99

FROM THE DEVELOPER

Click n' Talk is an augmentative communication app that allows the user to attach text and voice to individual pictures and organize photos in photo albums.

iREVIEW

iTunes is full of talking photo albums that are usually simple and inexpensive, providing a great way to display photos from a field trip, school project, task analysis, family, etc. *Click n' Talk* is a great example of a talking photo album that lets you easily create, present, and share your handiwork. Fun ways to use talking photo albums:

- Illustrate steps of a cooking activity.
- Chronicle your trip to the zoo.
- Show steps of a task analysis.
- Tell about friends and family.
- Create a visual schedule.
- Prepare a school presentation.

TALKING TOM AND FRIENDS
by Out Fit 7 Ltd.

http://outfit7.com/our-work/

FREE (nominal charge to remove ads)

FROM THE DEVELOPER

The company was formed by a group of creative minds and entrepreneurs. With a mission to bring fun and entertainment to all, these experts in the field of online search realized that direct engagement with users was key and that a new interactive and animated animal app would provide the fun and entertainment they were looking to create. Their first creation was *Talking Tom*. Our gang can hardly wait to talk to you and be your friends.

iREVIEW

Talking Tom and Friends encourages expressive language. Simply say a word or phrase, and Tom will repeat it. All characters are bright, colorful, and cute. The user can tickle, poke, and pinch the characters to make them respond. They were originally meant as novelty apps; however, they have become one of the best ways to inspire verbalizations and giggles from most students. With The Talkers, the user can record, save, and send messages via email or social networking. Moreover, these recorded messages can be used to communicate like a single-button communicator, put into an open-ended book app to build a story or make an electronic communication binder. The uses for these talking characters are endless and the motivation is high.

 Most Talkers will have a Child Mode. Turn on Child Mode to avoid burps, farts, and some naughty behaviors.

TALKING GINGER
by Out Fit 7 Ltd.

Little Talking Ginger will help out with some important hygiene routines. As your child helps Ginger with brushing teeth, taking a shower, blow drying hair, and sitting on the potty; these routines may become easier for your child.

FURRY FRIEND
by Plutinosoft

Lenord is a friendly, furry monster that can help a child learn how to produce air flow by blowing a pinwheel, balloon, and bubbles. There are also a couple of lessons on eating and drinking through a straw.

TALKING REX THE DINOSAUR
by Out Fit 7 Ltd.

Have you ever pet and fed a tyrannosaurus rex? Now is your chance to play with your own pet dinosaur.

TALKING TOM & BEN NEWS
by Out Fit 7 Ltd.

Breaking news—Tom and Ben can teach teamwork, turn-taking, and cooperative play. Join them in the TV studio to tell jokes, report stories (sequencing), or just chat. They can get rough with each other, so be sure child mode is turned on.

Success Story: Teddy

Transitions can be trying for children on the spectrum, but for Teddy, they were nearly impossible. He struggled to walk from the car to the classroom, from the classroom to the playground, from the playground back to the classroom, and so forth. Unfortunately, due to the significant amount of time taken in transitions, there was little time in Teddy's day for school work.

Teddy is a bright five-year-old boy who is learning to use AAC to communicate. He loves, loves, loves dinosaurs: enter *Talking Rex*. With the goal of making transitions easier and learning communication, I made a recording of Rex, asking, "Can I have your attendance?" Teddy's job was to go to each classroom and use *Talking Rex* to request the attendance.

Have you ever had something work way better than expected? *Talking Rex* was the motivation Teddy needed, quite frankly, to forget about his anxiety with transitions. We spent the next two hours sprinting around campus delivering messages from *Talking Rex*. Teddy now moves around campus freely and can use AAC to express himself. He still prefers *Talking Rex* and has made a book of *Talking Rex* phrases.

ANIMATEANYTHING
by MotionPortrait, Inc.
www.motionportrait.com
FREE

FROM THE DEVELOPER

Animate your pets, a drawing, or any object that you'd like to give an animated face and voice to. Using your voice you can create animated avatars to send personalized birthday messages, let somebody know you miss them, or to just give your pet rock some character. Super easy to email, text, or share to social networks.

iREVIEW

The iPad has made communication more fun than ever, and communication should be fun. *AnimateAnything* is so appealing that kids want to talk; isn't that the goal? Simply take/choose a picture, designate eyes and mouth, record your message, and share via email, text, or social network. Easy, motivating, and free!

MOVIE SOUND EFFECTS (PRO)
by GearSprout

www.gearsprout.com/index.html

$0.99

FROM THE DEVELOPER

With hundreds of high quality movie sound effects from action, comedy, kids', and sci-fi movies, you can play the perfect noise or song at the exact right time! Have you ever wanted to walk into a room and play the perfect movie sound effect for everyone to hear? You have hundreds to choose from!

iREVIEW

Everybody enjoys using sound effects to make a statement. One sound effect can communicate 100 words. The sound of crickets, a yawn, or snoring all convey a very clear message. *Movie Sound Effects (Pro)* gives everyone, verbal and non-verbal, the opportunity to be a comedian!

 Movie Sound Effects (Pro) is the most kid-friendly sound effect app I could find. Unfortunately, the sounds are labeled with words only, and some are vague (Crowd 01, Sound 13). Rest assured, users will soon learn and remember where to find favorite sounds and eventually read the labels. Imagine that; sounds effects can support literacy development!

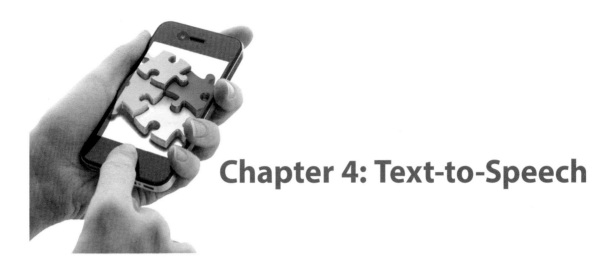

Chapter 4: Text-to-Speech

With text-to-speech applications, you can convert written text into spoken words, spoken words into text, thoughts to text, or text into a talking bald guy! Being proficient at text-to-speech will free you from icons, pictures, and symbols. Say anything to anyone without hunting through hundreds of pictures that make awkward sentences with bad grammar. When text-to-speech is combined with "smart word prediction" that grows with the learner, true expression of thoughts and ideas can be shared quickly without boundaries. The goal of all of my students who have communication challenges that require AAC is to become proficient at text-to-speech.

 ## Success Story: Hanna

Students are learning speech intelligibility from their text-to-speech apps – I have seen this on more than one occasion among students who have emerging expressive language skills and are learning to use text-to-speech.

Hanna is a bright, nine-year-old who has been struggling with speech production her entire life. She is a whiz at using the iPad and operates several apps with ease to communicate. I recently introduced her to *Predictable* and text-to-speech as a means to express her thoughts. She immediately liked using text-to-speech and soon quit using her picture-based apps. I expected that; however, what I didn't expect was the additional use of *Predictable* Hanna devised for herself. As Hanna would type words or phrases, she would listen to them over and over and over again. Soon she began to make attempts to imitate the words until her production matched the text-to-speech production. This technique, of imitating a model, is something she has had significant challenges with in face-to-face therapeutic interactions. OMG, Hanna just figured out a way to teach herself intelligible speech. Not only was her speech & articulation improving, but also her literacy skills and ability to decipher words in both written and spoken phrases/sentences increased.

This is nothing I had taught her to do, I'm embarrassed to say. My students are truly amazing in their ability to find their own path, strengths, and learning style(s).

PREDICTABLE
by Therapy Box Limited
www.therapy-box.com/predictable.aspx
$159.99

FROM THE DEVELOPER

Predictable is an exciting text-to-speech application for the iPad, iPhone, and iPod touch. Offering customizable AAC functions with the latest social media integration, *Predictable* provides a new benchmark. Using a word prediction engine and switch access, Predictable meets the needs of a wide range of people using AAC. Many different people are using *Predictable*, including those with MND/ALS, Cerebral Palsy, and those with communication difficulties after a stroke or head injury.

iREVIEW

It's hard to ignore how important apps have become where communication is concerned. *Predictable* is perhaps one of the most robust and important apps in this category. With incredible smart word prediction, voice output, switch access, and scanning capabilities, *Predictable* is much more than text-to-speech, but a sophisticated assistive technology app that allows the user the flexibility and tools needed to communicate more naturally in a variety of environments. Among the many features users have at their fingertips are the three modes of access (scan and switch, direct touch, and touch anywhere), a customizable phrase bank, dyslexia support, nine adjustable voices, social network access, and email capabilities. This app must be considered when making assistive technology decisions. See for yourself by viewing the introduction to *Predictable* on the therapy-box website. Are you still not sure? Read through the downloadable user guide, which is also provided on their website.

 Impressive picture/symbol support for a number of features—text-to-speech, frequently used words, and common phrases—make this a fantastic choice for either those who are transitioning from pictures to written words or who continue to need some visual cues.

 **ASSISTIVE EXPRESS** *by assistive apps*

www.assistiveapps.com

$24.99

FROM THE DEVELOPER

Assistive Apps presents *Assistive Express*, an affordable Augmentative Alternative Communication (AAC) device catered to people with speech difficulties. In many cases, the biggest challenge for these AAC users is the number of keystrokes or hits required to construct sentences, causing these individuals to communicate too slowly for typical conversational environments. To overcome this challenge, Assistive Express is designed to be simple and efficient, allowing users to express their views and thoughts quickly with the help of natural-sounding voices.

iREVIEW

Assistive Express is an excellent, reasonably priced, word prediction/text-to-speech app. Some features of Assistive Express are word prediction, adaptive vocabulary learning, three-voice selection, a favorites list, and a quick list. Word prediction supports individuals who have challenges retaining ideas, difficulties with spelling, and motor impairments which make it difficult to use a keyboard effectively. No picture support is offered with *Assistive Express*.

ROCKETKEYS *by MyVoice*

http://myvoiceaac.com/app/rocketkeys

$159.99

FROM THE DEVELOPER

RocketKeys is an amazingly customizable talking keyboard for people with speech disabilities. This powerful app lets you build the perfect keyboard by choosing the exact keys, size, layout, colors, prediction, and voices you want. And because *RocketKeys* understands touch input from users with unsteady or imprecise hands, it is very physically accessible.

iREVIEW

If you, your child, or your student is having difficulty with a standard keyboard, design your own using *RocketKeys*. Select any size, color, or location for the keys, then activate them by tapping, hovering, or touching the screen with a finger or a fist. A unique word prediction engine, based on nine million tweets, guesses misspelled and incomplete words including popular names, terms, and news. No picture support is offered with *RocketKeys*.

PROLOQUO4TEXT *by AssistiveWare*

www.assistiveware.com/product/
proloquo4text

$129.99

FROM THE DEVELOPER

Proloquo4Text is a text based communication app that gives a voice to people who cannot speak. It offers a customizable single-screen layout for easy conversation, free natural-sounding voices in 15 languages, word and sentence prediction, social media sharing, and more.

iREVIEW

The makers of *Proloquo2Go* have delivered another excellent communication app. So many features—word prediction, a phrase bank, and a customizable keyboard—make communicating your ideas and thoughts more accessible than ever. Proloquo4Text is an excellent choice for those who are literate yet have challenges with verbal communication. *Proloquo4Text* doesn't feature picture support.

QUICK TYPE AAC *by Digital Scribbler, Inc.*
http://digitalscribbler.com
$1.99

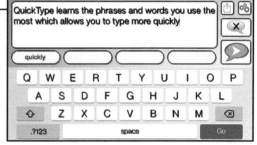

FROM THE DEVELOPER

We designed *Quick Type* as an affordable, easy-to-use alternative to many of the typical Augmentative and Alternative Communication (AAC) apps and devices currently available. We have included an intelligent word prediction tool that learns the words and phrases you use the most to enable the user to speak even more quickly. The more you use it, the better it gets at predicting what you want to say! You can also delete a word prediction by simply holding the word—a feature not available in other AAC apps.

iREVIEW

Smart word/phrase prediction for under two dollars, Wow! *Quick Type AAC* is everything it claims to be: affordable, simple, and smart with a clean user interface. This is one of those apps that should be on every iPad.

iBALDI *by Psyentific Mind, Inc.*
http://psyentificmind.com/apps/language-instruction-with-baldi
$1.99

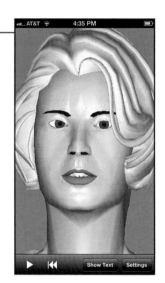

FROM THE DEVELOPER

Watch and listen to *iBaldi* or *iBaldette*, 3D-animated characters who can read text using extraordinarily accurate mouth and face movements while displaying convincing emotions. You can import any text to have *iBaldi* or *iBaldette* speak it to you. You can also save your favorite texts in your Notes app for *iBaldi* to read at any time. You can control iBaldi's facial look and emotions. Take your content with you and enjoy *iBaldi* offline.

iREVIEW

I still love this guy and gal! *iBaldi* is much more than a great text-to-speech app, it is an articulation coach and language tutor. iBaldi provides the user with an optional inside (medial) view to the articulators as he is speaking. Pretty cool tool for a speech pathologist. I was thrilled; however, some students did not share my excitement. They thought *iBaldi* was kinda creepy, however enjoyed having him say silly things. *iBaldi* is incredibly interactive, as you can change his emotions, rate of speech, and head position in space. All in all, this is one of the best, coolest apps around. I wish I would have had iBaldi when I was in grad school; maybe if I had, I would have gotten a better grade in my articulation/phonology classes. *iBaldi* and now *iBaldette* are recommended for everyone, even grad students.

DRAGON DICTATION *by Nuance Communications*
www.dragonmobileapps.com
FREE

FROM THE DEVELOPER

Dragon Dictation is an easy-to-use voice recognition application powered by Dragon® NaturallySpeaking® that allows you to easily speak and instantly see your text or email messages. In fact, it's up to five times faster than typing on the keyboard.

iREVIEW

Dragon Dictation is not just for business productivity. It is a seriously good assistive technology speech-to-text transcription application. Speech-to-text allows users to give commands and enter data using their voices rather than a mouse or keyboard. Individuals with motor or vision challenges can take notes, write reports, tweet, use Facebook, and send emails. Check the *Dragon Dictation* website for languages supported.

 For best results, the user must have clear speech and pronounce each word separately to use *Dragon Dictation* effectively.

 # Success Story: Bret

Bret has perhaps the most poignant success story of all and provides proof of why we must all continually strive to do better.

Bret was a new student in one of my junior high classrooms. He was considered non-verbal because his speech was very low and unintelligible. Bret would usually sit with his arms crossed with a look of frustration on his face. His communication goals were simply to use two- to four-word utterances to convey information via picture exchange and/or verbalizations. During a language group in which the students were describing wax paper, I saw Bret attempting to make a comment. Each student had a chance to give one or two descriptors about wax paper. I heard correct descriptors such as thin, smooth, clear, crinkly, etc. Bret again attempted to make a comment. The classroom teacher prompted Bret, "Speak up so that we can hear you." This prompt did not help. Bret then crossed his arms and sat back in his chair with no further attempts to make a comment. Clearly he had heard this prompt way too often.

Luckily, I had my iPhone within reach. I opened a text-to-speech app and handed it to Bret. He immediately began to type the response, "Moisture resistant due to a thin layer of wax." OMG! The classroom fell silent, and Bret smiled with pride. I think we should rethink and rewrite some goals for this young man. My students surprise me every day.

Chapter 5: Producing Voice

Many individuals with autism are unable to speak fluently or produce sounds volitionally. Some children are silent and make few attempts to use their voices while others produce many vocalizations or repetitive sounds that appear to lack meaning. When asked to make a sound or say a word, many children with ASD will struggle to respond, as if they can't initiate the process. In severe cases, some children on the spectrum remain silent. What is the cause of this? We can hypothesize that a combination of auditory processing and motor planning may be culprits, but nobody really knows why some children on the spectrum can speak and others cannot.

In this chapter, I will present some very engaging apps that can help children learn to harness their voices and eventually shape voiced sounds into words. This group of apps focuses on oral awareness skills, from producing airflow to forming first syllables, using activities such as chewing, blowing, sucking, and—yes—spitting! Although these non-speech activities have shown little efficacy with many communication-delayed children, new studies are challenging this view when it concerns individuals on the autism spectrum. UK-based philanthropy Autistica funded research which revealed that emphasizing motor skills alongside speech and language intervention has produced promising preliminary results. These new findings are key because they help to expand our understanding of motor behaviors' role in the development of communication and social interaction.

VAST PRE-SPEECH ORAL MOTOR
by SpeakinMotion
www.speakinmotion.com
$12.99

FROM THE DEVELOPER

VAST Pre-Speech is designed for individuals on the autism spectrum who are non-verbal or have minimal verbal skills due to a motor speech planning disorder such as apraxia. Children with apraxia of speech have difficulty planning speech movements of the tongue, lips, palate and jaw (articulators), hindering their development of verbal speech. Some children on the spectrum may have challenges with everyday activities such as blowing their nose, spitting out toothpaste, or pocketing food.

VAST Pre-Speech utilizes the highly effective concept of video modeling and auditory cues to promote awareness of oral structures, coordination, strength, tone, chewing, swallowing of food and saliva, and speech clarity; it eventually works towards enabling students to gain the ability to speak for themselves. In clinical trials, the *VAST* videos have been highly effective in increasing a child's ability to attend to a communication partner's mouth in the natural environment.

iREVIEW

Each movement has two to three examples of different children performing the target activity. Users can choose from a pre-selected group of videos that target a specific deficit or make a playlist that fits the needs of their child. *VAST Pre-Speech* also includes a mirror feature that encourages self-monitoring along with information on each activity and how/why it is important for oral motor development.

iTunes user mammakbare offers the following review: We absolutely LOVE this app!! We practice a little every day, some days more than others. My nephew's face lights up seeing the other kids doing the variety of activities. This is a great app to help realize sensory and actions. I have been trying to get him to blow kisses for a year now, and with no prior interest in it, he shocked me by blowing me a kiss out of the blue!!! I am so happy I discovered this app. There are no words to describe my gratitude for what you are doing and offering people like us!! You're our angels and an extended part of our team. Thank you, thank you, thank you!

SINGING FINGERS *by Beginner's Mind*

http://singingfingers.com

FREE

FROM THE DEVELOPER

Singing Fingers lets you finger-paint with sound. Just touch the screen while you make a sound, and colorful paint appears. Touch the paint to play back the sound again! You can paint your own musical instrument and play it, play with your voice, experiment with sounds, or create whatever else you can imagine.

iREVIEW

Singing Fingers brilliantly combines motor movement with voice and vice versa. Embed sounds, words, and messages into your finger paint projects, then play them back by tracing your masterpiece. Use your imagination to focus on goals or just have fun playing with your voice. Take a look at the Demo Video website for tons of inspiration.

PAH! 2.0 *by Labgoo Ltd.*

http://ahhhpah.com/

$0.99

FROM THE DEVELOPER

The *PAH* game returns with new twists and laughs— amazing new version! Use only your VOICE. Say *Ahhh* to control the ship. Shout *Pah* to shoot.

iREVIEW

Pah! 2.0 is like playing Asteroids with your voice! Prolonged phonation, air flow, and plosives are just a few of the skills that can be improved by playing *Pah! 2.0*. The user is not limited to *Ahhhh* and *Pah*; any prolonged sound and sudden shout will do, making this versatile app perfect for practicing articulation or phonological processes. This is a true example of "gamification" at its best.

Pah! 2.0 is available on iTunes under the category "iPhone Only."

AH UP *by ttgan.com*
www.ttgan.com
$0.99

FROM THE DEVELOPER

ATTENTION!!! You need to prepare a glass of water before playing this game Voice activated and iPhone accelerometer controlled! Extremely funny and addictive! Shout "Ahhh" and fly "Up"!

iREVIEW

Having the ability to see that your voice can make something happen—like making a rocket fly—gives children feedback from what they are doing. *Ah Up* is a bright, colorful game that keeps motivation high while teaching how to not only produce voice but also prolong phonation. That's not all; the child needs to also guide the rocket around obstacles by tilting the iPad left to right, therefore working on bilateral coordination.

Ingenious mom Pami Jean shares this creative use of Ah Up *on iTunes:* I have a daughter with a severe brain injury. This app is awesome to motivate her to practice and strengthen breath support with a visual display and a score to show how well she did. Thanks for your creativity.

 Ah Up is available on iTunes under the category "iPhone Only."

BLA | BLA | BLA

by Lorenzo Bravi

www.lorenzobravi.com

FREE

WAVES

by Aestesis LLC

www.aestesis.net:8080/waves

$0.99

FROM THE DEVELOPER

Bla Bla Bla is a sound-reactive application for iPhone and iPad.

FROM THE DEVELOPER

Waves generates real-time colorful and unique visuals based on sound.

iREVIEW

Witness cause and effect using your voice—see what your voice can produce with these two fun and beautiful cause-and-effect apps. This is a great way to motivate a student to vocalize. The more fun they have, the more they will practice turning their voice on and off. *Bla Bla Bla* gives us 16 expressive faces to choose from. Each will react to sound in a unique way that is both funny and engaging. *Waves* produces six different effects and unique visual patterns using your voice.

 Both *Bla Bla Bla* and *Waves* will react to any sound; for that reason, have a quiet environment when working on producing vocalizations only.

Chapter 6: Articulation

Articulation is the production of speech sounds. The American Speech-Language-Hearing Association defines Articulation Disorders as follows:

> Most children make some mistakes as they learn to say new words. A speech
> sound disorder occurs when mistakes continue past a certain age. Every sound
> has a different range of ages when the child should make the sound correctly. An
> articulation disorder involves problems making sounds. Sounds can be substituted, left off, added, or changed. These errors may make it hard for people to
> understand such children. Adults can also have speech sound disorders. Some
> adults continue to have problems from childhood, while others may develop
> speech problems after a stroke or head injury.

Articulation treatment may involve demonstrating how to produce the sound correctly, learning to recognize which sounds are correct and incorrect, and practicing sounds in different words.

In The Spotlight:

An Articulation Activities that Children Want to Practice

By Erick X. Raj, M.S., CCC-SLP

www.erikxraj.com

As a practicing speech-language pathologist who works primarily within the elementary school setting, a large percentage of my caseload consists of children who are working towards improving their articulation abilities. These are the youngsters who have difficulty pronouncing tricky sounds such as /r/, /s/, /th/, and more. Thankfully, school-based clinicians have a plethora of tips, tricks, and strategies that, when taught to students, can help to bring them one step closer towards crisp and clear talking. We do everything we can during our speech therapy sessions to increase their growth as verbal communicators, but the determined students who practice at home are the ones who usually meet and surpass their articulation goals and objects much faster than those who do not.

So how can we persuade children to actually WANT to practice at home?

Over the years, I have brainstormed with parents and caregivers in an attempt to discover what home activities their children enjoyed most. I thought that, by figuring out those activities, maybe I would encounter a wonderful opportunity for us to intertwine some articulation practice into those favorite home activities.

So what did I find out?

Time and time again, parents confessed to me that that their son or daughter simply could not get enough of the family iPad. Interacting with an iPad was the MOST enjoyable activity. In addition, my elementary-school-aged students clearly confirmed their love for this digital device, as they would always clap and smile at the slightest mention of my iPad in speech therapy. Thankfully, the iPad allows for many educational experiences to be had, both inside and outside of the classroom. So with that being said, I have made it a personal mission of mine to help educate adults in the home setting on the subject of using an iPad as a means for effective AND fun articulation practice outside of school.

Below, I will illustrate to you a pair of my favorite iPad home practice activities that have been described to me by parents and caregivers of students in my caseload during our brainstorming sessions. These ideas have all been successfully implemented and have truly helped to increase the students' willingness to practice their articulation goals at home after school. It is my hope that, by sharing these diverse scenarios with you, you might be able to incorporate some of these ideas into you and your child's after-school routine.

Home practice activity #1— a few minutes after dinner.

I created an app called *Multiple Choice Articulation*. In short, it's an app that is filled with hundreds of silly and thought-provoking audio questions and answers that are organized by articulation sound. For example, if a student was working on her /s/ sound, this app would present /s/ questions to her, such as:

- What kind of sandwich would you rather eat—a sandwich that fell on the floor or a sandwich that a fly landed on? Why?
- Where would you rather live—in a ham sandwich home or in a peanut butter and jelly sandwich home? Why?
- What kind of sandwich would you rather feed a dog—a bone sandwich or a cheese sandwich? Why?

Parents have reported that they have taken this app out after the meal has ended in order to introduce additional lively and fun family conversation at the table. I firmly believe that keeping your family together at the table for a bit longer, after the meal is complete, helps to build a communication culture that celebrates sharing verbally with one another and caring about communicating. So this app, which asks interesting multiple-choice questions, not only gives that student working on her /s/ sound an opportunity to properly pronounce it within sentences, but also encourages her to justify her decision or course of action, which helps to increase her overall ability to communicate effectively with other listeners at the table.

Home practice activity #2—while walking the dog.

Students and parents have both mentioned to me how much they enjoyed walking the family pet together after school. It always makes me so happy when I hear this, because I love any situations that provide my students the opportunity to get outside for some fresh air and exercise. When one of the parents of a student mentioned how she used my app called I Dare You Articulation with her son while they were walking their dog, I was ecstatic.

I Dare You Articulation is an app that allows, encourages, and celebrates getting up and moving around while practicing proper pronunciation. It has more than 600 child-friendly sound-specific dares that are perfect for students to do at home. The app has an audio presentation of the sentence, so the student can say the sentence and then do the dare.

- Working on initial /r/ sounds? Consider this sentence: I dare you to pretend like you're wearing red roller skates. Show off some really cool moves.
- Working on medial /l/ sounds? Consider this sentence: I dare you to pretend like you're a smiling shark about to attack a sailboat.
- Working on final /ch/ sounds? How about this sentence—I dare you to pretend like you're eating a rotten peach for lunch.
- Working on /s/ blends? Try this sentence: I dare you to pretend like you're a scary vampire with scary vampire teeth.

When we are walking our dogs, we are in movement. Movement is key; it gives us the perfect opportunity to think about our articulation in ways that we probably have never thought about before. I am an educator who believes in the power of using our arms and our legs during all learning instances, especially during speech therapy. Children, by nature, are active learners, and this is the reason I have heard so many success stories from parents who have used this app during home practice.

These ideas aren't just for those with articulation difficulties!

I suppose what I love most about these ideas is that I have been told by numerous moms and dads that these ideas have been a huge hit, because not only are the described apps fun for the child to practice articulation, but both apps also have been adopted happily by other siblings (those who aren't even enrolled in speech therapy). Because those siblings want to actively ask and answer the given multiple choice questions or participate in the child-friendly dares, they help the student working on articulation not to feel as if he or she is the "odd man out." Thus, these apps effortlessly craft a fantastic family-centered approach to home practice.

I hope that, with these ideas, you can see that not only are we, as adults, able to help our youngsters increase their articulation abilities, but we can also increase their imagination at the same time. Imagination helps children grow up to be adults who are creative thinkers. Adults who were imaginative children often become excellent problem-solvers and amazing innovators. Imagination starts in the home setting, and thanks to devices such as the iPad, growing a child's articulation and imagination has never been easier to do at home.

—Erik X. Raj, M.S., CCC-SLP

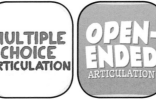

by Erik X. Raj
www.erikxraj.com/apps
$2.99

FROM THE DEVELOPER

The structure of this group of articulation apps is a departure from traditional articulation drill work and is effective for students from ages six and up. With these games, clients have a blast challenging their friends and classmates outside of the speech therapy room, further practicing their articulation skills and thereby facilitating the sometimes-difficult stage of carrying over newly acquired skills. By playing articulation games with the client, paraprofessionals in the classroom and/or parents at home can reinforce the client's skills while sharing a fun activity. Practicing communication skills in environments outside the speech therapy setting increases opportunities for generalization of communication skills. These articulation apps are intended to aid in the remediation of articulation impairments as well as language difficulties, because clients often need practice in more than one area of communication.

iREVIEW

Finally, articulation remediation is fun! Speech, language, and communication are meant to be enjoyable and something you want to do. This is a fantastic group of articulation apps that can be used to target language, auditory processing, memory, and much more! Thank you, Erik Raj, for breaking the "boring" mold. Your unique collection of articulation/language apps gives students an entertaining way to learn while providing the therapist with a powerful tool for speech therapy.

VAST AUTISM 1 – CORE *by SpeakinMotion*

www.proactivespeechtherapy.com (for further information on Autism 1-Core)

www.speakinmotion.com (for further information on Speakin-Motion)

$4.99

FROM THE DEVELOPER

VAST™-Autism 1-Core provides unprecedented support for spoken language, combining evidence-based best practices and technology to deliver remarkable results. *VASTTM-Autism 1-Core* is a groundbreaking tool that provides state-of-the-art therapy to students with autism and motor speech programming disorders such as apraxia.

VAST™-Autism 1-Core combines the highly effective concept of video modeling with written words and auditory cues to help individuals acquire relevant words, phrases, and sentences so that they can speak for themselves. For children and individuals with strong visual skills, this can be the key to developing speech.

Videos are organized into a hierarchy of five categories, beginning with syllables and ending with sentences. Each video gives a spoken target utterance that is preceded by the written word(s). Each word, phrase, and sentence is comprised of core/functional words and has meaning that can be generalized and practiced throughout the day. Providing the written word will prevent a student from labeling a picture of a frog jumping as "go," a person lying on a mat as "break time," or labeling a swing as "weee." The ability to recognize the written target word(s) will increase functional communication and enhance acquisition of spoken language. The progression of *VAST™-Autism 1-Core* Videos is as follows:

1. Syllable Repetition
2. Single Syllable Words
3. Multi-Syllabic Words
4. Phrases
5. Sentences

iREVIEW

I designed this app to work for individuals who have motor speech challenges and/or autism after seeing how extremely effective the *VAST Autism* technique is for those with adult-acquired apraxia and non-fluent aphasia. My colleagues and I have had amazing results with students on the spectrum as well as students with motor speech programming disorders.

Individuals who have challenges with eye contact usually have difficulty looking at a person's face and can miss the visual input that is so important when learning how to articulate. However, on an iPad, students will watch very intently as each word is pronounced by the model. Interestingly, after using *VAST Autism* for a few sessions, students begin to look more carefully at my face and mouth as I talk. Some even try to put their hands into my mouth as I am talking. At that point, I can combine *VAST Autism* with a more traditional apraxia therapy such as imitation and repetition. Because *VAST Autism* uses written words combined with the video production of those words, many students are now able to read target core words.

SUNNY ARTICULATION PHONOLOGY TEST KIT

by Smarty Ears

www.smarty-ears.com

$49.99

FROM THE DEVELOPER

The *Sunny Articulation Phonology Test* (*SAPT*) is able to provide a very detailed picture of a child's articulation skills immediately after the assessment. Standardized assessment provides a limited picture of a child's pho-

netic and phonemic inventory (Elbert & Gierut, 1986). The *SAPT* can be used to identify articulation error patterns in children as well as adults while supplementing data obtained from standardized assessments.

The *SAPT* is an individually administered clinical tool for screening, identification, diagnosis, and follow-up evaluation of articulation skills in English-speaking individuals. The *SAPT-R* has 42 targeted /r/ phonemes. Of these, 12 are r-blends, 10 are prevocalic /r/, two are "rl" words, and the remainder are the six vocalic /r/ in all positions of words (e.g., "airplane, stairs, and mare" complete the "air" vocalic /r/).

Bravo Smarty-Ears! *Sunny Articulation Phonology Test* makes the life of a speech pathologist a little bit easier and saves trees. The *SAPT* is easy, portable, and clear cut; it even analyzes data. This app can be used as a screening tool or full test. Smarty Ears provides anyone interested in this app with access to a video tutorial and downloadable manual. This is the future of testing, screening, data analysis, protocols, and clinical efficiency, recommended for busy speech-language pathologists who need an easy tool for testing or screening speech production.

ARTIKPIX – FULL *by Expressive Solutions LLC*
http://expressive-solutions.com/artikpix
$29.99

FROM THE DEVELOPER

ArtikPix-Full is an engaging articulation app with flash card and matching activities for children with speech sound delays. Among the many features in *ArtikPix-Full*, group scoring is available for collecting scores on flash cards of up to four children at a time. A group of students can collect data as they practice sounds in words and sentences.

Utilizing fun and modern graphics, *ArtikPix-Full* has all 24 decks with 40 cards each (113 cards in the r deck, 1,033 total cards) for the following sounds: th, w, y, h, f, v, ch, sh, k, g, s, z, l, r, s-blends, r-blends, l-blends, p, b, m, n, t, d, j. The decks can be combined, selected for sound group (e.g., beginning th, er), and then practiced in full-featured flash card and matching activities. Features include recorded audio, voice recording, and scoring (aka data collection).

iREVIEW

Students learn correct articulation, labeling, and self-monitoring skills. Therapists and teachers get the luxury of having data taken automatically. *ArtikPix-Full* has some cool new features like video recording and custom cards combined with the same great features it always had: sound and visual settings, two modes of learning (flash card and matching), audio recording, and data collection options. *ArtikPix-Full* is great app to utilize at home, school, and/or independent practice to assist with delayed speech.

 Take advantage of *ArtikPix*'s free version to see if this is the right app for you.

 **SPEECH TUTOR** *by Synapse Apps, LLC*
http://pocketslp.com
$9.99

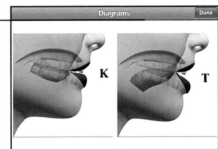

FROM THE DEVELOPER

A first of its kind in the field, *Speech Tutor* brings the latest in technology and animation to the world of speech. The animations inside Speech Tutor take the areas of the face that impede the view of tongue placement and positioning and make them transparent. Now one can literally see inside the mouth as the sounds are being made!

Speech Tutor offers a "Side View" and a "Front View" of each sound production, both of which can be viewed at three different speeds (slow, medium, fast). The movies can also be paused at any given point. With 132 animations in all, *Speech Tutor* is sure to offer a helpful view and speed for anyone in need.

iREVIEW

Get an inside look at articulation with *Speech Tutor*. This is a super tool for any therapist who has been trying to explain to her students where the tongue goes while making a target sound. *Speech Tutor* will show how individual sounds are made from front and side views at three different speeds. Detailed written explanations describe how sounds are made. Other features include articulation milestones and tips to improve speech production. Consider *Speech Tutor* for visual support of single-sound production.

POCKET PAIRS *by Synapse Apps, LLC*

http://pocketslp.com

$19.99

This application from *Pocket SLP* is a state-of-the-art Minimal Pairs application designed to target the twelve most common phonological processes. *Pocket SLP – Minimal Pairs* offers two different activities to help improve phonological processes.

The "Receptive Mode" requires students to identify which of the words in the pair contains their target sound(s), and an "Expressive Mode" cues students to say both words. Data tracking buttons are provided for therapists, parents, and teachers to enter whether the response was correct, incorrect, or approximate. Highly detailed diagrams provide side-by-side images that highlight correct/incorrect tongue positioning.

iREVIEW

Articulation apps are notorious for crunching your data, and *Pocket Pairs* is no different. To simplify my life even more, *Pocket Pairs* provide "homework text," which describes specifically what and how to practice at home—comment boxes for parents and therapists are provided, too! Many of our students on the spectrum have auditory processing challenges that can be improved with minimal pair practice through which they can both see and hear (picture, written word, recording or diagram) subtle differences in words.

SPEECHPROMPTS *by Handhold Adaptive, LLC*

www.handholdadaptive.com

$19.99

FROM THE DEVELOPER

SpeechPrompts™ provides speech therapy exercises to help those with autism practice rate, rhythm, stress, and loudness of speech (prosody). The U.S. Department of Education's IES SBIR program funds research and development of *SpeechPrompts*, a collaborative project with the Yale Child Study Center.

iREVIEW

With *SpeechPrompts*, users will receive both auditory and visual feedback on their speech production to self-monitor precision, rate, loudness, and stress. The user is given a choice of 50 teaching waveforms and the opportunity to add his or her own. If the goal is to teach self-monitoring of speech production, then take a look at *SpeechPrompts*.

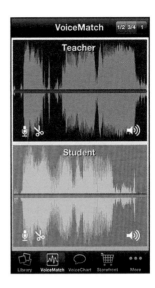

Chapter 7: The Power of Edutainment

By the age of three, most children are able to use language to communicate their wants and needs and make comments. Children with autism have difficulty with spoken language and struggle with communication throughout their lives. Encouragement to attempt verbalizations using innovative and highly motivating methods can make a significant positive impact on the eventual display of talent. And since children are often more willing to communicate about things that interest them, utilizing high-interest, and encouraging apps will ensure a tremendous level of motivation and accomplishment. A little encouragement goes a long way. There are *so many* apps that can fit into this category, and each individual will have their own group of favorites that work, no matter what.

Toca Boca apps are some of the best examples of combining fun, learning, and play. Björn Jeffery, CEO of Toca Boca, reveals his incredibly successful secret formula for building quite possibly the most engaging apps in the iTunes Store today.

In the Spotlight:

Björn Jeffery, CEO of Toca Boca

When Emil and I started Toca Boca in 2010, I must admit that we didn't pay specific attention to kids with special needs. Looking back now, I wonder if that isn't why our apps have been so well received by the community. Let me explain what I mean.

Our approach has always been to make digital toys as opposed to games. It came about by looking at kids and the different ways they play. There are many models you can use, but the one we chose divided play into five areas: active play, make-believe play, manipulative play, creative play, and learning play. The last area is constituted of books and games and is considered learning because it is linear—it has a beginning, middle, and end. You learn the right way to go through the process.

When we looked at the App Store, we found that most apps were in the learning category. It didn't really make sense, though, since kids don't prefer that way of playing more than the others. It started to dawn on us that maybe this was because app developers had looked at themselves as opposed to looking at kids. For instance, adults are more likely to read books and play games than play with dolls.

Turning this on its head, we looked at the other end of the spectrum instead. If we completely remove linearity, game mechanisms, and time constraints, what could we make then? In a way, this was the complete opposite of what everyone else was doing at the time. We were ungamifying instead of gamifying. Games are fine and fun, of course, but kids like other things just as much.

When doing this, the only way of knowing what works is to play with kids directly and to watch, learn, and play together. In that way, we know that our apps genuinely work, because if the kids don't like them, we either cancel the project or we keep going until they do. The process starts and ends with kids.

So how does this relate to kids with special needs? I think that sometimes products that are specifically designed with kids in mind overly focus on developing a certain skill or trait. And although the products probably do what they advertise, simply put, they might not be fun. An app that isn't fun isn't used. And no matter how well intended it might be, the app must be used for any kind of learning to take place. Since this is the starting point for everything that we do, we know that we get that part right. If it's not fun, it's wrong.

The second part is the way in which you can play. Since you can't win with our apps, you also can't lose. Since there are no high scores or timers, there is no frustration or failure. And since there are no rules, all kids decide for themselves how they want to play. There is no right, there is no wrong. It lets all kids – regardless of age, gender, and developmental level – play in any way that they want to. Thus, it treats all kids as equals.

—Björn Jeffery, CEO of Toca Boca

TOCA DOCTOR
$2.99

Let your kids be a doctor for a day! Examine a patient and solve fun puzzles and mini-games that take place in the human body.

TOCA HAIR SALON ME
$2.99

Toca Hair Salon Me lets you be the customer and the stylist! Curly, straight, or purple? Create a funky hairdo any way you like.

TOCA HOUSE
$2.99

Welcome to *Toca House*! Help the five friends to do fun chores around a cozy house. Let your kids do the dishes, ironing, sweeping or planting flowers in the garden.

TOCA KITCHEN
$2.99

Ever wanted to play with your food? Now you can! Pick any ingredient and prepare it in your own way! Slice, boil, fry, cook, microwave, or mix? And wait for your hungry friend's response.

by Toca Boca AB

FROM THE DEVELOPER

Toca Boca is a play studio that makes digital toys for kids. We think playing and having fun is the best way to learn about the world. Therefore, we make digital toys and games that help stimulate the imagination and you can play together with your kids. Best of all, we do it in a safe way without advertising or in-app purchases.

Anything Toca Boca! That's my response when asked, "What are the best apps to engage my child?" Play, laugh, giggle, and learn all at the same time with the apps from this developer. Who said learning had to be structured and boring with flash cards and workbooks? Not the folks at Toca Boca; they have developed some of the best, most intuitive, friendly apps available today. Without a word of instruction (verbal or written), children can amuse themselves while learning how to cook dinner, clean their room, comb their hair, build a town, and mend a boo-boo. Without a doubt, Toca Boca apps should be on every child's iPad.

 Still having reservations? Try one of their great free versions/apps.

SHAPE BUILDER - THE PRESCHOOL LEARNING PUZZLE GAME *by Darren Murtha Design*

http://touchscreenpreschoolgames.com/games/shape-builder-iphone-toddler-game

$0.99

FROM THE DEVELOPER

Shape Builder educates & entertains your little one with easy to move shapes that snap into place on top of silhouette puzzles. Each puzzle has five to 10 pieces, and after positioning all of the pieces, the real image

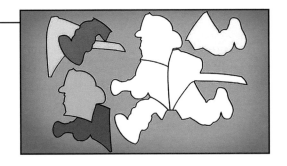

is revealed along with a professional voice recording of the word spoken by a licensed speech therapist that specializes in early child development. *Shape Builder* encourages cognitive thinking and fine motor skills and exposes young minds to new music instruments, animals, produce, objects, and the alphabet in a fun and engaging format with LOTS of sound effects!

iREVIEW

Shape Builder is my first go-to app to get a student's attention and engage them. No one can resist that click/tick when a piece fits into the puzzle and the joys of seeing the puzzle come to life after all the pieces are fit together. The puzzles are quick and easy to put together, making *Shape Builder* the perfect task reinforcement or tool for turn taking when sharing is the goal. *Shape Builder* has so many therapeutic and recreational uses that I recommend this app be on every iPad.

 Try the Lite version to see this amazingly simple app in action.

PROFESSIONAL
$9.99

Help your students develop pre-reading, early reading, and language skills. They'll giggle with delight all the while learning how letters correspond to sounds and how letters' sounds form words.

SIGHT WORDS
$9.99

With over 300 of the most common words in the English language, this app focuses on the core vocabulary your children will need throughout their lives.

ANIMALS
$1.99

More than just a game, it is a sophisticated learning tool that engages your child, encourages exploration, and helps them begin building a deep understanding of the relationships between letters and words.

VEHICLES
$1.99

Kids can play this game by themselves, but they also enjoy bringing their adults along, talking about the vehicles, saying the names of the letters, and watching them spin and make their vehicle noises.

FIRST WORDS *by Learning Touch LLC*
http://learningtouch.com
$9.99

Our goal is to create the highest quality games for toddlers, running on the iPhone and iPod touch. We are making games that are fun and smart, entertaining, and educational. We are making games that let kids explore and there are no wrong moves, but the right move will reveal, reward, and teach.

iREVIEW

What, a literacy app that children want to play? Yes! *First Words* apps have replaced skittles and chips as reinforces. Merely drag the letter to the corresponding square and spell a word with error-free learning. I can adjust the difficulty, speed, phonics, and word length as their skills improve. The "Professional" versions let me choose the target words and categories I want to work on. Older students who have been working on the ABCs for years can immediately begin matching letters and spelling real words with *First Word* apps. This group of apps is recommended for all students of every age and ability.

THE MONSTER AT THE END OF THIS BOOK – STARRING GROVER! *by Sesame Street*

www.sesamestreet.org

$4.99

FROM THE DEVELOPER

The Monster at the End of This Book enhances the classic Sesame Street book with a completely immersive experience that draws children right into the story. Join lovable, furry old Grover as he tries his very hardest to tie down pages and build brick walls—all to keep readers away from the monster at the end of this book. The all-time favorite you loved as a child comes alive for today's young readers with interactive play, plus touch-point animation.

iREVIEW

Just the sound of Grover saying, "Hello everybodeee!" gets my students sitting in the chair next to me excited to read a book. They can't wait to turn the page or knock down the brick wall, all the while learning how to read. When they get good at reading *The Monster at the End of This Book*, I hand them the hardcover edition, and they begin to read through the pages, just like Grover. Then I send the book home and let them read *The Monster at the End of This Book* to mom and dad, thus transferring skills learned on the iPad into the real world. Time for a library card!

 ## Success Story: Zeke

My students amaze me every day! Zeke is a beguiling young man who has significant auditory processing and expressive language challenges. He has worked his whole life to acquire a handful of verbalizations that are intelligible. He communicates via a combination of text-to-speech, picture exchange, and verbalizations. Zeke works extremely hard during therapy sessions, and for reinforcing, he loves the app, *The Monster at the End of This Book*, narrated by Grover. He will read it twice after every session.

For Zeke's birthday, I gave him a hard copy of *The Monster at the End of This Book*. I thought we might be able to read it together, and I could teach him how to hold a book and turn the pages. To my surprise, Zeke was extremely excited; he took the book, unprompted, went to the front of the classroom, and read it to his classmates, keeping the same tone and vocal inflections as Grover. We all sat in disbelief for a few seconds, just before giving him a standing ovation.

 **DINOSAURS EVERYWHERE! A JURASSIC EXPERIENCE IN ANY PARK!**
by Useless Creations Pty Ltd.
http://uselessiphonestuff.com/?app=dinosaurs-everywhere
FREE

FROM THE DEVELOPER

See dinosaurs in the *real world* for the first time ever! See them walking all around you in their REAL SIZE, just as they were when they ruled the Earth! Hold your iPhone, iPod, or iPad as if you were taking a photo, and

look around you. Keep your fingers away from the lens! *Dinosaurs Everywhere* uses amazing Augmented

Reality technology to place dinosaurs in the real world. You'll believe they're really there!

iREVIEW

We all have one or two kids who love dinosaurs. I have three on my caseload right now. *Dinosaurs Everywhere* is a totally open-ended app that allows me to work on many goals, such as shared attention, counting, "wh" questions, articulation, and history. Most of all, I have a super-motivated student in the chair next to me.

 Be aware, every now and then, the dinos eat each other.

Part II

Building Language

In the Spotlight:

Building Language with Apps

by Patti Hamaguchi, M.A., CCC-SLP (www.hamaguchiapps.com)

When we think of language, we tend to think of talking with people, certainly not computer software. And when we think of speech-language "therapy" or instruction, it was previously difficult to imagine how a tablet device could possibly be of any value. My, how things have changed!

When I first became a speech-language pathologist many, many years ago, my speech room was stocked with carefully organized picture cards, worksheets, games, and toys. As the years went on, I would carefully draw and create individualized games with a child's target verb ("ran") or devise simple activities to show sentence structure, using a card to show each part of the sentence. Although they were great activities, the amount of time it took to put them together for one thirty-minute session (let alone put them all back in the correct box when we finished!) was overwhelming. As caseloads grew and prep time all but disappeared, individualizing games and copying pictures for a single lesson became a huge challenge.

The appearance of the iPad and tablets several years ago opened up a whole new world for those of us whose lives revolve around the teaching of language. Has this technology replaced people? Certainly not. Toys and play? No way. But it has given us a very valuable tool that we can use to help teach a variety of concepts in a way that grabs a child's attention long enough to get the information "in there" so that we can integrate it into everyday language tasks. In particular, for children with autism, learning language in a visual way is a key component to their intervention. With one touch, we can access hundreds or even thousands of pictures, customize lessons, and provide repetitions of language tasks that are so vital to the learning process.

Another key feature of apps is the way we can use animation and video clips. Language is dynamic. Think about it. The girl is riding her bike. How does a static picture properly convey that action? Riding is something that is happening, but it can be hard to reproduce and show. With app technology, we can use video clips or animations to show just about anything.

Apps for teaching language are often produced by speech-language pathologists. For many of us developers in the special needs/speech field, we felt like the proverbial "kid in a candy store" when we realized that we might very well be able to create games and activities that would captivate the attention of so many of our children with ASD who learn just a little differently.

That said, the nature of language offers us the ability to take just about any app activity and turn it into a language-learning opportunity. So how do we do that? That's where we come in—the people. Think about it. Using apps is always best done as a joint-sharing activity, especially for our children with autism spectrum disorders who may be inclined to grab the iPad/tablet and play in isolation. A simple cupcake-decorating activity app can elicit unlimited language opportunities. *I'll put some pink frosting on this one. Do you think we should put some sprinkles on it? I like that!* Consider apps to be another way to engage, not DIS-engage!

—Patti Hamaguchi, M.A., CCC-SLP

www.hamaguchiapps.com

Hamaguchi & Associates Pediatric Speech-Language Pathologists Inc. & Hamaguchi Apps for Speech, Language & Auditory Development, Cupertino, CA

 ## Success Story: Joshua (by Patti Hamaguchi)

Consider four-year-old Joshua (name has been changed). His mother emailed us at Hamaguchi Apps to share a story about his triumph with one of our apps, *First Phrases HD*. Joshua had been using primarily single words but had not yet put them together to form a two-to-three word phrase. After playing the app for just one afternoon, he walked over to a door and said, "Close the door!" just as he had been shown in the app animation. That kind of transfer of language is why we make apps and why so many professionals and parents have incorporated them into their language-building activities.

But remember, apps merely give us the tools to do what we do best—talk, play, and learn together!

Chapter 8: Language Comprehension & Auditory Processing

Listening to something or someone and hearing them are two very different concepts. Just because we have heard a sound, word, or sentence doesn't mean it has registered in our brains. This is why teaching of listening and auditory processing skills are so acutely important to the development of speech and language.

FUN WITH DIRECTIONS HD

*by Hamaguchi Apps for Speech, Language &
Auditory Development*

http://hamaguchiapps.com

$15.99

FROM THE DEVELOPER

Fun with Directions is a ground-breaking app for the iPad, designed to provide a fun and engaging way to practice listening, following directions, colors, spatial concepts, auditory memory, and auditory processing. From the simplest of directions ("Touch the cat") to the more complex ("With your orange crayon, color the large one that is a furry pet and likes to chase mice") your child can grow and learn with this game over time. Colorful vivid art and animations against a white background combine to create a complete game experience without visual clutter. Sound effects and surprises keep the game engaging! This app is a great choice for a toddler/preschooler or any young child who would like to practice listening to or reading directions (concepts include give, touch, open, close, top, middle, bottom, push, color, and erase).

iREVIEW

It won't be long before your students are following even the most complex set of directions. For about the same price as a deck of flash cards, you can get an interactive therapy eTool that will accommodate up to 75 children, will never get destroyed, and will receive updates—and your students won't get bored! *Fun with Directions* gives the educator/therapist tons of options and collects your data in the background. Adjust difficulty level, interaction, prompts, and reinforces to fit your students' goals.

   To challenge my students' auditory comprehension further, I cover the face of the iPad while the direction is given, count to five, then uncover and let them follow the direction. Students love a challenge, and I get to target both auditory and memory skills.

 Check it out on YouTube! www.youtube.com/watch?v=EXCe1fETCnc or purchase the lite version for $0.99

PROCESSING POW WOW *by Synapse Apps, LLC*

http://pocketslp.com

$19.99

FROM THE DEVELOPER

Processing Pow Wow targets auditory processing and memory skills. It is appropriate for ages five and up. There are a total of six levels and a barrier game activity. Each level has up to 50 different stimuli that are presented in a randomized order. Wait time is embedded in the app, following the presentation of auditory information, in order to give the user time to process the information before using it. Data tracking capability is also included.

iREVIEW

Processing Pow Wow is a must-have tool for working or playing with children who have auditory processing challenges. There is a nice progression from easy to difficult and a piggy bank to keep children interested. The wait time accompanied by an on-screen countdown – "3-2-1!"—is the feature that sets this app apart. Wait time is designed to give the user processing time; however, wait time can also increase working memory.

QUESTIONIT *by Language Learning Apps, LLC*

http://languagelearningapps.com

$24.99

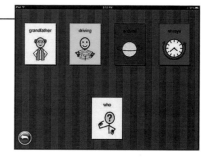

FROM THE DEVELOPER

QuestionIt is an educational app for children with autism or other significant language disorders that provides systematic instruction for answering "wh" questions. Activities include sorting words by the type of question they answer, answering questions about sentences, and answering questions about paragraphs. The app uses faded color cues and errorless learning techniques. The data manager records responses for each type of question at every level of each task. Data reports can be emailed from the app. The student is intermittently reinforced with a fireworks display for correct answers.

iREVIEW

Teaching "wh" questions is one of the most difficult goals an educator faces with students on the spectrum. Having engaging visual supports with levels that are color coded makes the process easier and more enjoyable.

 Try the lite version to see if *QuestionIt* is right for you.

SOUNDSWAPS *by Language Learning Apps, LLC*
http://languagelearningapps.com
$9.99

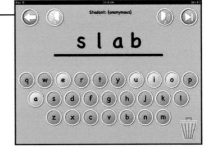

FROM THE DEVELOPER

Designed for students with dyslexia, the goal of *SoundSwaps* is to assist students to improve decoding and encoding skills through improved auditory conceptualization. (It's great practice for all students but was originally designed for students with dyslexia and auditory processing disorders.) Students will practice seeing and hearing words and learning where and when sounds are deleted, added, or moved to make new words.

Some students have difficulty developing awareness of individual sounds in words, of whether two sounds are the same or different, and of the order in which to put them to form a specific spoken (or written) word. These students have difficulty discriminating speech sounds in sequences and perceiving and comparing the different patterns in sequences within words; they often cannot judge the differences between sounds and may delete or add sounds and syllables from words. *SoundSwaps* provides visual support to auditory processing within words, providing great spelling practice for all kids.

SoundSwaps was obviously designed by a speech pathologist. Being able to hear subtle differences in words is such an important foundational skill. *SoundSwaps* uses visual processing strengths to boost auditory processing challenges, brilliant! Plus, *SoundSwaps* builds literacy by using a keyboard (consonants in blue and vowels in yellow) and focusing on word families/sounds. If your child or student has a basic knowledge of the ABCs but struggles with auditory processing challenges, this app will not only improve his or her spelling but also overall literacy skills.

AUDITORY PROCESSING STUDIO   AUDITORY WORKOUT

by Virtual Speech Center Inc.
www.virtualspeechcenter.com/Default.aspx

$29.99 $19.99

FROM THE DEVELOPER

Created by a certified speech-language pathologist, *Auditory Processing Studio* is for adults and children, ages seven and up, who exhibit Central Auditory Processing Disorder or other auditory processing disorders. This research-based app implements the bottom-top approach to the treatment of auditory processing disorders and focuses on improving auditory processing through auditory discrimination, auditory closure, and phonological awareness activities. Users can also introduce background noise to help children or adults practice their listening skills in a noisy environment. *Auditory Processing Studio* employs a bottom-up approach. To complement this app, speech pathologists may consider *Auditory Workout* which targets the top-down approach to auditory processing disorder.

The duo of auditory processing apps is packed with lessons that break down the skills and level of difficulty from easy to very challenging. I really like the fact that Virtual Speech Center apps are based on Central Auditory Processing research and hands-on experience. Use *Auditory Processing Studio* and *Auditory Workout* together for students who exhibit central auditory processing disorder.

AUDITORY FIGURE GROUND AFG *by Foundations Developmental House, LLC*
www.speech-ez.com
$24.99

FROM THE DEVELOPER

Welcome to the *Auditory Figure Ground AFG* app! This app aims to improve an individual's ability to accurately perceive speech in the presence of background competing noise. This skill is important in situations such as a noisy classroom, busy restaurant, etc. The inability to understand speech in the presence of background noise is one of the most common auditory complaints of students who have language and learning problems.

iREVIEW

Classrooms can be noisy places. If you have auditory processing challenges, you may not be able to recognize a voice from background noise. *Auditory Figure Ground AFG* can help you learn how to attend to a voice in various noisy settings. Learning to listen and attend is a very important foundational skill for success in school and life.

SOUND TOUCH

VIDEO TOUCH LITE

by SoundTouch

https://www.facebook.com/SoundTouchInteractive

$4.99

FROM THE DEVELOPER

The app opens right to the activity, without a main menu. It's broken into six categories, which are shown at the bottom of the screen as pictures—animals, wild animals, wild birds, vehicles, musical instruments, and household items. Each page has 12 items displayed in bright, cute cartoon images. Tap a picture, and a real-life photo of the item pops open, accompanied by the sound it makes. Tap the picture anywhere, and it disappears.

While playing around with the app, you'll discover something even cooler: each item has not one, but five real pictures and sounds! Bringing up something new every time you tap is a great way to keep kids' attention. The photos are great, as is the sound quality of the recordings. *Video Touch* has 40 beautiful video clips of animals, vehicles, and musical instruments.

iREVIEW

The photos and videos in *Sound Touch* & *Video Touch* are fantastic, as is the sound quality. It is super simple to navigate, and it relies only on taps. Both are great for auditory processing or sound imitation activities. To support generalization, each sound has four different photos or videos and four different sound bites. This app is highly recommended for auditory processing, auditory discrimination, labeling, describing, imitating, and just plain enjoyment.

Children can explore the app independently to improve auditory discrimination, vocabulary, and listening skills or use it as a guessing game: "What is this sound?" When students get good at listening, two or three animal sounds can be played consecutively to increase the difficulty.

Chapter 9: Language Development

"The limits of my language mean the limits of my world."

—*Ludwig Wittgenstein*

anguage comprehension is the ability to understand communication from others. Understanding spoken language requires a complex series of auditory processing to translate speech into meaning. In this chapter, you will find apps to support comprehension of the spoken word, following directions, critical thinking, and concept imagery. Practicing these skills will help our students understand and express their thoughts in an organized manner.

FIRST PHRASES HD
$15.99

There are 17 simple verbs such as drink, eat, wash, and 12 verb + preposition forms such as jump on, take off, or turn on. Each verb form is paired with various nouns to make a logical phrase. Perfect for the child who is learning how to put two or three words together or any child who is learning basic English phrases.

FUN WITH VERBS & SENTENCES HD
$15.99

Fun with Verbs & Sentences is the next step up for children who are learning to speak in sentences, understand past and present verb tense, and formulate basic syntax structures. Select the verbs from 39 choices or select the random setting, and choose the target syntax structures.

PICTURE THE SENTENCE HD
$9.99

Practice language and auditory processing tasks at the basic sentence level. This app offers three different levels of difficulty so the child can learn how to attend to important elements of a sentence and "picture it," attaching meaning to the words and eventually forming mental pictures without visual support.

by Hamaguchi Apps for Speech, Language, and Auditory Development
http://hamaguchiapps.com

FROM THE DEVELOPER

Wouldn't it be great if there were actual games that did what we needed them to do for both the iPad and iPhone? Animation clips instead of frozen picture cards? A way to record and play back children's language productions? A way to make learning language FUN? Most importantly, wouldn't it be great if this technology were affordable? With the quest of fulfilling these goals in mind, Hamaguchi Apps was born in 2011. Of course, now there is a wide range of great apps for speech in the App store, so we recognize that the consumer has a great many choices. We believe our apps stand out because we bring a very solid theoretical framework to the layout and design of our apps. We bring studio audio quality, professional artwork, creativity, innovation, and state-of-the-art technology to our apps to give you the very best quality we can. We hope you and your child enjoy them!

iREVIEW

Patti Hamaguchi, a speech-language pathologist, has created some of the best, most engaging language apps available today. Hamaguchi apps are flexible enough to use in a speech therapy session and at home as a fun family game. If you have a child or student who has emerging verbal skills, this is the group of apps that will support language development, grammar, and auditory processing competences. Each app has levels of difficulty to grow with your child, choice of subjects, data tracking for multiple learners, and many other customizable features to make a perfect fit for each student's needs for about the same price you would pay for flash cards or a workbook.

 Try the Lite versions for $0.99 and watch the demo versions provided on the developer website www.hamaguchiapps.com

LANGUAGEBUILDER($9.99)
Language Builder offers a rich and fun environment for improving the ability to create grammatically correct sentences.

RAINBOW SENTENCES ($7.99)

Rainbow Sentences is designed to help students improve their ability to construct grammatically correct sentences by using color-coded visual cues.

TENSEBUILDER ($9.99)

TenseBuilder is designed to help students learn how to identify and use correct tense forms by playing movie-quality animated videos to demonstrate past, present, and future tense.

PREPOSITIONBUILDER™ ($7.99)

PrepositionBuilder™ is designed to help elementary-aged children learn the correct use of prepositions and learn how prepositions can change the meaning of a sentence.

by Mobile Education Store LLC
http://mobile-educationstore.com

FROM THE DEVELOPER

We are dedicated to providing cost-effective educational tools for parents of elementary age children. Our products take advantage of the mobile visual and touch mediums that are now available to the masses. By engaging the visual, audio, and tactile senses, our products help children learn faster and retain what they learn with greater ease. Helping users hone the basics of sentence construction in *LanguageBuilder*™, learn how to build grammatically correct sentences in *Rainbow Sentences*™, and master the use of prepositions in *PrepositionBuilder*™—our award-winning apps allow teachers and speech pathologists to help students overcome language and social difficulties in a fun and engaging way.

iREVIEW

I call these fun, engaging, and easy-to-use apps the "Builder Apps." Students can practice grammar and learn to answer questions independently. Levels can be set to match abilities. Animations are likeable, and the multitude of reinforcements keeps students engaged. Each app tracks data! All Builder Apps are recommended for students who have emerging language and literacy skills.

Diana Zimmerman, MS, CCC-SLP, has the following to say about Sentence Builder: I love so much about this app! The dial format is engaging. I love the quick animations for correct answers. The animations are cute, funny, and quick! There is a man's voice that reads the sentence aloud after the correct answer and tells you to try again if you get it wrong. He speaks slowly and clearly and sounds real (not like a computerized voice). The graphics are simple but interesting. This can be used to address a variety of syntax errors in speech therapy. This would also be a nice way for kids to practice their syntax (grammar) at home. As a speech therapist, I can also target vocabulary by expanding on these sentences and pictures. Basic concepts can be targeted (example sentence: He is skiing around the, up the, in the, before the, or down the hill.). This app could be especially helpful for ESL students and SLI students.

"DreamsofTomorrow" agrees with Diana Zimmerman If you have a high-functioning child with autism who is leaving off the small words of sentences, this is a great app for him or her to get accustomed to putting those small words in the appropriate [places]. I liked it enough that I bought an iPad and the

iPad version. As a foster parent with seven autistic children in the home, I love the work put into programs like this. Keep up the good work!

YOU'RE THE STORYTELLER: THE SURPRISE (HOME EDITION) HD

by Hamaguchi Apps for Speech, Language & Auditory Development

http://hamaguchiapps.com

$5.99 – Home Version for recording one child

$9.99 – Pro Version for recording up to 30 users

FROM THE DEVELOPER

In this beautifully animated, wordless story, the child watches each scene and can then record and/or write their very own narration! In this delightful story, a boy brings home a stray dog and attempts to hide it from his mother. Using body language, facial expressions, and carefully selected sound effects, the story unfolds, and we find out why this story is called "The Surprise!"

There are eight chapters in this story. Each chapter's animation clips run for an average of 15 seconds, allowing the child to describe and retell the story in small increments. The user may replay the entire narrated story from beginning to end via the Table of Contents. You can also watch the original story with or without music accompaniment, email your story including the voice file, or print it out!

iREVIEW

It's Monday morning, I'm late, and I have three students waiting for my arrival. Instead of panicking, I pull out my iPad, open the You're the Storyteller app, and begin my session. *You're the Storyteller* is a seemingly simple open-ended app that lets the user target speech, language, and/or social goals of up to 30 students (Pro version). Better yet, You're the Storyteller provides prompts such as challenge words and questions for each chapter, encouraging students to stay on topic while recording and/or writing their rendition of the story.

As a speech-language pathologist, I can use *You're the Storyteller* to focus goals such as vocabulary, articulation, verbal sequencing, turn taking, perspective, labeling, describing, and interpreting body/facial expressions. Occupational therapists can also use You're the Storyteller to encourage keyboarding and problem-solving skills.

All of my students have been highly motivated by the record feature; however, they may need some encouragement to produce the written portion. Parents and caregivers love receiving their child's story via email or in the backpack at the end of the day. "The Surprise" is the first story developed for the You're the Storyteller app. I hope there are many more to follow!

TELL ABOUT THIS *by RSA Group, LLC*
www.tellaboutapp.com

xxx

FROM THE DEVELOPER

Tell About This is an easy platform to inspire and capture children's thoughts and stories! They will love to explore and respond to any of the 100 interesting photo prompts using their voice. Craft custom prompts and add profiles to personalize the experience! Simple save/share options.

iREVIEW

What a wonderfully simple, yet effective concept. Show a thought-provoking picture, ask a thoughtful question, record your answer, re-play, and share. You can also choose to use your own photos and prompts to capture curiosity and imagination.

 Try the free version and check out the demo on the developer's website – www.tellaboutapp.com

SENTENCE MAKER *by GrasshopperApps.com*

www.grasshopperapps.com

$0.99

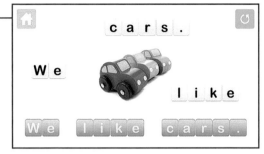

FROM THE DEVELOPER

Sentence Maker is an exciting interactive game that helps your children rapidly learn to make and complete their own sentences —all with just the touch of their finger. The interface is so easy to use that even a nine-month-old baby will delight in moving his or her first words around the page.

iREVIEW

Sentence Maker is one of the best deals in the App Store today! It comes with 30 pre-programmed categories that I can begin using immediately, or I can customize everything about this app—from the voice and fonts to the sounds and difficulty level. However, the best feature by far of *Sentence Maker* is the ability to add your own pictures, thus making learning personal, concrete, and motivating. Better yet, have your children take their own pictures of anything—friends, personal items, or family—then add two or five word phrases/sentence(s), and voilá—a customized, personal language tool perfectly customized for your child. This app is highly recommended for anyone with emerging language skills.

 Sentence Maker has a trial free version.

SPLINGO'S LANGUAGE UNIVERSE

by The Speech and Language Store LLP

www.speechandlanguagestore.com

$2.99

FROM THE DEVELOPER

While following Splingo the alien's spoken instructions, your children will practice their listening and language skills by interacting with the images and animations on the screen. As a reward, they will love helping Splingo build a spaceship, while completing the tasks, in order to get him home. His hilarious animated responses will capture your child's imagination. Splingo's instructions range from a very early level of language development (e.g., single-word recognition) to much more complex aspects of language (e.g., multi-step instructions).

iREVIEW

Students may think that they are playing a fun spaceship-building game, but they are actually focusing on language comprehension and auditory processing as well as labeling and describing. *Splingo* is extremely customizable and has thousands of word-sentence possibilities that are interactive and keep motivation high. *Splingo* uses the concept of gamification to keep children interested in an otherwise not-so-interesting subject.

LANGUAGE THERAPPY *by Tactus Therapy Solutions Ltd.*

http://tactustherapy.com/apps/language

$59.99

FROM THE DEVELOPER

Language TherAppy is a bundle of four great apps in one. Combining the receptive exercises of *Comprehension TherAppy* and *Reading TherAppy* with the expressive training of *Naming TherAppy* and *Writing TherAppy*, you get four of our best-selling language apps for aphasia and special needs in one convenient and cost-saving comprehensive app. All four apps use the same core functional vocabulary (nouns, verbs, and adjectives) and more than 700 clear pictures. Each app tracks data, sends professional e-mailed reports, and has built-in levels, cues, and options.

iREVIEW

Language TherAppy is an evidence-based language app that was originally meant for adult rehab, but it works very well for older students or students who are distracted easily. The images are real photos on a white background, and the audio is crisp and clear. There are two types of language apps—expressive (*Naming TherAppy* and *Writing TherAppy*) and receptive (*Comprehension TherAppy* and *Reading TherAppy*)—for aphasia, special needs, and language learners. All apps have the ability to add custom stimuli for training individualized vocabulary or foreign languages!

 For a free trial of the full suite of *Language TherAppy* apps, try it out with *Language TherAppy Lite*.

 ### LANGUAGE TRAINER *by Smarty Ears*
www.smarty-ears.com
$14.99

FROM THE DEVELOPER

Language Trainer was created specifically to help individuals improve their mastery of spoken language. Designed by a certified speech-language pathologist, *Language Trainer* is a perfect tool for those working on vocabulary, word finding, stuttering, and receptive or expressive language therapy. *Language Trainer* complements and facilitates the work of the busy speech-language pathologist or caregiver. *Language Trainer* includes four activities within one application. Activities include picture identification, picture naming, divergent naming, and sentence completion.

iREVIEW

Featuring four language tools in one app and incorporating a speech therapist's design insights, *Language Trainer*'s overall look and content seem to appeal especially to older students and young adults, yet this app can be used with any age group. The first activity is Picture Identification and, with nearly 300 high-quality images, it provides an opportunity to practice identifying commonly used items. The Picture Naming activity offers the option to practice labeling those items. The third activity, Divergent Naming, simply asks an individual to name items in a category such as "Name three things that have legs." Sentence completion is a close or "fill-in-the-blank" task: "The weatherman said it is going to _____ ."

 See the demo on the Smarty Ears website – www.smarty-ears.com

WHQUESTIONS *by Smarty Ears*
www.smarty-ears.com
$9.99

FROM THE DEVELOPER

WhQuestions is a multi-player game designed specifically to help kids answer and ask such questions as "what," "where," and "why." Children with language disorders often struggle to answer these questions in a meaningful way. In addition, many children with language disorders are unable to ask grammatically correct questions. Designed by a certified speech-language pathologist, *WhQuestions* features over 400 "Wh" opportunities to answer and ask real-world questions.

iREVIEW

WhQuestions offers settings that allow the educator or therapist to import students, choose settings for each student, and record/play back questions and answers through data collection. *WhQuestions* is a good fit for therapists working with multiple students on auditory processing, language, and social skills.

 See the demo video on the Smarty Ears website – www.smarty-ears.com

AUTISM LEARNING GAMES: CAMP DISCOVERY
by Center for Autism and Related Disorders
http://campdiscoveryforautism.com
FREE

FROM THE DEVELOPER

Camp Discovery creates fun learning opportunities for children with autism and offers learning games including objects, colors, shapes, community helpers, emotions, and more. New learning games are released regularly! *Camp Discovery* is an excellent therapeutic tool for children ages two and up.

iREVIEW

Evidence-based and influenced by the behavioral principles of prompting and reinforcement, *Camp Discovery* uses a flash card like format to teach language concepts such as emotions, actions, functions, and comparisons. Children are provided with many opportunities to repeat a target; however, they may not perform every repetition of a target word or concept with verbal instructions such as, "put the thing," "sort," and "which is _____."

 Camp Discovery "Colors" is free to try; however, an in-app purchase or purchase of the Pro version for $24.99 is required to unlock additional concepts.

Part III

Vocabulary and Concept Development

Learning vocabulary is important for any student, but it is doubly important for a student with autism. Individuals with autism find it difficult to express their feelings, thoughts, wants, and needs without having the specific words. An individual may be tired, ill, frightened, happy, or thirsty; however, without the vocabulary to express themselves, those feelings or desires may be expressed through behaviors.

Students with autism will learn more readily when material is presented in a simple, visual format. It is well known that, if pictures are presented repeatedly, the student will learn and retain the info. Add the motivation of using a cool iDevice, which an individual can freely explore, and you have successfully expanded his or her perception of the world. Remember the words of Aristophanes, "By words, the mind is winged."

Chapter 10: Vocabulary

A vocabulary is a set of words that an individual is familiar with and feels comfortable using while writing or speaking. Acquiring and expanding one's vocabulary is a life-long process and sometimes requires singular effort. Ultimately, the investment in vocabulary-building pays off, providing a richer, deeper, and broader understanding of the world around us while allowing us to make fine distinctions among concepts, from the concrete to the figurative.

Traditionally, educators taught vocabulary with flash cards, which showed one example of a target word, but these quickly became destroyed or thrown away. Today with eFlashcards, children learn not only how to label but also how to spell and read, without wasting paper or losing materials!

MARTHA SPEAKS DOG PARTY *by PBS KIDS*

http://pbskids.org/mobile

$9.99

FROM THE DEVELOPER

A U.S. Department of Education-funded study found that target vocabulary improved up to 31% for children ages three through seven who played this Parents' Choice-recommended app over a two-week period. *Martha Speaks Dog Party* includes four fun-filled games, starring Martha the Talking Dog from the popular PBS KIDS TV series, *Martha Speaks*™.

iREVIEW

Martha Speaks Dog Party is evidence-based! Students learn vocabulary by engaging in three games and a pop quiz. Each game is led by Martha the Talking Dog. Martha teaches vocabulary development through engaging games and activities. But that's not all; Martha also supports auditory processing, sequencing, creativity, and motor control. The audio and graphics are excellent. *Martha Speaks Dog Party* is enthusiastically recommended for individuals with vocabulary and auditory processing goals.

KIDS LEARNING - LITTLE SPELLER 3 LETTER WORDS *by GrasshopperApps.com*

www.grasshopperapps.com

$0.99

FROM THE DEVELOPER

Little Speller is an exciting interactive game that helps your child rapidly learn to read, write, and spell words—all with just the touch of a finger. The interface is so easy to use that even nine-month-old babies will delight in moving their first letters around the page.

I do not know one student who does not find *Little Speller* irresistible. Students who show limited interest in the traditional flash card type app will often spend an entire session with *Little Speller* apps. Labeling, spelling, reading, hand-eye coordination, motor control, and smiles are all incorporated in one app! Users can customize their settings for images, speech/sounds, letter order, case, speed, and length. The audio is great and images are crisp on a white background. My students and I have experienced such amazing results from *Little Speller* that I downloaded *Sight Words* by Little Speller and Preschool Games, too.

So much more than a flash card! Have your child or student take pictures of friends, classmates, clothing, family, or objects, then personalize Little Speller with those photos. Your child learns not only how to label the picture but also how to spell the item or person's name in the photograph. These are must-have apps for every iPad to supplement vocabulary, literacy, and concept development.

 Free versions are available!

BITSBOARD PRO - THE BEST EDUCATIONAL LEARNING GAMES AND FLASH CARDS IN 1 APP

by GrasshopperApps.com
http://bitsboard.com
$4.99

FROM THE DEVELOPER

- *Bitsboard* offers access to a catalog that includes tens of thousands of gorgeous flash cards and carefully curated lessons, covering hundreds of topics.
- *Bitsboard* is ideal for learning languages, mastering vocabulary, learning to read, learning to speak, becoming the next spelling champion, and so much more.

- *Bitsboard* is fully customizable to meet your specific learning needs.

iREVIEW

Bitsboard PRO is an amazing fully customizable vocabulary-language-literacy app that comes with hundreds of pre-loaded lessons, which you can modify with your own personal images. Each board or topic (animals, sight words, emotions, etc.) offers 19 learning games that take students from labeling a flash card to reading, spelling, and keyboarding along with Word Search, Sort It, Photo Hunt, BINGO, and much more to ensure their knowledge of a concept or word group. Bitsboard keeps track of every answer and makes it easy for you to see what words and boards you have mastered and which ones you need to study more. Bitsboard makes it easy and enjoyable for a student to learn new words and word groups while giving the educator the flexibility to tailor each lesson to meet goals and maintain interest.

 Try the free version and only purchase what you want through in-app purchases.

FIRST WORDS INTERNATIONAL HOME HD
by Hamaguchi Apps for Speech, Language & Auditory Development
http://hamaguchiapps.com
$5.99

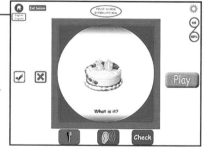

FROM THE DEVELOPER

Apple! Manzana! Pomme! How many ways can you say it? Just select the language of your choice and start playing! This beautifully illustrated and photographed multi-language app is perfect for the toddler or speech-delayed child who is learning how to label common nouns as well as for any child who wants to learn the names of basic objects in the following seven languages: English, Chinese, Spanish, French, Japanese, Hindi, and Russian.

The app has a core of 50 objects which are shown 10 or more ways so the child with special needs can more readily generalize their meaning. For example, "chair" is represented as a wooden chair, a blue plastic lawn chair, an overstuffed upholstered chair, a rolling desk chair, and even a plastic toy pink chair.

iREVIEW

First Words International comes in "Pro" and "Home" versions. The Pro version supports up to 30 children, while the Home version is for a single user. Both versions are excellent for building vocabulary and reinforcing each target word with multiple examples, trials, and activities. Hear-the-word tasks as well as find-and-say-the-word activities for each target will ensure that your child has learned a word's meaning. *First Words International* is entertaining enough to entice your child to play with it and powerful enough for use in therapy or classroom settings.

SEE.TOUCH.LEARN. *by Brain Parade*
www.brainparade.com
FREE

Pro Version ($24.99) has data tracking

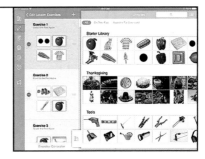

FROM THE DEVELOPER

A Picture Card Learning System replaces all of your physical flash cards. Create custom lessons using the starter library or purchase any of 50 individual libraries with over 4,400 pictures and 2,200 exercises developed by professionals. Subscribe to the Brain Parade Community for access to thousands more lessons shared by your peers around the globe. Save hundreds of dollars on flash card purchases and eliminate the need to carry around all those cards!

iREVIEW

See. Touch. Learn. is an interactive flash card app that lets users customize their learning experience and, if desired, record their own voice. Download See. Touch. Learn. as a free trial, then buy only what you want via in-app purchases. If you need more powerful features, get the Pro Version with the entire 4,400 images, 2,200 lessons, and 40 libraries.

Verbs

A verb is a word used to describe an action. Children with autism are concrete visual learners who tend to focus on one aspect of a picture or a flash card. Therefore, when teaching a verb like "jump" using a flash card, we do not necessarily know what aspect of the picture the child is focusing on. For example, the child may be attending to the girl's hair, not the fact that she is jumping, and wrongly label her hair as "jump." As educators, we need to be mindful of children's learning styles and challenges and provide the most appropriate approach to fit each individual. Dr. Temple Grandin recommends the following teaching approach for children on the autism spectrum: "[When children] learn words like 'up' or 'down,' the teacher should demonstrate them to the child."

The following apps are meant to support the teaching of verbs, using short video clips rather than static pictures, that draw attention to the action being performed, not an unknown aspect of the picture.

ACTIONS IN VIDEO – FULL *by Geraldine Moran*
www.actionsinvideo.com
$33.99

FROM THE DEVELOPER

Actions in Video is unique in that it combines a number of traditional therapy strategies to work on both the user's comprehension and production of key action words. These include visual strategies, video modeling, and color-coded systems, which support an array of language skill development, all in one easy-to-use app. The app does this by using videos of real people performing these actions. This app is also a great resource for schools and therapy clinics.

iREVIEW

Excellent, simply excellent! Videos that depict real people performing real actions in regular every-day environments are an obvious way to teach verbs and actions. *Actions in Video* targets 49 core action words that are color coded to visually support sentence structure. Other features include self-monitoring via audio recording, levels of difficulty, three representations of each action and an in-app tutorial.

Actions in Video builds verb knowledge in addition to literacy and language skills. This is a terrific new app that takes advantage of the great features the iPad has to offer.

 Try the free sample action pack, then buy only what you need via in-app purchases.

 **NOODLE WORDS HD - ACTION SET 1** *by NoodleWorks*
http://noodlewords.com/index.html
$2.99

FROM THE DEVELOPER

Not all children learn to read the same way. Exposure, repetition, and context all help build relationships to vocabulary and understanding. *Noodle Words* is a word toy designed to offer emerging readers a playful modality for language acquisition and word comprehension. Kids of all ages can explore at their own pace and develop a love of word play through direct interaction. It's even designed to draw in the most hesitant early reader.

iREVIEW

Through play activities, *Noodle Words* demonstrates word meanings for 18 action words with animated expressions and antics.

Check out this iTunes review from Teach Tots: When I first laid eyes on this, it didn't excite me. But when I actually watched how it worked, I was very impressed. The greatness of this app lies in its simplicity and its ability to do all the right things in a simple but effective manner. It's fun, educational, and entertaining—simply a very well-thought-out design. This is well worth every penny!" We are all waiting for the release of more interactive action word sets!

SPEECH WITH MILO: VERBS *by Doonan Speech Therapy*

www.speechwithmilo.com

$2.99

FROM THE DEVELOPER

Speech with Milo: Verbs is centered on an adorable and energetic mouse named Milo. Milo performs over 100 actions, such as "bounce," "count," and "play." This provides an engaging way to build up a child's action-word vocabulary. Flash cards are typically used for this type of exercise, but the animation that comes with Milo will keep any child focused and attentive. And most importantly, it is fun!

iREVIEW

Speech with Milo is simple and fun to use for both the young and the young at heart. Select target actions, or activate all actions from the settings. Touch Milo to see the target word while he performs its action, then hear a phrase to support the action word. That's it—simple, fun, and engaging.

Chapter 11: Concept Development

Once your child or student has a vocabulary of 50-100 words, it is time to introduce organization, or concepts. Individuals should begin noticing that words have patterns and relationships to one another and that there may be more than one meaning for a word and sometimes words don't mean exactly what they say (figurative language). I have attempted to organize this chapter from basic to complex concepts.

MINY MOE CAR *by Blinq*

http://blinq.se

$1.99

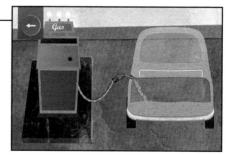

FROM THE DEVELOPER

Put your kids behind the wheel of their very own car. *Miny Moe* car-driver simulator lets them drive just like you do. They can steer, accelerate, brake, and use real dashboard functions like tuning the radio and using the windshield wipers, all with amusing yet realistic sounds. They also get to wash the car and perform simple maintenance tasks. There's even a racetrack they can zoom around!

iREVIEW

Learn how to drive and repair an automobile with *Miny Moe Car*. This close-to-real-life, delightful open-ended app will let the user target basic receptive and expressive language concepts like stop, go, faster, clean, dirty, broken, fixed, and turn on/off. *Miny Moe Car* is completely intuitive (no directions given) and a great example of how edutainment can teach functional life skills while building language concepts through play.

THE HUMAN BODY *by Tinybop Inc.*

http://tinybop.com

$2.99

BRAINS MY BODY *by Blinq*

www.blinq.se

$1.99

FROM THE DEVELOPER

Explore a working model of the body. Every part is animated and interactive: the heart beats, guts gurgle, lungs breathe, the skin feels, and eyes see.

FROM THE DEVELOPER

Kids can build working skeletons or identify and position major organs. They'll soon pick up key basics like food digestion, blood

Designed for kids to discover what we're made of and how our bodies work.

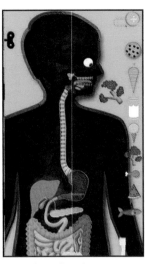

To enrich your learning experience, a free handbook full of facts and guides for interactions is available on our web site.

Download *The Human Body Handbook* here: http://tinybop.com/handbooks.

A seventh system, the urogenital system, is available through in-app purchase via the parents' section.

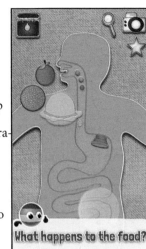

circulation, and even how the brain works! Fun facts pop up throughout operation of the app. There is even a memory game to challenge children's powers of recall. And, of course, they can build virtual models of their very own bodies and take, save, and mail snapshots of their creations! Boost your kids' awareness of how their body works. It's a sound start to a strong and healthy life!

iREVIEW

Both *The Human Body* and *Brains My Body* are highly interactive and effective in teaching bodily functions while building language skills. Children on the spectrum often face difficulty localizing pain, thus making it difficult for adults to provide help. Teaching your child the anatomy and physiology of the human body may be a good start in helping them to pinpoint their discomfort, therefore allowing an adult to properly comfort them or provide appropriate relief. *The Human Body* and *Brains My Body* complement and reinforce each other in teaching important life skills to your child. Using a combination of both will teach healthy eating, bodily systems, and fun facts while infusing any language concept goal desired.

MY PLAYHOME ($3.99)   **MY PLAYHOME STORES** ($1.99)

by PlayHome Software Ltd.
www.myplayhomeapp.com

FROM THE DEVELOPER

My PlayHome is the original and best doll house app. Massively interactive, your kids can explore and use everything in the house. The characters eat, sleep, shower, brush their teeth, and more. Want the room to be darker? Close the drapes! Fancy a change in music? Pop a different CD into the stereo! No other doll house app compares to *My PlayHome* in terms of interactivity, detail, ease of use, and just plain fun! "My PlayHome Stores" allo w your child to explore an open play world and play store without making a mess of your house! Take a walk down the street and look around four beautifully hand illustrated stores, all in stunning retina-display clarity.

IREVIEW

This app provides a digital play home and digital play store where everything is interactive and nothing ever gets broken or lost. Everything from shared attention, sequencing, and spatial relations to colors, quantities, pronouns, and action words can be taught while using *My PlayHome* and *My PlayHome Stores*.

 My PlayHome has a free trial version—try it with your child.

 **WORDTOOB: LANGUAGE LEARNING WITH VIDEO MODELING** *by John Halloran*
http://wordtoob.com
$5.99

Video Modeling made simple and fun! *WordToob* is designed to make learning words and new skills fun and engaging through pre-stored and customized videos. People of all ages and intellectual levels enjoy watching videos. With *WordToob*, they can now play an active role in learning while doing what they love. Customizing the app with personalized videos is easy, but the learning experience is powerful!

iREVIEW

This app is totally open ended and customizable to age, difficulty level, and personal interest. Target any language concept using the evidence-based practice of video modeling. Have fun while creating one or multiple short videos for each concept. Creating multiple visual supports for a concept will reinforce and support the generalization of knowledge. *WordToob* is easy to use and has countless functional applications for therapy, education, and communication; I recommend that it be installed on every iPad. *WordToob* also has a terrific speech recognition feature that lets the user activate cells saying the words, thus allowing the user to practice articulation and clear speech while learning crucial language concepts.

POCKET LEXI *by Synapse Apps, LLC*
http://pocketslp.com
$9.99

FROM THE DEVELOPER

Pocket Lexi is a unique eBook reader application designed specifically for educational and therapeutic purposes; however, the entertainment value of the books will serve those who have no educational deficiencies and will strengthen language skills. *Pocket*

Lexi comes with its own eBook store containing books prepared with features supported by the reader application. Reading functionality is provided with swiping gestures. The app also includes an index for moving to different pages, and it also allows for bookmarking. Each eBook contains interactive features targeted for specific language skills. The first eBook is embedded in the application and concentrates on figurative language, word replacements, and reading comprehension. Each interactive activity is scored in the background as the reader progresses. Quantitative reports are provided which can be viewed and analyzed within the application. Student record keeping is supported with all books.

iREVIEW

Pocket Lexi is "the cat's meow" for presenting figurative language and opposites visually while building language/literacy skills. If you know and love Amelia Bedelia, then you will love Jude Sky, as he encounters the strangest day in his life. Help him fix all of his strange encounters and watch them change before your eyes. Oh, don't forget to search for hidden hotspots on the pages. If you find them, an audio reinforcement confirms the find. Once you purchase *Pocket Lexi*, you will have access to the bookstore, where you can download eBooks that focus on a specific language concept expertly presented. Pro versions are available for educators to access comprehension, crunch data, and email reports.

CIRCLE TIME (GROUP TIME) *by Visual Edvantage*
http://visualedvantage.com
$2.99

FROM THE DEVELOPER

Circle Time, also called *Group Time*, refers to any time that a group of people are sitting together for an activity involving everyone. It is a special time to share finger-plays, perform chants and rhymes, sing songs, play rhythm instruments, read stories, and participate in movement games and relaxation activities. *Circle Time* provides a time for listening, developing attention span, promoting oral communication, and learning new concepts and skills. It is a time for auditory memory, sensory experiences, socialization, and a time for fun. Teachers have the power to make group time more effective and enjoyable for all involved. It also has roots in social group work and in solution-focused therapeutic approaches.

The *Circle Time* app is a tremendous visual support for, well, circle time. *Circle Time* is also an excellent tool to use with students in an individual session to reinforce the concepts that are discussed in daily circle time and build confidence to participate. Guide your students (one though ten) through subjects such as the calendar, weather, attendance, feelings, and finally to YouTube video for a circle song.

DESCRIBE IT (SLP) *by Synapse Apps, LLC*
http://pocketslp.com
$8.99

FROM THE DEVELOPER

Describe It is a game application designed by certified speech and language pathologists to make the process of learning to describe fun and easy. Use this tested method of improving describing skills utilized by speech and language therapists around the world and watch as the describing ability of your student improves effortlessly. Often children have difficulty describing because they do not have a proper "framework" to reference when trying to find words. *Describe It* provides children with such a framework by giving them audio clues in seven of the most important parameters for describing: taste, touch, function, sight, hearing, smell, and category. Describe It provides a "Study" section and two games to help generalize learning: "Pass It" and "Guess It."

iREVIEW

When asked to describe something, many people will use their sense of vision to describe it, such as color, size, and shape. However, we have five senses that we can use to describe a person, place, or thing. *Describe It* encourages students to use all of their senses as well as function and category. Once your student(s) has used the study feature of this app, they can choose from two games to play. The Pass It game is designed for two groups/teams of students, and the Guess It game can be played by one or more students.

GUESS 'EM *by GameWeaver*
http://guessem.gameweaver.com
FREE

FROM THE DEVELOPER

Guess 'em is a guessing game in which the user tries to find out which face your friend has selected by asking a series of questions, such as "Do they have big eyes?" and "Are they wearing purple?" Two people must download a version of the game to their iPhone/iPod/iPad touch to play.

iREVIEW

If you like to play "Guess Who?" then you will love *Guess 'em*. This game is meant to be played with two devices; however, it can be easily modified to use with one device. Simply have one student choose a picture, write it down (for a reminder), and have the second student ask a question to deduce who the first player selected. This game is very language rich and gets students interacting and asking questions. *Guess 'em* also targets problem-solving skills and categorization. *Guess 'em* comes with one free character pack to get you started, with additional packs sold for only $0.99 to keep them guessing. Choose from Insects, Jungle, Pets, Robots, and other character packs to keep interest high and costs low (buy only what you want). This app is highly recommended as a must-have for speech-language pathologists.

DESCRIBING WORDS *by The Conover Company*
www.conovercompany.com
$0.99

FROM THE DEVELOPER

Describing Words covers 80 simple adjectives and adverbs necessary to describe people, places, and things. This program can be used in conjunction with our nouns' and verbs' programs to help users create simple sentences. It includes such words as *ahead, behind, clean, closed, empty, hot, large, open, smooth,* and *tall*.

iREVIEW

Part of the Functional Skills System, *Describing Words* focuses on descriptors. The user is provided with a multi-modality mode of learning for each descriptor. A short video defines the word and uses it in a sentence along with the correct spelling and pronunciation. The Functional Skills System apps are a very well-thought-out and developed set of learning tools. *Describing Words* and all the Conover apps feature young adults in a more mature format.

FIRST GRADE AND SECOND GRADE ANTONYMS AND SYNONYMS *by De Abitalk Incorporated*

www.abitalk.com/

$3.99

FROM THE DEVELOPER

First Grade and Second Grade Antonyms and Synonyms is a fun educational game to help children to learn antonyms and synonyms and improve their vocabularies. The app includes four different activities; flash

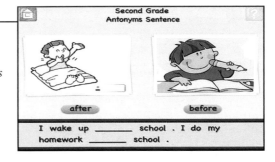

cards, matching game, memory game, and sentences. The app includes about 250 pairs of antonyms and synonyms. Teachers and parents can also create customized content worksheets from the app. You pick the word list and create matching worksheets or sentence worksheets.

iREVIEW

If you are targeting synonyms and antonyms, then this is the app for you. It offers great opportunities for practice with four activities, 250 pairs of antonyms and synonyms, and accompanying worksheets.

  There is a free version of this app for you to try out.

HOMOPHONES - ENGLISH LANGUAGE ART GRAMMAR APP *by Abitalk Incorporated*

www.abitalk.com

$2.99

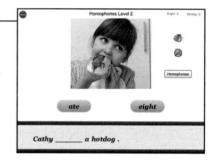

FROM THE DEVELOPER

Homophones are words that sound alike, even though they have different spellings and meanings. This app allows each student to work at his or her own level. It is ideal for self-paced learning or home schooling.

iREVIEW

Homophones and multiple meaning words are abstract, difficult-to-master language concepts. *Homophones – English Language Art Grammar App* will give the user practice in understanding that sometimes words have more than one meaning. *Homophones – English Language Art Grammar App* is in a quiz format with two levels of difficulty with 31 homophones. At each level, the child picks the correct homophone from two possibilities. Level one offers a picture and audio support, and in level two, the student reads the sentence independently for understanding.

 Try the free version before you buy.

Part IV

Pragmatics and Social Skills

According to the American Speech-Language-Hearing Association (ASHA), an individual may say words clearly and use long, complex sentences with correct grammar, but still have a communication problem if he or she has not mastered the rules of social language known as pragmatics. Pragmatic disorders often coexist with other disabilities and can lower social acceptance. Peers may avoid having conversations with an individual with a pragmatic disorder.

Individuals with pragmatic challenges may say inappropriate things in conversation, be disorganized, have poor personal hygiene, have difficulty reading or displaying body language, and demonstrate poor eye-contact. These impairments are not always obvious to an outsider. Often, individuals with poor pragmatic skills get labeled as "weird" or "geeky." As we think back on our lives, we can all remember those of our peers who just didn't fit in. It is my sincere hope that one or all of the following apps can help alleviate some of the stigma and heartache that go along with poor social pragmatic skills.

In the News:

Using the iPod to Teach Freedom and Independence

by Mike Schmitz

We live in an exciting time. Technology is making it easier and easier for people with disabilities to function inde¬pendently in their homes, workplaces, schools, and communities. Things that were once considered impossible are now possible with the aid of these innovations. Every day there are new tools available to assist in the transition toward independent living, but none have had as big an impact as the iPod touch. When most people think of an iPod, they think of a portable music player. It is actually also an amazingly, powerful assistive technology tool that allows the learner to take instruction out into the community. Using the iPod touch, one can:

- Plan the day

- Create a shopping list

- Follow directions

- Go to a restaurant

- Use public transportation

- Handle difficult social situations

- Perform work activities

- Much, much more!

- Go to school, work, shopping, etc.

The possibilities for the use of the iPod are endless. With the right content, you can use the video and audio abilities of the iPod touch to teach freedom and independence in new ways and, most importantly, give learners the motivation they need to learn.

Thinking in Pictures

The concept of thinking in pictures is nothing new. In fact, The Conover Company has been teaching skills of freedom and independence using this philosophy since 1982. At that time, research was very limited on the topic of computer-based software using pictures and audio to teach functional survival skills to youth and adults with significant disabilities, but The Conover Company was at the forefront of that research. We developed a software program called *Survival Words*. *Survival Words* teaches 60 functional survival skills in a picture format with full audio. The program was targeted to individuals with no reading skills.

We began a process of software development incorporating pictures with various levels of audio, including English and Spanish languages, to teach basic survival words concepts such as "stop," "go," and "caution," all critical terms needed for independence in our society. The software concept is simple – present the picture along with an audio track saying the targeted word; for example, "stop."

The next step showed the word or sign in context, as it is used in real life, with an audio track describing the situation.

Our design back then was just as valid as it is today. A picture—or better yet a video —is worth a thousand words. We called this the Instructional Phase. In the Instructional Review, we began to bring in distracters, both auditory and visual, to make sure the learner understood the concept. Finally, a Generalization Phase is implemented. This phase allowed the sign or the word to be generalized in everyday use in the community.

This basic design worked well for us back in the early days of software development, but it had its limitations. For example, each picture had to be hand drawn, one pixel at a time. We used the True Apple Tablet, using a stylus to draw pixilated lines, which required a lot of skill and patience. The audio was recorded and then converted to a poor-quality, robotic-sounding voice. It was crude but better than anything else at the time, and it provided an effective method to teach these important skills.

During the first year we released *Survival Words*, we sold six programs for the Apple II computer. So much for that or so we thought. Out of the six programs that were sold, two were used for graduate-level research on whether this new computer-based technology could improve upon the traditional, teacher-led format for teaching survival skills. The results were very promising and showed that yes, students with significant disabilities could and did learn survival skills from a software program if it was designed to accommodate their particular learning needs. More importantly, information learned through this computer format could be easily transferred to functionality within the community.

Today, all our programs use digital pictures, video, and human-quality audio. The video format takes the "thinking in pictures" concept to a whole new level, and with the advancements in digital video, we are able to move to more complex activities. This led to the development of our *How To Series*. The *How To Series* uses the same instructional format as our Signs and Words Series to teach basic activities requiring a variety of sequenced steps, such as crossing the street or brushing your teeth.

As we developed these programs, we continued to shoot thousands of short video clips that are now used in our iPod applications to reinforce these crucial independent living skills. *Our Functional Skills System* now offers more than 3,500 video clips. This series now includes 42 programs covering functional life and social skills, literacy, math, and work skills, with more programs under development.

Motivation to Learn

Many research studies have been conducted since our original *Survival Words* program was released over 25 years ago for the Apple II, and studies were done on the effects of computer-based instruction for individuals who have significant learning difficulties. Many theories have been presented regarding the effects of computer-based instruction for teaching functional life and social skills, literacy, work, and math skills. When you boil all of that research down, it points to one single element that is the most important factor in this large body of research. This factor is motivation. Learners with special needs are no different than any other learners in this regard. The desire to learn new skills is fueled by motivation, and this motivation makes learners with special needs appear to be no different from anyone else in our society. Correctly designed computer software provides individuals with an opportunity to learn like their peers.

I will never forget the beginning of the software revolution in education. In those days, classrooms seldom had computers for special needs' students, so it was necessary to carry a computer into the school and set it up in order to do a demonstration. When it came time for me to leave and carry the equipment back out, I never lacked for volunteers to assist me. It did not take long to realize that these students wanted to be seen in the hallways carrying that Apple II computer.

This early computer revolution has evolved to the iPod revolution of today. Motivation to learn is dramatically enhanced when these skills are reinforced on the iPod. Learners with special needs WANT to be seen carrying an iPod, because they desire to be like everyone else. The iPod itself is a "cool" tool for learning, and the best thing about the iPod is that it is small and portable and fits easily in your pocket.

In the last few months, we at The Conover Company have launched a movement which has taken the industry by storm. We have taken all 42 of our Functional Skills System software programs and created iPod applications for each program. (You can download our apps from the iTunes App Store. Simply search for "Conover" and you will find them.)

Getting Parents Involved

Perhaps one of the most exciting advantages of our iPod applications is that parents can now be involved in their son's or daughter's education process. Our apps are currently selling for 99¢ each—less than a cup of coffee. These very affordable applications provide a great way to review at home what's being taught at school, because parents can now access the same technology that we make available in the schools. The apps are easy to use with our unique user interface, provide direct access to any of the videos in the application, and can be used over and over again.

While the apps do not have all of the functionality of our *Functional Skills System* software, they do include all the videos from their software counterparts—approximately 80 video clips in each app. With the use of these applications, there is no longer a disconnect between what is being taught in school and what is being reinforced at home. The tools available to parents today will enable parents to help their sons or daughters learn these key life and social skills, literacy, math, and work skills essential to function more independently in their homes, workplaces, schools, and communities.

See for yourself how The Conover Company's iPod applications can make learning new skills fun while making a dramatic difference in the lives of your children.

Chapter 12: Video Modeling

Video modeling has proven to be a highly effective, evidence-based method used in teaching social skills and desired behaviors to individuals on the autism spectrum and those who require visual supports to not only learn, but also generalize and maintain skills as well.

Using mobile technology, video modeling has become easier than ever. Basic video modeling involves recording yourself or another performing a target behavior, skill, or task and then playing it back to the learner as a therapeutic technique to acquire that skill, behavior, or target task. Video modeling is a powerful learning tool for individuals on the spectrum of every age and ability. This chapter includes a list of apps that make using video modeling techniques a breeze. Each app has unique feature(s) that can be considered when determining the best fit for your needs.

FLUMMOXVISION *by Flummox Labs LLC*

http://flummoxandfriends.com

FREE

FROM THE DEVELOPER

FlummoxVision is an offbeat, live-action comedy that works to help kids navigate the social and emotional world. Join Professor Gideon T. Flummox and his friends as they put their minds to work on inventions to help them understand the most perplexing scientific mystery of all: other people! The show is designed with the help of experts in the field of social communication to engage and support kids (ages six to 12) who experience social and emotional struggles, cluding kids with attention or sensory challenges, kids with an autism diagnosis, and kids considered "bright but quirky." The laughs are designed to entertain kids and families of all kinds.

iREVIEW

FlummoxVision is super cool in every way! Settings give teachers, parents, and therapists the power to discuss social skills with built-in prompts and scene selection with additional curriculum support on the Flummox and Friends website.

An *iTunes review from kamazonmom really says it best:* I have so much appreciation for the creation of this app! For those not familiar with Flummox and Friends, all I can say is GET FAMILIAR! I have been working with children on the autism spectrum and their families for 25 years now, and this app is a great tool for me to be able to carry a fun lesson right into their homes. And the lesson is in an area so many of my clients struggle with – social skills! I love that there is a setting for discussions during the episode. It gives me the opportunity to pause the show and talk about the question that is being posed, which helps me to help the child really apply what they are watching to their own life and experiences. I also bought the in-app purchase, "the alternate method," and can't wait to share it with the parents of my clients. Many kudos to the creators for this much needed resource!"

 The pilot episode of *FlummoxVision* is free; additional episodes can be purchased through in-app purchases.

SOCIAL SKILLS SAMPLER HD

by The Conover Company

http://education.conovercompany.com

FREE

Cloud based and can be used on any device!

FROM THE DEVELOPER

This sampler includes 62 of the most common topics in the *Functional Social Skills System*. Included in the program are the topics of meeting/greeting people, taking responsibility, being polite and courteous, joining others in groups, apologizing/excusing oneself, following directions, and handling criticism. Please view our support site for help logging in to the application: www.conovercompany.com/mobile/apps.

iREVIEW

Finally, I can take social skills into the community where they belong and practice in real time and in natural situations. Video modeling has proven to be a fast, effective training method for teaching tasks to individuals with autism and those who require visual supports for success. Students on the spectrum are often unable to absorb information or maintain attention through a one-on-one or classroom demonstration. *Social Skills Sampler* provides individuals on the spectrum the visual support they need to practice a skill until it is mastered. And now it is easy to practice at home, school, and with parents and educators to encourage generalization and success.

MODEL ME GOING PLACES 2 *by Model Me Kids, LLC*

www.modelmekids.com

FREE

FROM THE DEVELOPER

Model Me Going Places™ is a great visual teaching tool for helping your child learn to navigate challenging locations in the community. Each location contains a photo slide show of children modeling appropriate behavior.

Locations include:

- Doctor
- Playground
- Hairdresser
- Mall
- Restaurant
- Grocery Store

iREVIEW

This app is so important to all students on the spectrum. *Model Me Going Places* features six functional social stories. The stories are read in book style with music in the background. My students watch these stories over and over again. Students with a limited ability to talk can read along with *Model Me Going Places*. They eventually begin using the language in their daily lives. The narration could be more articulate. Some of the words are difficult to understand without the graphics to support meaning. However, I liked the app so much, I bought the DVD collection. Sometimes the best things in life are free!

 ## Success Story: Alex

Alex is a handsome, 12-year-old boy with autism. His verbal language consists of echolalia, ritualistic speech, and unintelligible lines from movies and TV. Alex can read at the kindergarten level. He memorizes certain rhythmic books and may repeat lines at inappropriate times. Alex likes social attention; however, he does not know how to get it in a positive manner. Alex instantly took the iPod touch, like a fish to water.

His first app was *Model Me Going Places* by Model Me Kids, LLC. He would read all the social stories and look for more. In a few weeks, we began hearing phrases from the social stories make their way into his language. After using the social stories he began to play *First Words Deluxe*. This app facilitates spelling and vocabulary development. Now Alex can spell and label all of the animals on this app. He will occasionally draw on *Doodle Buddy* and is fascinated by iHourglass. He will now complete his classroom goals and earn tokens for time on the iPad. Just today, he began sharing his time with a friend and turn-taking. *Predictable* is next followed by *First Phrases*! Mom and Dad are going to buy Alex his own iPad soon. Great work, Alex!

VIDEO SCHEDULER *by MDR*

www.look2learn.com

$12.99

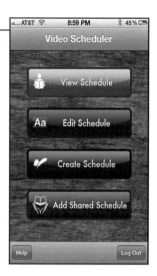

FROM THE DEVELOPER

Scheduler offers a variety of features in an easy-to-use interface allowing maximum customization. These features include various orientation locks, which prevent students from engaging in stimulatory behaviors with the video. Users can also select from three video and picture sizes. There's also a pass code function, which can be applied to prevent users from skipping around to preferred aspects of their schedule. After creating, share your schedules/modeling for free with other users.

iREVIEW

This app uses not just pictures, but—excellent! Use *Video Scheduler* to create just about any visual support needed to promote independence and learning. A combination of pictures and/or videos can be combined with text to create task analysis, schedules, and steps to an activity or sequence a daily routine. The addition of videos and video modeling to any visual support defines the activity or task, making it easier to follow-through. *Video Scheduler* is highly customizable and therefore can be used with any age or ability.

THERAD FOR AUTISM *by Marz Consulting Inc.*

www.behaviortrackerpro.com/products/
therad/therad-for-apple.aspx

$14.99

FROM THE DEVELOPER

TherAd for Autism allows a student to watch "motivating" media (movies) that are occasionally paused by *TherAd* at an interval that the parent or teacher sets. A short video self-modeling clip is then presented to the student, who watches the short clip of themselves engaging in some behavior that the parent or teacher wishes to encourage. After the video self-modeling clip finishes, the student is automatically reinforced by being returned to the motivating content.

iREVIEW

This app is simply ingenious, embedding a lesson within a favorite movie to ensure that the lesson will be viewed multiple times. It's like watching your favorite show with commercials about yourself. Lessons can be just about anything, from manners to spelling your child's name. And like the lines of the movie will be memorized, so will the messages that have been cleverly hidden within a favorite movie. *TherAd for Autism* can be customized for multiple students, using favorite movies and individual goals with data collection and export. The parent or educator sets the time and duration of leisure versus instructional content to match the attention span of each the student. This app enables us to take advantage of every minute possible to teach our children important life skills.

AURASMA *by Aurasma*
www.aurasma.com/#/whats-your-aura
FREE

FROM THE DEVELOPER

Aurasma—a new way to see and interact with the world. *Aurasma* is an augmented reality app that's changing the way millions of people see and interact with the world. Bring tagged images, objects and even physical locations to life with interactive digital content, such as video, animations, and 3D scenes we call auras.

iREVIEW

Aurasma was originally intended to serve as a marketing/social media tool, but it can provide unique, highly personalized visual support for individuals on the spectrum. Once you get past the learning curve, you will love the distinctive "auras" that can be generated with *Aurasma*. Here is how it works: A user creates a short video of a task such as tying a shoe or using the microwave. Next, the user captures a trigger image (make sure it relates to the video), like a shoe or microwave dial. He or she then imports the video and image to *Aurasma* when prompted. Here is the cool part: when the user locates the trigger image on the *Aurasma* screen, the video will begin to play. Using the microwave example, when the user locates the microwave dial, using the *Aurasma* search screen, the video of how to use the microwave will play. Theoretically, you could make how-to "auras" of equipment, chores, tasks, or even fun items in your home and have your child find the trigger image to see the video. It's like a scavenger hunt on the iPad!

 There is a learning curve and you probably won't need or want the pre-stored "auras," or to share yours; however, the option is available.

 ### iMOVIE *by Apple*
www.apple.com/ios/imovie
$4.99

FROM THE DEVELOPER

iMovie puts everything you need to tell your story at your fingertips, with a beautifully streamlined interface and Multi-Touch gestures that let you enjoy your videos like never before. Browse your video library, quickly share favorite moments, and create beautiful HD movies and Hollywood-style trailers. And with iCloud, you can enjoy them in iMovie Theater on all of your devices.

iREVIEW

Let your students create their own movies and visual supports with *iMovie*. It is quick and easy, and has great-looking end results. Choose a theme, and then add music, enhancements, and a trailer for a more professional looking video that your student is proud to share with friends, with family members or on social media. *iMovie* is totally open-ended to focus on any goal, task, or special interest.

Chapter 13: Social Skills Group Activities

Social groups are intended to build social interaction techniques to provide individuals with an array of skills from engaging in basic conversations, sharing, practicing non-verbal language and eye-contact, and nurturing complex and subtle skills like those applied in relationships and dating.

SOCIALLY SPEAKING™
by Socially Speaking LLC
http://sociallyspeakingllc.com/
my-socially-speaking-app.html
$9.99

FROM THE DEVELOPER

This app is an early detection screening/lesson plan template for young children at risk for behavioral/social issues (autism, special needs, immaturity, sensory processing deficits, and learning differences).

iREVIEW

Socially Speaking is an invaluable tool for assessing social skills and identifying goal areas. The entire evaluation is quick and easy, and the entire evaluation as-well-as recommendations can be exported to team members. A checklist provides ages for skill mastery when determining early intervention and goals. This app can be used as a screener for both regular education and special education students! While it is geared toward younger children, it can be used to fill in the blanks when evaluating older ones, especially those with autism!

 Take a look at the demo video available on the developer's website.

BETWEEN THE LINES LEVEL 1, 2 & ADVANCED HD *by Hamaguchi*
Apps for Speech, Language & Auditory Development
www.hamaguchiapps.com
$15.99 each

FROM THE DEVELOPER

Hamaguchi Apps for Speech, Language & Auditory Development presents this groundbreaking app for the iPad, designed for older elementary students and older who would benefit from practice of interpreting vocal intonation, facial expressions, perspective-taking, body language, and idiomatic or slang expressions. Using real photographs, voices, and short mini-video clips of a variety of social situations and expressions, this app provides a dynamic way to help learn and practice interpreting the messages that are "between the lines" and simply can't be replicated with worksheets and static flash cards. Scenes for the body language activity include a shopping mall, kitchen, restaurant, park, bedroom, school, gym, and a birthday party. THIS IS NOT A SOCIAL SKILLS MODELING APP. Some people say and do things that are rude, such as interrupt a conversation, say something that is insensitive, and lie. That is why we suggest adult coaching to supervise and provide input regarding situational language use.

iREVIEW

Levels one and two are for elementary-aged to adolescents; advanced is for adolescents to adults. Each *Between the Lines* app gives you practice with three social pragmatic activities: Listening & Facial Expression, Body Language & Perspective Taking, and Idioms & Slang. *Between the Lines i*s an essential app on the iPad of anyone working with or living with a student who has challenges with social pragmatic skills. Educators & therapists can customize lessons and track data for up to 75 students for about the same price as a workbook.

 See for yourself how great *Between the Lines* is. Try the Lite version for $0.99 and check our demo on YouTube: www.youtube.com/watch?v=rRy4QF1E1Y8.

 **CONVERSATIONBUILDERDELUXE** *by Mobile Education Store LLC*
http://mobile-educationstore.com
$19.99

ConversationBuilderDeluxe™ is designed to help elementary-aged children learn how to have multi-exchange conversations with their peers in a variety of social settings. The content for *ConversationBuilderDeluxe*™ is identical to that of the IAP's of the award-winning *ConversationBuilder*™, but is available in a stand-alone app. The auditory pattern of conversation is presented in a visual format to help students recognize and master the flow of conversation. Students will learn when it is appropriate to introduce themselves, ask questions, make observations and change the subject of the conversation.

iREVIEW

ConversationBuilder prepares your child to interact appropriately with peers and develop relationships through fun and engaging practice. Use *ConversationBuilder* individually or with a group to build turn-taking, initiation, and responding skills. My students stretched their imaginations and took *ConversationBuilder* one step further by pretending to have conversations as their grandparents, pirates, or toddlers. They even used corresponding voices and mannerisms and then archived the conversation and emailed them to their parents.

 Take a look at the short tutorial to get a better idea of how *ConversationBuilder* works. http://mobile-educationstore.com/video-tutorials/conversationbuilder-teen-video-tutorial

CONVERSATION COACH *by Silver Lining Fingerpaint, Inc.*
www.silverliningmm.com
$29.99

FROM THE DEVELOPER

When playing the *Conversation Coach*, two players sit facing each other with the iPad between them. The first player chooses something to say, then passes the ball to the other side. Choices for player two will appear oriented such that player two can read them. For students who are not ready for back-

and-forth conversations or for individuals who need to use the *Conversation Coach* to make statements, there is a one-way mode available. Two-way conversations can also be practiced in a "play-against-the-computer" mode.

iREVIEW

"Get the ball rolling!" *Conversation Coach* comes with more than 1,400 images and 150 premade conversations, or you can add your own. *Conversation Coach* will prompt the student(s) through interactions with another person by providing picture and/or graphic support to keep the conversation going. *Conversation Coach* is a great choice if your student is ready to learn the intricacies of back-and-forth communication.

 Conversation Coach has a Lite version available for $2.99.

SOCIAL SKILLS *by MDR*
www.look2learn.com
$3.99

"My turn." The girl raises her hand.

FROM THE DEVELOPER

Social Skills (S2L) offers parents and educators the ability to practice interacting with six social narratives, broken into two levels, providing a possible total of 12 social narratives, designed to help individuals improve their social ability. With *Social Skills (S2L),* the stories contain targeted instruction in the following core areas: joint attention, non-verbal communication, greetings, structured game play, turn-taking, classroom rules, and imitation.

iREVIEW

Given the ability to customize over 100 photos with audio and text, *Social Skills* can target individualized social skills. *Social Skills* come with six stories that are divided into basic and advanced levels, thus offering educators, parents, and caregivers the ability to pinpoint and build upon acquired skills. In addition, users can customize pictures and audio for even more flexibility. This app is recommended as a multimodality tool to enhance social skills in the school environment and beyond.

CHOW CHAT *by Shoe The Goose*
www.shoethegoose.com
FREE

FROM THE DEVELOPER

Chow Chat is an engaging, educational app that brings the family closer while encouraging critical thinking, language development, and the sharing of diverse ideas. *Chow Chat* provides a year's worth of thought-provoking discussion cards. Each card starts with an interesting fact, quote, or proverb that helps stimulate the thought process. The related questions that follow (and most cards actually have more than one question) encourages children and adults to share ideas and opinions, not just by answering the questions, but also by responding to the engaging nature of the facts, quotes, and proverbs.

iREVIEW

What a great way to spark imagination while learning something about your friends and family! *Chow Chat* provides thought-provoking facts, quotes, and proverbs followed by related questions to encourage individuals to share thoughts, ideas, and opinions. I use *Chow Chat* for social groups to encourage topic maintenance, conversations, and friendships. *Chow Chat* is excellent practice for anyone who has difficulty initiating and maintaining social interactions. Users have the ability to edit pre-existing information or add their own facts, thoughts, and proverbs. Rating and grouping settings help keep all facts organized for easy access. All material is rated "E" for Everyone.

QUIZZLER DATING *by Perkel Communications*
www.pcommapps.com
$0.99 (iPhone Only)

FROM THE DEVELOPER

Quizzler Dating is the question game that breaks the ice by acting as an immediate conversation starter. Thought-provoking, funny, yet simple questions stimulate insightful answers that help you learn about someone quickly and figure out if you're a good match. You'll have fun and learn a lot about each other answering questions like:

- Would you rather go to the ballet or a ballgame?
- Describe your ideal vacation.
- Most impressive hidden talent?

iREVIEW

Quizzler Dating will help break the ice on a first date, start a conversation, or just get acquainted with another human. With *Quizzler Dating*, you can customize your own questions, create a "favorites" play list, or choose to answer all of the questions randomly. This app is recommended for getting to know someone. It is rated "E" for Everyone.

QUIZZLER FAMILY *by Perkel Communications*
www.pcommapps.com
$0.99

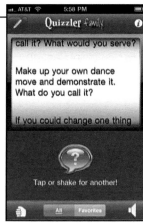

FROM THE DEVELOPER

Quizzler Family is the fun question game that turns "down time" into "quality time" as everyone answers fun, insightful, and silly questions. No matter where or when you play, *Quizzler Family* is guaranteed to amuse, and you'll get to know your kids in ways you might not have ordinarily. Questions range from silly to thought-provoking.

iREVIEW

Start a conversation anytime, anywhere, or just get to know someone better with the help of *Quizzler Family*. Social skills groups are a breeze with this app, and educators do not have to worry about inappropriate questions. *Quizzler Family* questions are also great story starters for written assignments..

YOU MUST CHOOSE! *by Indigo Penguin Limited*
Website currently unavailable
FREE (iPhone Only)

FROM THE DEVELOPER

You MUST CHOOSE! is like the board game, *Would You Rather?*, in the form of an app. It is rated "E" for Everyone.

iREVIEW

The questions in *You MUST CHOOSE!* are simple, yet they make you think about your answer. Students can answer the questions for themselves or predict what another might choose and why. Here are some examples of the thought-provoking questions you may get asked. You Must Choose:

- Be a superhero? or Be a supervillain?
- Eat a hairy pizza? Or Eat a saliva sandwich?
- One wish granted today? Or five wishes granted in three years' time?

I use the *You MUST CHOOSE!* in social pragmatic groups to encourage the development of peer interaction, topic maintenance, and turn-taking skills. Because it is a motivating game to play, it generates good participation and cooperation. I could do without the spinning choice wheel and advertisements.

WAY NO WAY™: AMAZING FACTS
by Spinapse, Inc.
http://spinapse.com/details.html?id=1015
$0.99

FROM THE DEVELOPER

Way No Way is a new trivia game with a twist, a spin, and a truckload of facts. We worked hard to make sure that the trivia is 100% true and the game play will stimulate the mind.

Way No Way is the perfect app for a social group. Students take turns, maintain topics, and learn interesting facts at the same time. Up to five single players can be entered into profiles, or the game can be played in teams. The first player spins to determine points. Then he is asked a quirky trivia question that he answers by touching either the "Way" or "No Way" button. Instantly the game provides feedback and additional information about the question. *Way No Way* also provides users with a scoring system that lets them compare scores locally or worldwide. Great game for .99 cents!

MR. PEABODY & SHERMAN *by Ludia*
www.ludia.com/en
FREE

FROM THE DEVELOPER

Mr. Peabody & Sherman is a fun and fast-paced trivia game hosted by that loveable genius, Mr. Peabody. The game also features Sherman and his friend, Penny, who will help you answer questions along your journey.

iREVIEW

Mr. Peabody & Sherman is a lighthearted trivia game that can be used to develop social groups, turn-taking, and topic maintenance skills. *Mr. Peabody & Sherman* features thousands of light-hearted trivia questions, historical events, space explorations, movies, famous people, and virtual rewards. The app is fun and challenging for all ages: Wrong answers are slowly eliminated and optional power-ups keep gameplay accessible for all knowledge levels. Users can learn and play at the same time.

ESTEEM BUILDER *by Justin Okun*
http://okunariumlabs.com
FREE

FROM THE DEVELOPER

Feeling down or defeated? Feel that way no more. Thanks to modern technology, you can receive words of encouragement anytime, anywhere. With the press of a button, you will hear an uplifting message intended to build your esteem and confidence. All phrases are narrated by a professional voice talent to be uplifting, yet lighthearted and humorous.

iREVIEW

Esteem Builder is here to save the day for those of us who occasionally suffer from low self-esteem. One user called this app "cheesy." I would have to agree; however, many individuals with disabilities suffer from low self-esteem. These messages put a smile on many faces and encourage a better attitude. I like it. *Esteem Builder* is like a "Big Mac" for feeding self-esteem.

 It will cost $0.99 to remove the ads and acquire over 100 new phrases.

Chapter 14: Eye Contact and Body Language

Body language is the second form of communication that humans use to express themselves. An individual with autism has difficulty deciphering what a person is saying with facial expressions or body language. Most people with autism also have a hard time making eye contact. They appear to be in a world that is centered in themselves and the nuances of a gesture or facial expression is lost. Visual supports and practice, practice, practice can help individuals navigate the confusing world of facial expressions and body language.

EYE CONTACT-TOYBOX   **LOOK IN MY EYES—RESTAURANT**

by FizzBrain

www.fizzbrain.com

$2.99 each

FROM THE DEVELOPER

Eye contact is a social skill that some children find challenging. This game helps these kids practice the skill while earning fun rewards. The game is similar to those in our *Look in My Eyes* series, but the rewards are easier to obtain and more immediate. We developed this easy reward in response to the parent feedback on our previous games. Some parents who loved the eye contact practice in our *Look in My Eyes* series expressed the desire for a reward that was simpler. The game rewards players for quickly focusing on a person's eyes. Through repeated practice, we attempt to develop a habit that families can transfer to real-life settings as they remind children to use the skills they have practiced in the game.

iREVIEW

Eye Contact–Toybox is similar to the *Look in My Eyes* app but is easier to master. It is recommended for slightly younger students. Both apps are good at encouraging eye contact and imagination. Students with more severe deficits will not complete or understand the task. Both apps require the user to look into the eyes of a series of faces to discover the correct answers to number-based questions. Users can earn rewards for correct answers. *Look in My Eyes–Restaurant* is a helpful app to encourage generalization of eye contact. This game is recommended for high functioning or Asperger's students. I have had parents tell me that their child thought it was creepy at first but was lured in with earning rewards and has demonstrated improved eye contact. Try the entire *Look in My Eyes* collection—Zoo, Undersea, Dinosaur, Car Mechanic, and Stream Train—for better eye-contact skills and the added bonus of improved working memory.

SMILE AT ME *by FizzBrain*

www.fizzbrain.com

$2.99

FROM THE DEVELOPER

Smiling can be difficult for many children. Some children, particularly those with autism spectrum issues, may feel uncomfortable and resist smiling when it is appropriate. They may also smile when it is inappropriate to do so. Some children also have difficulty interpreting the social cues that signal when a smile is or is not appropriate. *Smile at Me* provides quick, repeated practice in interpreting these social cues and rewards children for practicing appropriate smiling.

iREVIEW

Many individuals on the spectrum have difficulty interpreting and displaying facial expression. Smile at Me is a delightful way to practice the most basic facial expressions of smiling and frowning. The student is shown a picture that will elicit a smile or frown and is encouraged to hold the iDevice like a mirror (to see their reflection in the glass) and to compare their mouth to that of the child in the picture. The picture on the app dims every few seconds to allow the student to view his own facial expression and practice making smiles or frowns to match the pictures. The student then decides if the child in the picture is smiling or frowning and touches the corresponding image. If the response is correct, the student earns a star. A virtual trip to the zoo is earned after acquiring four stars where more social skills are practiced and generalized. The developers of *Smile at Me* make no promises that practicing this game will affect real behavior; however, they do believe that smiling is a cultural norm that can be learned with practice.

 See the YouTube demo at www.youtube.com/watch?v=aV9TNzpVhZE

MORFO 3D FACE BOOTH
by SunSpark Labs
www.sunsparklabs.com
$0.99

FROM THE DEVELOPER

Use *Morfo 3D Face Booth* with a photo of a friend, celebrity, pet, or just about any object you can imagine, and quickly create a talking, dancing, and life-like 3D character! Once captured, make your character say anything you want, wear wigs and makeup, speak in a silly voice, rock out, disco dance, suddenly gain 300lbs, and more. Want to show off your awesome 3D creations to the world? Easy! Record a video of your talking, dancing character and email or post right to Facebook! Surprise your friends with the coolest Party Invite or Happy Birthday message ever.

iREVIEW

Watch your photos come to life with *Morfo 3D Face Booth*! Better yet, add emotions, tweak facial features, customize a costume, and you are ready to make a recording that can be shared via email or social media. Morfo 3D Face Booth will get your child's attention and make a game out of exploring emotions, vocal prosody, and facial expression. Use *Morfo 3D Face Booth* to draw attention to subtle changes in facial muscles and use this action as a springboard into a more structured social pragmatic activity. To access the facial expression, activate the "Record" button.

 The free version also offers many opportunities to explore facial expression and emotions.

MICRO-EXPRESSION TRAINER *by Mario Micklisch*
http://favo.asia/METrainer
$3.99

Micro-Expressions express the seven universal emotions: anger, contempt, disgust, fear, happiness, sadness, and surprise. This app shows brief, involuntary facial expressions on the face according to emotions someone is experiencing. They can occur as fast as 1/25 of a second, which makes them very hard to see. With this trainer you will improve your recognition of facial expressions and the interpretation of all seven expressions. In your training, you will see all expressions with many different characters. You can modify the expression durations to match your reading ability, enabling you to learn them at your own speed.

iREVIEW

By accessing both the written explanation and the visual input, with *Micro-Expression Trainer*, individuals can practice (using a mirror) making these expressions themselves. There is no audio or sound effects, only beautiful faces making expressions. To repeat the facial expression, the user taps the small circle-arrow in the bottom right corner. I thought one would tap the face for a repetition. I have found that Micro-Expression Trainer is also good for encouraging eye contact as the user must look at the face for approximately five seconds to see the entire expression loop when the expression duration is set to maximum.

AUTISMXPRESS *by StudioEmotion Pty Ltd. Inc.*
http://autismspectrum.org.au/iPhone
FREE

FROM THE DEVELOPER

The *AutismXpress* iPhone app has been created to help promote greater awareness about autism spectrum disorders. It is designed to encourage people with autism to recognize and express their emotions through its fun and easy-to-use interface.

This app is hilarious, silly, and free. My students really like AutismXpress. The exaggerated facial animations and sounds entice the students to mimic expressions and feelings. AutismXpress features 12 faces with common feelings. Choose one and see the delightful animation and sound effect that accompanies the feeling. *AutismXpress* is perfect for the segment of circle time discussion of, "How are you doing?" "Gassy" is a favorite among the boys. I recommend AutismXpress for all students as a learning tool or reinforcement.

 The free version also offers many opportunities to explore facial expression and emotions.

MAGIC EYEBALL *by Joy Entertainment LLC*
http://joyentertainmentllc.com/Joy_Entertainment_LLC/
Home.html
$0.99

FROM THE DEVELOPER

This app is like the old Magic 8 ball but is more beautiful and more fun! Just consult the all-knowing, all-seeing mystical eye, and all of your questions will be answered. Take a deep breath, ask a question, and press the pupil of the all-knowing, all-seeing eye. It will blink and give you your answer. Press the pupil again and it will blink, and you can ask another question. Very simple, yet very powerful and fun!

iREVIEW

Just like the "Magic 8 Ball," *Magic Eyeball* inspires question-asking and social interaction as well as eye contact. Just ask a yes/no question, tap the eye, and get the answer. When the *Magic Eyeball* is not answering questions, the eye follows the user from side to side—kinda eerie! *Magic Eyeball* has been responsible for some lively social group interaction in my classroom!

 The free version also offers many opportunities to explore facial expression and emotions.

Chapter 15: Hygiene, Pre-Vocational & Safety

Even though adulthood may seem far away or may be just around the corner, it is never too late or too early to work on independent life skills, pre-vocational skills, and self-care. There are things everyone can do, and starting early is the key to success.

An early study from Australia, "iPod Therefore I Can: Enhancing the Learning of Children with Intellectual Disabilities Through Emerging Technologies," tracked the progress of ten autistic children who were using iPod touch devices. Results indicate that corrective behavior was reinforced in children with autism who, in one case, couldn't wash their hands, by combining images and voiceover. An amazing 60% of the study's goals were achieved.

 ## Success Story: Earl

Earl is a very interesting teenage boy. He is able to spell, follow multi-step directions, and communicate well via picture exchange. Yet, he is unable to talk. He is a full-sized young man who has intense likes and dislikes. Family members have warned the staff about Earl's dislike for brushing his teeth. As a matter of fact, Earl's grandpa is the only person Earl allows to brush his teeth.

This year at Earl's IEP, his family was deeply concerned about his oral hygiene, as Grandpa had fallen ill. The occupational therapist and I took it upon ourselves to support Earl with his goal for independent oral hygiene. After lunch, we demonstrated brushing teeth with the *Brush Teeth Free* app and had Earl practice. After that, we walked him to the sink, gave him a toothbrush and toothpaste, showed him the app again, and with hand-over-hand prompts brushed his teeth. The next day, he required set-up and some verbal prompts, with review of the app. By the third day, we switched apps to *Ed Meets the Dentist* (for generalization), set him up, and he completed the task. Earl needed to see why brushing was important. *Brush Teeth Free* and *Ed Meets the Dentist* gave Earl the visual support needed to understand the task. Goal met!

BRUSH TEETH FREE *by Runic*

www.runicdev.com

FREE

FROM THE DEVELOPER

Love brushing teeth? Who doesn't? HILARIOUS app!

iREVIEW

Brush Teeth Free seems like a novelty app, yet it has proven to be terrific in giving students on the autism spectrum the visual input they need to support good oral hygiene. Once they have completed the task on the app and we have had a few giggles, students feel more confident putting the toothbrush into their mouths. Please read Earl's success story (previous page) to get a better understanding of the power of visual supports.

 There is no audio or graphic toothbrush with this app.

ED MEETS THE DENTIST *by Holt IP Holdings, LLC*

www.kidsdentalonline.com

FREE

FROM THE DEVELOPER

Join Ed, the young rabbit, on his trip to the dentist! The perfect app to help prepare your child for the first trip to the dentist! Interactive games familiarize children with the dental experience by reinforcing each step that might be encountered during a check-up visit. Kids are less anxious about the dentist when they have already experienced the unfamiliar with Ed!! Created by Jeffrey D. Holt, DDS, MS.

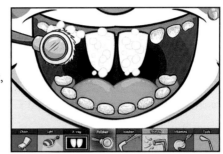

iREVIEW

Ed Meets the Dentist will show your children what to expect when they go to the often "dreaded" dentist. Expose them to all the sights, sounds, and dental concepts, from X-rays and the dental chair to drills and suction straws. A cute animated video of Ed and his mom going to the dentist is also included. Knowing why and what to expect on a dental visit can ease the anxiety associated with going to the dentist and make the process less "painful" for everyone.

SEE ME GO POTTY ENGLISH
by AvaKid Productions
www.avakid.com
$0.99

FROM THE DEVELOPER

The unique, distinctively useful, and exceptionally fun potty trainer. Fifteen actionable potty training tips included: The app includes concrete advice about preparation, behavioral reinforcement, behavioral shaping, when to continue vs. take a break, and more. This app allows teaching with positive reinforcement and fun: The Go Potty scene ends with your child's avatar happily celebrating a successful "I did it!" potty experience. In contrast, the Accident Scene ends with your child's avatar being disappointed by the "uh-oh".

iREVIEW

Using the potty is one of the most important and challenging self-care tasks we can teach our children. The key to success is showing your child what to do, but if you have ever been responsible for creating the visual supports for potty training, you know how daunting and sensitive this task can be. *See Me Go Potty* really works! There are no complicated settings or features just an animated child that you can customize to look like your child, will walk you through the entire routine from; "Go potty please," to "I did it!" Auditory prompts are paired with written cues via a simple voice-over narrative for step-by-step instructions that your child will instantly memorize. Yes, there is actual pee pee, poo poo and wiping; however it is very tactfully done. Recommended for anyone and everyone who has the goal of independence.

 See the demo video on the developer's website. http://www.avakid.com/products.html

 **PEPI BATH** *by Pepi Play*
www.pepiplay.com
$1.99

FROM THE DEVELOPER

Pepi's hands are dirty, her hair stands up, and there are grass stems and leaves between her teeth. Should Pepi clean herself? Why is she frowning? Have you soaped her nose by accident? Try popping soap bubbles, or maybe help Pepi wash her clothes. And do not forget to hang them out to dry. There is much to do! *Pepi Bath* is a role-play game in which children learn about hygiene in a fun way.

iREVIEW

Learn about important hygiene routines with Pepi Bath. Tiding up does not have to be a chore, but rather enjoyable and an action that keeps us clean and healthy with a sparkly smile. That is the message Pepi delivers. *Pepi Bath* has four parts for different situations in which this character, Pepi—a boy or a girl—appears at the sink, washing clothes, going potty, and taking a bath, which can be incorporated in a structured pre-set sequence or free play.

 There is a free Lite version of *Pepi Bath* available with two day-to-day activities.

DIALSAFE PRO *by Little Bit Studio, LLC*
http://littlebitstudio.com/dialsafepro.html
FREE

FROM THE DEVELOPER

Teach your child proper phone usage and safety with an app that lets them actually practice it! *DialSafe* is designed to teach these critical skills in a kid-friendly manner through the use of animated lessons, skill-building games, practice sessions, and even a realistic phone simulator. *DialSafe* helps provide a comprehensive learning experience in a safe environment where the child can both explore and learn. International Users: 000, 911, or 999 will be taught based on your device country code or can be selected in settings for Australia, Canada, Ireland, United Kingdom, or United States.

iREVIEW

Learning how to use the phone is an essential skill for every child. *DialSafe Pro* gives your child the opportunity for guided practice in learning how to call for help, dial family members, even order pizza. Teach your child how to operate a phone keypad and what to say if a stranger calls, with a simulator that works like a real phone.

FIND MY FRIENDS *by Apple*
www.apple.com/apps/find-my-friends
FREE

FROM THE DEVELOPER

Find My Friends allows you to easily locate friends and family using your iPhone, iPad, or iPod touch. Just install this free app and sign in with the Apple ID you use with iCloud. Adding a friend is easy; just choose from your contacts or provide an email address to send an invitation. When your friend accepts your invitation using the *Find My Friends* app on their device, you can start following their location. Your friends can request to follow your location the same way. *Find My Friends* also lets you set up location-based alerts that can notify you automatically when a friend arrives at the airport, a child leaves school, or a family member arrives home safely. You can notify friends about your current location or changes to your location at any time. *Find My Friends* works even when the app is in the background (a passcode lock on your device is required) and has been optimized to avoid draining your battery.

iREVIEW

Get this app! *Find My Friends* not only lets you keep track of your loved ones, but also locate a lost iPhone or iPad. *Find My Friends* is not usually thought of for safety; however it is a superb app for personal security and should be on every iDevice. This is worth repeating: location-based alerts will automatically notify you when a child leaves school, arrives at daycare, or enters/leaves any area that has been set up with location alerts.

 Find My iPhone will also work for keeping track of those who may wander or an iDevice that has been misplaced, lost, or stolen.

The user will need to set up iCloud accounts for each family member (free for up to five accounts). Apple gives full instructions on use of *Find My Friends* on their website.

HYGIENE HD & GROOMING HD
by The Conover Company
http://education.conovercompany.com
$1.99

FROM THE DEVELOPER

Hygiene & Grooming are two programs in our *How To* series on personal hygiene, grooming, and dress. The program provides step-by-step instructions on how to take a bath or shower, floss and brush your teeth, use deodorant, wash your face and hands, and control germs.

As our children grow older, their hygiene routines change, *Hygiene HD & Grooming HD* teaches important cleanliness routines to pre-teens, teens, and young adults. The highly effective evidence-based concept of video modeling is utilized to show individuals step-by-step routines to manage personal needs.

LIVING SAFELY *by AbleLink Technologies, Inc.*
www.ablelinktech.com/index.php?id=27
$29.99

FROM THE DEVELOPER

Living Safely provides self-directed learning sessions for 27 important safety skills topics based on proven content developed by the Attainment Company. *Living Safely* provides an accessible learning tool that is specifically designed to be used directly by individuals with autism and learning or other developmental disabilities at their own pace on the coolest technology platform there is – the iPad! *Living Safely* is powered by Visual Impact, AbleLink's highly effective cognitively accessible learning tool.

iREVIEW

Living Safely sessions include a series of vector pictures narrated by a human voice that gives step-by-step training regarding home and personal safety topics. The user can stop, replay, move forward, or move backward in the app. Safety topics include fire safety, bathroom safety, kitchen safety, swimming safety, relationship safety, getting lost, and much, much more.

 Watch the demo video on the website to know exactly what to expect with *Living Safely*. www.ablelinktech.com/index.php?id=27

iDRESS FOR WEATHER *by Pebro Productions*
www.pebroproductions.com
$1.99

Customize the closet and customize the temperature range; *iDress for Weather* is for anyone, at any age, and with any ability anywhere in the world! *iDress for Weather* can serve as assistive technology for individuals with disabilities, an educational tool for children, or just plain fun for everyone! Everyone interprets temperatures differently. *iDress for Weather* takes this into account by allowing individual settings of temperature ranges that define hot, warm, cool, cold, and really cold.

iREVIEW

This app offers up-to-date weather information with a full set of clothing suggestions at the swipe of a finger: *iDress for Weather* offers concrete information for those individuals who have difficulty matching clothing and accessories to the daily weather conditions. Parents now have visual support to reinforce the connection between weather and clothing for their children. Parents and caregivers can also customize the closet contents. Simply snap a picture of the clothing that goes with a weather condition and add it to the corresponding closet. Users enjoy the ability to configure temperature ranges to personal preferences and the opportunity to customize extended info like humidity, wind, location, and units of measure (Fahrenheit or Celsius) within the settings. *iDress for Weather* is fantastic for supporting individuals in making appropriate clothing choices for the day.

DRESS-UP *by Fishdog.net*
http://fishdog.net/dress-up
$0.99

FROM THE DEVELOPER

Awesomely original, creative fun for boys and girls ages two to six. Kids choose outfits, colors, and patterns by tapping and moving items on the screen. Boy and girl dolls are included. No ads, no score-keeping, no repetitious music, no makeup, or immodest clothing are present. Kids focus on their task, show their designs to siblings or parents or save them to the photo album, then tap the arrow to start a new doll. Clothes snap into place, so finger accuracy is not required.

iREVIEW

What should I wear today? *Dress-Up* can help individuals make appropriate clothing choices by providing visual input. A plethora of choices are given for gender, tops, bottoms, shoes, accessories, glasses, hair, and skin color. In addition, *Dress-Up* is a superb app in terms of labeling, categories, and increasing use of descriptors (people, places, and things). Think of *Dress-Up* as a digital paper doll that never gets lost or torn.

SAFETY SIGNS AND WORDS *by The Conover Company*
http://education.conovercompany.com
$0.99

FROM THE DEVELOPER

There are dangers everywhere! This program covers 80 of the most common safety signs and words used in our communities. Knowledge of these signs and words could save a life. Don't let experience be the harsh teacher of these key signs and words. Some of the safety signs and words included in this program are crosswalk, danger, do not eat, do not touch, fasten your seat belts, keep off, keep out, and watch your step.

iREVIEW

I had no idea there were so many signs in the environment. Each safety sign has a short video to explain its meaning with an example. *Safety Signs and Words* contains 80 signs with accompanying videos that are arranged in alphabetical order. Safety Signs and Words is a great resource for young adults or teens learning life or independent living skills. Two more noteworthy apps available from Conover Company are *Information Labels* and *Emergency Signs and Words*.

WHAT'S NEXT? (GETTING A JOB) *by Sacramento County Office of Education*

FREE

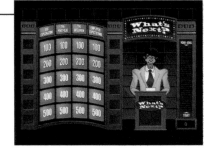

FROM THE DEVELOPER

What's Next? (Getting a Job) is an entertaining and informative app to help users learn vital tips for finding the job that's right for you! Couched in a humorous game show format, you'll find yourself laughing while you learn insider tips on job exploration, building a strong portfolio, making the best impression during a job interview, what employers are looking for, and more!

iREVIEW

What a fun and creative way to open up the (usually boring) discussion about job interviews. Students love the game-show format with lights, sound effects, scoring, and a "cheesy" host. *What's Next? (Getting a Job)* can double as a social pragmatic game, as it requires turn-taking and topic maintenance. I have had more than one student design their own "game show" after playing *What's Next? (Getting a Job)* and do a great interpretation of the host. *What's Next? (Getting a Job)* is free, thoroughly entertaining, and teaches life skills, all from the palm of your hand.

WHAT'S THE RIGHT JOB FOR YOU? *by Anxa Europe Limited*

www.anxa.com

$0.99

FROM THE DEVELOPER

At one time or another in our lives, we have asked the question, "What's the right job for me?" This test examines in detail your dominant personality traits at work in order to give a specific answer to that question. Knowing your personality is an invaluable tool in identifying the jobs that best match your temperament, lifestyle, and attitude towards others. This test allows you to form an accurate profile of your assets and professional behavior.

iREVIEW

What's the Right Job for You? will open up a discussion into careers and personalities. The user answers a set of questions that provide a personality type with career options based on the answers given. I have used the questions productively during discussions regarding career opportunities and how they may or may not fit into individual personality types. *What's the Right Job for You?* is a good tool to open up discussions about personality and good career options; however, it is only part of a larger process of determining individual career choices.

Part V

Visual Aids & Organizers

Every individual has a unique style of learning. For some, learning comes easily through traditional methods. Others have challenges and need to use different techniques to access information. A highly effective technique used for the visual learner is the use of graphic organizers. Studies have shown that using graphic organizers can help to improve recall, cut down on boredom, stimulate interest, organize thoughts, and enhance understanding of subject matter. Graphic organizers and visual aids such as storyboards, mind maps, contingency maps, charts, and schedules are traditionally assembled with Velcro, lamination, cardboard, and/or contact paper and then placed in obvious locations so that the user can refer to them throughout their day.

With advancements in technology, graphic organizers and visual supports can be made in minutes, personalized, taken to any location easily in a pocket or purse, and shared with family (via email). It is just that easy to provide your child/student with the supports they need to cope with each day, feel secure, and, in many ways, feel proud.

Chapter 16: Visual Supports

No longer are visual supports a major construction project of expensive Boardmaker PECs, sticky Velcro, lamination, or contact paper. Today, visual supports are inexpensive, convenient, personalized, and a cinch to make. Here are some of my favorite tried-and-true apps to support the visual learner.

iCOMMUNICATE *by Grembe Inc.*
www.grembe.com
$49.99

FROM THE DEVELOPER

iCommunicate lets you design visual schedules, storyboards, communication boards, routines, flash cards, choice boards, speech cards, and more. It is customizable to your needs.

iREVIEW

iCommunicate makes storyboards, schedules, menus, and voice output effortless and is a breeze to customize. After becoming familiar with the app, one can create a wonderful portable storyboard, choice-board, visual schedule, flash cards, or talking picture album in only a few minutes. Visual supports can be printed via AirPrint. *iCommunicate* offers a Google image search feature, making finding great images a snap, plus the option of using 10,000+ NTY SymbolStix images. Before this app was available, I remember cutting, laminating, and Velcroing well into the evening, but this drastically changes that routine.

STRIP DESIGNER *by Vivid Apps*
www.mexircus.com/Strip_Designer/
index.html
$2.99

FROM THE DEVELOPER

Impress your friends with your own personal comic strips, created on your iPad, iPhone, or iPod, using photos from your photo album or iPhone camera. Select one of the many included page templates. Insert photos into the cells. Add a couple of words with fun comments. Add additional effect symbols (stickers) with action phrases like "Boom," "Splash," or "Bang" to spice up the story. When you are happy with your new graphic novel, share it with friends and family.

iREVIEW

The ability to create wonderful visual schedules, memory books, and social stories while keeping a sense of humor and creativity is *Strip Designer*'s specialty. Thanks to *Strip Designer*, visual supports do not have to be boring. Begin by selecting from over 100 templates. Resize and rotate photos within the template cells, add text balloons, insert captions, and/or make cartoon exclamations. *Strip Designer* gives users the ability to be clever, innovative, and original. After your masterpiece is complete, share it with friends and family via email or social networking.

 Visual supports do not have to be boring!

 ## FTVS HD-FIRST THEN VISUAL SCHEDULE HD
by Good Karma Applications
http://goodkarmaapplications.com
$14.99

FROM THE DEVELOPER

FTVS HD gives you five different options for adding images: take a picture using your device's camera or grab one from the camera roll, use the Internet search feature to look for an image, use one of the stock images in the app, or access one of 10,000 Smarty Ears symbols. All of the stock images and Smarty Ears symbols are searchable by name. Set a timer for either an entire schedule or for individual steps within it.

iREVIEW

FTVS HD is one of the best apps for individuals who need visual input to increase independence, promote understanding of upcoming events, and decrease anxiety during transitions.

Listed are five formats to view your unique visual schedule, they are:

| One single image at a time | Two images in a First Then board format | Scroll through a checklist | Drag and drop an image to the opposite column when step is complete | Drag and drop completed step into an envelope |

The ability to embed video or a choice board into any step combined with Google connectivity makes this scheduling app an excellent choice for any individual who benefits from visual input.

 Attach a choice board or video to any step.

PICTURE PROMPT TIMER (PPT) *by MDR*

www.look2learn.com

$3.99

FROM THE DEVELOPER

While such a visual tool is helpful, the *PPT* adds a new dimension: an auditory prompt that allows you to customize messages that will be delivered at intervals of your choice! For example, if you want Johnny to stay on task and he needs to be reminded every 30 seconds, just simply set up an audio reminder and tell it how frequently to play. The end result is that Johnny has a constant reminder of what he needs to do.

iREVIEW

The best feature of the *PPT* is the audio timer that gives customized audio reminders at targeted intervals during the task and an auditory completion message/reinforce when the time is up. The *PPT* allows you to display two photographs in a first/then format (First you do this, then you get this) with a corresponding bar that shows the individual how much time is left on the task. If your child or student needs picture support for first/then along with auditory reminders to "keep going," or to stay on task, the *PPT* is a great choice.

ALL ABOUT ME STORYBOOK	**I CREATE ... SOCIAL SKILLS STORIES**	**iGET... MY SCHEDULES AT HOME SOCIAL SKILLS STORIES**	**PLAN IT, DO IT, CHECK IT OFF**
$2.99	$4.99	$4.99	$2.99
Create your own personal information storybooks by using your own CUSTOM photos, text and audio.	Totally customize sequential steps of a storyline for individuals who need help building their social skills.	Social skills story for individuals that need support in understanding the process of their morning and evening routines.	Plan It, Do It, Check It Off is a real photo "To Do" app that can be fully customized by the user.

by i Get It, LLC
http://igetitapps.com

I Get It! is dedicated to developing educational applications that can be utilized by diverse populations. From the *i Get* series to the *i See-quence* collection, each app is designed for all ages, with real photo images for contextual support, personalized text options for visual support, and recordable audio capabilities for auditory support. The apps are designed with photo templates attached. However, the user may easily modify the samples or create their own pages to customize the app for their student/child's individual learning needs.

iREVIEW

Everything is customizable for multiple users of every age and ability. The *I Get It* apps come with preloaded pictures, sequences, and stories that you can personalize or start from scratch, making it as super simple or complex as you need.

 Take a look at the video tutorial(s) on the developer's website to get an idea of how to customize and use this app before you purchase: http://igetitapps.com/video-tutorials

FUNCTIONAL PLANNING SYSTEM
by The Conover Company
www.conovercompany.com/mobile/apps
$4.99

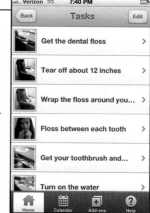

FROM THE DEVELOPER

Our *Functional Planning System* provides a visual approach to daily planning. Think of it as a cross between a video playlist and a calendar. Activities can be scheduled, alarms can be set, and step-by-step videos prompt the user through the completion of each activity. Videos for many activities are available via in-app purchase, with over 4,000 images and videos to choose from.

iREVIEW

Mobile technology has made it easier than ever to keep ourselves organized and provide visual and auditory support throughout the day, giving users freedom and independence. *The Functional Planning*

System is a powerful tool in teaching daily routines such as shopping, transportation, and hygiene in daily environments. It is completely customizable for any age or ability with video/pictures, addition or subtraction of steps to a routine, visualization of tasks in day/week or monthly view, and connection to the entire video Functional Skills Video Library. *Functional Planning System* has an adult look and feel; however, it can be used by all to attain optimum independence.

 According to a recent study at Virginia Commonwealth University (VCU), mobile technology such as Apple's iPod touch, can be the key to successful employment for people with autism (Gentry, T., and McDonough, J. (August 2011), Research to Practice Brief No. 1: Could an iPod touch be the key to successful employment for people with Autism? Autism of the great functions on the demo video - http://education.conovercompany.com/mobile/apps/fps/

iREWARD *by Grembe Inc.*
www.grembe.com
$2.99

FROM THE DEVELOPER

iReward is a motivational tool for your iPhone, iPod touch, or iPad. You can create a star chart or token board to help reinforce positive behaviors using visual rewards. Use of motivational charts is not limited to any one group. We all benefit from motivation to achieve our goals! This type of praise or approval will help parents of typically developing children and children with autism, developmental delays, ADHD, and anxiety disorders. We've updated the app to support multiple users and added more customizable options.

iREVIEW

Everyone wants to earn the Golden Ticket! *iReward* puts the effectiveness of a visual reinforcement chart in an easy-to-use app. Whether you choose an image from your camera roll or Google Image Search, *iReward* is a snap to customize to reflect individual likes and motivators. Lock out unintentional taps in the Lockable settings using a password. *iReward* is a highly recommended visual reinforcement system for students with autism, developmental delays, yourself, or anyone who could use a little motivation to achieve their goals. Verbal praise and/or a cute cat video are given after completing a set number of stars. Check out the iTunes review by miker1972:

My students love this app the best because they get to earn stars! I am an SLP who uses *iReward* to help my students with autism anticipate the end of an activity or to provide incentive to complete a difficult task. It is very easy to customize.

 Demos and videos are available on developer's website: http://www.grembe.com/demos.

 **GOALTRACKER** *by Twiddly Bits Software LLC*
www.appedgellc.com
$0.99

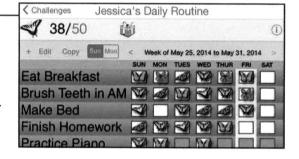

FROM THE DEVELOPER

Create a set of daily tasks, chores, good behavior, medicine, or things to do. Give yourself a sticker for each task you complete each day. Set up a reward for reaching your goal. You can also set goals for improving your eating habits, taking medicine daily, drinking enough water, or whatever you choose. You earn trophies as you complete your goals, and you can set up rewards for completing goals.

iREVIEW

GoalTracker is useful for parents, educators, and therapists to visually track progress. If you or your child needs structure, consistent routines, and tangible, visible feedback on his or her progress toward goals, then *GoalTracker* is for you. Users can personalize a challenge according to ability, set a reward, and place stickers as each task is completed.

CALENDAR AND REMINDERS *by Apple*

www.apple.com/ipad-air/
built-in-apps/?cid=wwa-us-kwg-ipad-com

FREE

FROM THE DEVELOPER

Calendar—Manage your busy schedule with Apple's *Calendar* app. You can view events by day, week, month, or year. Switch from portrait to landscape to get a broader view. Even your Facebook events are integrated into *Calendar*, so you can see what your friends are up to. *Reminders*—iPad never forgets, so you won't either. The *Reminders* app lets you set location- or time-based alerts for all the things you need to get done—even recurring tasks. And iCloud keeps *Reminders* in sync on all your devices, so you can make a list on your iPad and be alerted on your iPhone.

iREVIEW

Don't forget that Apple has some mighty fantastic apps that come pre-loaded onto your iDevice. My students use both *Calendar* and *Reminders* extensively to organize their day or review the details of past days. Apple continually updates all of its apps with cool features that not only support the busy business person, but students and parents as well.

 Both *Calendar* and *Reminders* are already on your iDevice.

Chapter 17: Open-Ended eBook Apps

Highly customizable, open-ended eBook apps let you be the storyteller. Today's eBooks give our children interactive storytelling with audio narration, auto page-turning, animation, songs, dance, and pride in accomplishment. Any goal, any activity, and any favorite silly, scary, or fantastic thing your child can think of can become an eBook. Let's encourage our children to become digital authors (or at least co-authors), put some eBooks on the iBookshelf, and share their achievements with friends and family.

There are many choices for open-ended eBooks at the iTunes Store. They all function in about the same way: load an image, record audio, write something cool, save, and share. It's the "extra" features that you should be aware of when deciding which one to purchase. The following is a list of common features to consider when deciding which eBook is best for you:

- Take pictures from within the app
- Can you import videos?
- Text-to-speech
- Recording features
- Type text and draw

- Can you import music?
- How do you share?
- Can they be stored on iBooks bookshelf?
- In -app Google image search
- Sharing capabilities with the community & vice versa

In the News:

Making Leo Digital Versions of His Favorite Books—on the iPad, of Course

Thank you, Shannon Des Roches Rosa

www.squidalicious.com

I put Leo on the bus this morning, and Seymour and I drove Mali to school. Iz and I leave for Ghana in less than an hour. I think Mali will be fine—she'll have Daddy, she'll have Grandma—but I am worried about Leo, because we're tight, we two. So I've done as much as I can to guarantee I'll "be" there for him, even while I'm away.

How? I've used the iPad app *Kid in Story* to make Leo digital versions of his favorite books, with my voiceover. That way I can "read" him his favorite books, even if I'm not present. (I also used *Kid in Story* to make a "Mommy & Izzy Went to Ghana" social story; that's a given.)

Making the books was easy-peasy, because with *Kid in Story* you can take and insert photos from within each photo page (though you could also use stored iPad photos, if you like). Even a 30-page book only took about 20 minutes to make.

Even better, I could then upload the customized books to the cloud storage service Dropbox and keep copies of them there, so I have backups if Leo decides to delete the resident versions (deleting and/or duplicating media is a favorite iPad pastime of his). And with the free *Kid in Story Reader*, I can even import and Leo can read the stories on my iPhone, even though the primary app is iPad only.

Of course, one should respect copyrighted material. Ahem.

These custom digital favorite books make Leo so happy. He uses them to keep himself calm when we're at medical appointments (there have been a lot of those lately). He can page through them at whatever pace he likes. And there's no danger of him loving the digital books to pieces, which he has done on occasion with their board-and-paper versions.

The ability to make Leo these custom digital favorite books is as thrilling to me as when Ocean-house Media came out with the ability for users to add their own voiceovers to their Dr. Seuss OmBook iPad apps; I believe that ability to control repeated readings contributed to Leo's performance yesterday, during which he read/recited the paper version of Dr. Seuss's *I Can Read With My Eyes Shut* to me *in its entirety* (!!). It is so great to have so many options to support his reading.

While I hope there will be sufficient wifi for me to FaceTime with Leo (and Mali, and Seymour, and my mom) while Iz & I are in Africa, there's no guarantee there will be. But I can guarantee that Leo will hear my voice while I'm away. I really hope that will help make it less hard for him that I'm away.

KID IN STORY BOOK MAKER
by Locomotive Labs

http://locomotivelabs.com

$6.99

FROM THE DEVELOPER

Kid in Story Book Maker templates come to life when you place your child or student's picture on every page. The 12 story templates cover a variety of practical and fanciful topics, from promoting good hygiene by washing your hands to a playful exploration of emotions and facial expressions and a fantasy visit to San Francisco! You can also write your own custom story or modify any of the templates as you see fit.

iREVIEW

Just as the title indicates, put your *Kid in Story*. Better yet, after a few demonstrations, your kids will put themselves in stories or lessons. Imagine you are in high school learning about the judicial system; kinda boring, right? Now, with *Kid in Story*, you can put yourself into the judge's seat or the jury box and create an entire book in which your child is the central character. The possibilities are endless with this easy-to-use eBook.

Watch the demo - http://bit.ly/ZshJPB *Kid in Story Book Maker* combined with the new free *Kid in Story* reader enables teachers, therapists, and parents to share stories they create with students, friends, and family.

PICTELLO *by AssistiveWare*

http://www.assistiveware.com/pictello

$18.99

FROM THE DEVELOPER

Pictello is a simple way to create visual stories and talking books. Each page in a *Pictello* story can contain a picture, a short video, up to 10 lines of text, and a recorded sound or text-to-speech using natural sounding voices. *Pictello* offers an easy visual story creation wizard so everyone can use pictures, video, and sound to share important moments in their lives. An advanced editor gives full control of the editing capabilities. **Stories can be shared with other *Pictello* users with iTunes File Sharing or via WiFi through Dropbox or a free account on the Pictello Sharing Server. Stories can be shared with non-*Pictello* users as PDF files through email, Dropbox, or iTunes File Sharing.

iREVIEW

Pictello is an exceptional app that allows users to capture outings, personalize social stories, create talking books, and share interests and memories with others. Students can create stories at school to share with family members or create stories at home to share with friends at school. Pictello comes with a choice of natural-sounding text-to-speech voices in 26+ languages. A record option allows the user to personalize adventures using their own voices. Other settings include Expert or Wizard mode, and both come with the ability to add videos to any page.

MY STORY - BOOK MAKER FOR KIDS
by iDef Web Solutions
www.causelabs.com
$3.99

FROM THE DEVELOPER

Create and share eBooks and stories by adding drawings, photos, and stickers. Then record your voice on every page and share your story with friends, family, and classmates. We've made My Story super teacher friendly by adding multiple authors and syncing across multiple iPads! So now you can have all your classroom iPads in sync! *My Story* is perfect for the home or classroom.

iREVIEW

Everyone can be an author! My Story is terrific for creating social stories, memory stories, concepts, and story boards. Combine pictures, drawings, stickers, and text with audio recordings to make a personalized eBook to share via email or social network and store in iBooks. All customizations, drawings, and audio features are at your fingertips and super easy to use.

BOOK CREATOR FOR iPAD
by Red Jumper Studio
www.redjumper.net/bookcreator
$4.99

FROM THE DEVELOPER

The simple way to create your own beautiful iBooks, right on the iPad. Read them in iBooks, send them to your friends, or submit them to the iBooks Store. Ideal for children's picture books, photo books, art books, cook books, manuals, textbooks, and more!

iREVIEW

Instantly create eBooks with *Book Creator*. You can create your own story—write some text, illustrate with a picture or drawing, and/or record your own words and sounds. You can even import videos and music to the pages. The app is easy to use with all the bells and whistles you could want, and the price is right. If you desire videos and music, *Book Creator* is a marvelous choice.

 Watch the short demo—www.redjumper.net/bookcreator—and/or check out the free version to see if *Book Creator* is right for you.

BOOKABI *by Tamajii Inc.*
http://tamajii.com/bookabi
FREE

FROM THE DEVELOPER

The beauty of *bookabi* is that everything children need to tell their stories is already there—no drawing skills needed. *bookabi* has a collection of 2D and 3D characters, fanciful backgrounds, and fun stickers and objects that you can place, resize, and rotate with the swipe of a finger. Children can add speech bubbles, create text, and even design the cover. You can also use your own photos as elements of the story or backgrounds (wait until you see how your living room looks with a spaceship in it!). Using *bookabi*'s fun and colorful characters, backgrounds, and stickers; it's easy for kids of almost any age to bring worlds and fantasies from their imaginations to life.

iREVIEW

The unique feature about *bookabi* is the preloaded and/or in-app content that is available in addition to the ability to import your own images. There are tons of people, backgrounds, characters, and stickers available to create any story. If you are looking for an open-ended book app that has 2D and 3D characters, speech bubbles, and comic-book-like exclamations, this is the app for you. *bookabi* is free to try, and then you buy only what you want via in-app purchases.

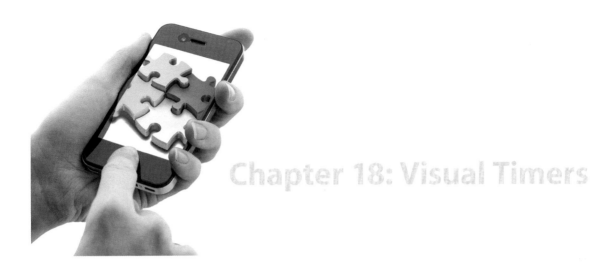

Chapter 18: Visual Timers

Visual timers are used to support time prediction challenges and transition difficulties at all ages and ability levels. One can see the time elapse and judge time without having to know how to tell time. I have chosen two very different yet highly effective timers to include in this chapter. There are countless others to choose from. Check them out and choose the most fitting for your needs.

CLOCK *by Apple*
www.apple.com
FREE with every device

iREVIEW

Apple installs on every iDevice an elegant clock with a countdown timer embedded. It is beautifully simplistic with a solid red line that counts down with the timer for those who need additional visual support or have challenges reading numbers. The user sets the time in one minute increments up to 24 hours, chooses a tone, and starts the timer.

It is already on your iPad if you have iOS6 or higher.

TIME TIMER *by Time Timer LLC*
www.timetimer.com
$4.99

FROM THE DEVELOPER

The *Time Timer* for iPad displays time as a red disk that quietly gets smaller as time elapses. Children as young as three understand that when the red is gone, time is up! And unlike many other visual timers, the I app has a professional look and packed features to help adults make every moment count. This app is highly recommended by experts in education, healthcare, ADHD, autism and parenting.

iREVIEW

Time Timer is the industry standard. This timer is used almost exclusively in schools and clinics. We all know it and love it. The time durations are easily changed and can be set for up to four children/tasks at a time. Time Timer can run in the background of other apps and offers a variety of tones/alarms and three modes to choose from.

IHOURGLASS *by Headlight Software, Inc.*
www.ftponthego.com/ihourglass.php
$1.99

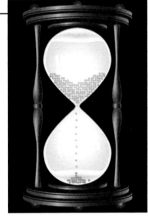

FROM THE DEVELOPER

It's a simple hourglass, intended for use with board games. Whenever we play, it is common that everybody gets so excited we forget to watch the timer. Using *iHourglass* will not be a problem. It activates a buzzer and even vibrates if everybody is yelling so the person "watching" the time will feel when time is up. The sand piles up, and turning it on the side to pause makes all the sand pour to the side. *iHourglass* instantly resets when you flip it upside down.

iREVIEW

Don't tell *Time Timer*, but my students like *iHourglass* better. iHourglass was originally designed for board games but works very well as a visual support timer. My students and I like to watch the sand fall through the hourglass. It even has a countdown warning when time is almost up (last five seconds). There are 12 stunning designs to choose from.

Try the free version, then decide if *iHourglass* fits your needs. Are you an artist and want to make an hourglass for potential inclusion in future versions? Go to the developer website for details: www.ftponthego.com/ihourglass.php.verbal

Chapter 19: Graphic Organizers

Graphic organizers such as knowledge maps, concept maps, Venn diagrams, cognitive organizers, and schedules are designed to help individuals structure their thoughts, problem solve, and understand the key points of ideas and relationships. Studies have shown that the process of converting information into a graphic map helps students develop increased insight, retention, understanding, and critical thinking skills.

For individuals on the spectrum, graphic organizers are essential visual supports that focus, structure, and arrange important information. Abstract information that is presented in a visual, concrete manner may be reviewed as needed and is more readily understood by students who may have auditory processing challenges. This chapter presents digital graphic organizers that can support a wide range of student goals, from completing a task and writing a report to planning their day and making transitions.

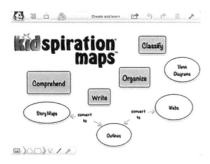

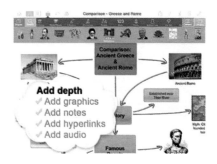

KIDSPIRATION MAPS

Kidspiration Maps

Kidspiration Maps helps young readers and writers in grades K-5 learn to organize and classify information, gain sight word knowledge, and expand their ideas into written and verbal expression. By creating story maps, Venn diagrams, and webs, students visualize what they are learning, thus improving their understanding and comprehension. Tap to transform visual diagrams into text—perfect for pre-writing.

by Inspiration Software, Inc.

www.inspiration.com

$9.99

INSPIRATION MAPS VPP

Welcome to *Inspiration Maps*™, the most intuitive and powerful visual learning app on the iPad. Build beautiful diagrams, graphic organizers, and outlines with ease! Getting organized has never been this simple. For Grades 4 and up.

FROM THE DEVELOPER

Visual thinking and learning strategies have been shown to increase academic performance for students of all learning abilities. Inspiration® Software's visual learning software is recommended for students with ADHD, autism, Asperger's, dyslexia, aphasia, and visual or auditory processing disorders. By providing multiple mediums for representation, expression, and engagement, Inspiration Software tools help students visually organize and outline ideas to structure writing and improve communication and expression, all while learning skills that enhance and make learning fun and engaging. With Inspiration Software's tools, students brainstorm using symbols and images to represent and sort their ideas and create visual diagrams and graphic organizers to break work down into manageable sections. Visual learning engages students of all abilities as they work together and contribute at their individual levels.

iREVIEW

Excellent visual supports for grade school students. *Kidspiration Maps* and *Inspiration Maps* have a gorgeous, easy to use interface that lets the students design their own visuals effortlessly. Features include a graphic library of 1400+ images, picture-to-text support that transforms visual representations into written words (*Kidspiration*), audio notes, and sharing options. Both apps come with additional templates and activities to get you started.

 Kidspiration Maps Lite and *Inspiration Maps Lite* are free previews of *Kidspiration Maps* and *Inspiration Maps*. Work with up to five diagrams to create maps, edit and stylize content, transform diagrams to outlines, and preview templates.

POPPLET *by Notion*
http://popplet.com
$4.99

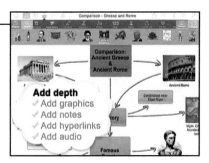

FROM THE DEVELOPER

Great for work and great for school, *Popplet* is a platform for your ideas. Popplet's super-simple interface allows you to move at the speed of your thoughts. With *Popplet*, you can capture your ideas, sort them visually, and collaborate with others in real time, quickly and easily!

iREVIEW

Visual supports are extremely important in the daily lives of individuals on the autism spectrum, and *Popplet* is an impressive piece of software that gives life to photo albums, maps, charts, schedules, boards, and more. A *Popplet* is like a corkboard or bulletin board on your iDevice that allows users to organize and visually create their ideas. The developers have made it super easy to add pictures (from camera roll), change colors, add text, or draw your own illustration. I have used *Popplet* to build visual supports for just about everything, from first-then schedules to complex outlines and essays.

 Start out by trying the free version to get an idea of how easy *Popplet* is to make use of. The only option that would make *Popplet* more versatile is an Internet image search (hint, hint).

iTHOUGHTS (MINDMAPPING)
by toketaWare
http://toketaware.com
$9.99

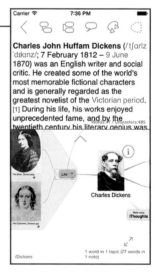

FROM THE DEVELOPER

iThoughts is a mindmapping tool for the iPad, iPhone, and iPod touch. *iThoughts* (mindmapping) enables you to visually organize your thoughts, ideas and information.

iREVIEW

Create large maps with many topics or simple lists with *iThoughtsHD*. Customize, colorize, size, cut, paste, and share visual supports for projects and thought organization. *iThoughtsHD* is great for junior high, high school, or college students who can visually organize information to complete classroom assignments.

Chapter 20: Sound Masking

Some individuals with disabilities, autism in particular, have a high level of sensitivity to noise. Seemingly quiet noises may cause an individual to cover his or her ears or run away or can contribute to a meltdown. Sound Masking works on the principle that disturbing noises can be reduced by constant noise in the background. Relaxing tapes, soothing sounds, or white noise can help with noisy settings and difficult transitions. Parents and caregivers have reported good success with noise masking apps when traveling or transitioning into loud environments.

SOUNDCURTAIN *by Andreas Raptopoulos*

www.futureacoustic.com

$4.99

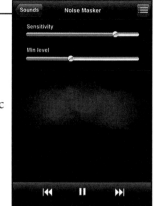

FROM THE DEVELOPER

SoundCurtain is an entirely new concept in sound control, using advanced adaptive masking technology, powered by FutureAcoustic's adaptive acoustic architecture (a3) engine. It works better than Active Noise Cancellation or traditional (steady-state) masking for blocking out fast-changing, informational rich noises, such as speech. The technology monitors noise in your environment through your headset mic and performs real-time spectral analysis to calculate the energy content across a number of perceptually important frequency bands. Sound is then generated in response, with its spectral content optimized to mask ambient noise. The sound is generated through a generative sound engine, using probabilistic rules to ensure that it is varied subtly over time and doesn't become tiring.

iREVIEW

Does your child cover his or her ears, run away, cry, or have meltdowns in noisy environments? If so, try *SoundCurtain* to make noisy transitions and rowdy environments tolerable. *SoundCurtain* adjusts to the noise in your environment by monitoring through your headset microphone and performing real-time analysis of the background noise. Individuals who are sound sensitive usually need to wear noise reduction headphones. These headphones usually do the trick, but they are large, expensive, and obvious. *SoundCurtain* helps the user tolerate noisy environments without looking different.

AMBIANCE *by Urban Apps*

http://ambiance.urbanapps.com/

$2.99

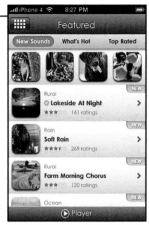

FROM THE DEVELOPER

Ambiance is an "environment enhancer" designed to help you create the perfect ambient atmosphere to focus, relax, or reminisce.

iREVIEW

With a huge collection of over 2500 downloadable sounds, *Ambiance* can help drown out the clamor around you. Sound-sensitive individuals may find it easier to transition into loud environments with the aid of *Ambiance*. Parents have had success using sound masking apps to help their children cope with environmental noise without using headphones or earplugs.

Part VI

Occupational Therapy

In the News:

Occupational Therapy and iPad

By Barbara Smith OTR/L, Author of *From Rattles to Writing: A parent's guide to hand Skills*

As the number of apps for the special education community grows exponentially, we occupational therapists are grateful to have *Apps for Autism* to help us choose the ones that promote specific OT skills such as scanning and eye-hand coordination. iPads will never replace the sensory stimulation and kinesthetic learning we all experience as we explore objects. However, children on the autism spectrum look at, touch, and manipulate objects and learn in atypical ways. They thrive when learning materials are exciting, predictable, and repetitive; don't feel slimy; and provide cognitive challenge while utilizing their incredible visual discrimination and memory.

All therapy begins with promoting engagement and some of the best ways to promote motor skills as simple as touching a screen or as complex as typing a word to reinforce (i.e., reward) with bright lights, colors, sounds, music, and animations. Most apps do exactly that! The apps in this section are of particular interest to occupational therapists because the iPad becomes more than a screen. It is manipulated in ways that help develop bilateral coordination, motor planning, and finger dexterity. Learners tilt their devices to navigate through obstacles in *Doodle Jump & Temple Run* or *SCOOP* ice cream. They develop finger control while playing *KNOTS* and pre-writing skills by painting on *Doodle Buddy*.

Occupational therapists have especially come to love the handwriting apps that teach correct letter formation. *Letter School* is one of my favorites because it requires accurate sequencing and tracing-followed by fun animations. Handwriting apps such as *Ready to Print* enable children with pencil control difficulties to first practice letter formation using only the finger with the option of using a stylus as skill progresses.

The "Apps for Occupational Therapy" section wouldn't be complete without addressing activities of daily living. Brady includes some of the best apps to encourage using the potty, choosing weather appropriate clothing, sequencing to prepare meals, and putting some fun into the tough subject of personal hygiene

Now that iPads are widely accepted and used to help individuals with special needs and of all ages, this revised edition becomes even more important. Occupational therapists can learn about the pros and cons of the selected options and integrate them into treatment plans. It's an exciting time to be an occupational therapist!

Chapter 21: Handwriting

Individuals with disabilities face an extra hurdle; they often lack the fine motor coordination required for handwriting, which will likely lead to problems with self-esteem and academic performance. Occupational therapists have tried many different programs to encourage students to write better. The programs are good; however, students sometimes lack motivation. Then came the iPad; students will literally wait in line for a chance to practice writing. Some students will work and earn time on the iPad so that they can practice their writing and fine motor skills. Students can use their finger or a stylus, whichever fits their individual needs and abilities. There is an abundance of highly effective handwriting apps on the market. Many of these handwriting apps can also be used for learning literacy as spelling is incorporated. Choose one or more to meet your goals. I guarantee no tears.

Success Story: Bonnie

I have worked with Bonnie for many years. She is a nine-year-old student with autism who frequently has challenging behaviors due to anxiety and frustration. She can read and type at around the first grade level. Her speech is mostly unintelligible with movie, TV lines, and scripting. She uses, but does not carry, a traditional voice output device to communicate wants (computer, swing, outside, and Jump Start). Initially she refused to write and was averse to the sight of a writing utensil. I introduced Bonnie to the iPad, and she instantly chose *LetterSchool*. She sat in a beanbag and completed each letter, upper and lower case. She is a perfectionist, so every letter had to be perfect. Bonnie now writes (pencil and paper) in phrases and has another modality to communicate. Bonnie will also frequently use *Quick Type, Little Speller, Lunch Box, Feed Me, Listen to Music, Read a Book* and will flip through the apps with ease. Bonnie knows her limits with the iPad and will give it back when finished, after about 30-40 minutes. Bonnie's teacher is using the iPad to introduce math concepts. Bonnie will carry her iPad to any destination with no protests. Fantastic!

LETTERSCHOOL *by Sanoma Media Netherlands B.V.*
www.letterschool.com
$2.99

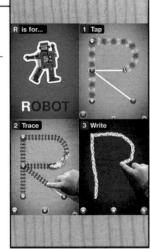

FROM THE DEVELOPER

This app offers an amazing, intuitive game to learn all about letters and numbers through writing, counting, phonics, and more. Kids practice essential skills as they play four exciting games per letter/number.

iREVIEW

I have heard folks say that their child learned to write using *LetterSchool*. I agree; *LetterSchool* is amazing at engaging students and keeping their attention. Some of the many excellent features include choice of typeface, levels of difficulty, scoring for up to three students, and stunning animations. Students can use a stylus to practice letter/number formation while using a writing utensil to improve generalization to paper-pencil tasks. The audio is clean while the sound effects are crisp and complement the graphics.

Check out this review from UltimateAutismGuide.com: This intelligently designed app will captivate the user through entertaining animations and an easy to navigate interface.

 If you are not sure if your student/child will enjoy this app, try the free version.

READY TO PRINT *by Essare LLC*
http://readytoprint.essare.net
$9.99

FROM THE DEVELOPER

Ready to Print is a comprehensive tool for parents, therapists, and educators to help teach pre-writing skills to children in order to build a strong foundation for beginning printers. *Ready to Print* progresses through the pre-writing skills in a specific order so that children can master the visual-motor, visual-perceptual, and fine motor skills necessary for correct printing patterns. It is designed to teach children the correct patterns for printing, and to avoid bad habits that are difficult to change as the child gets older. *Ready to Print* features 194 separate levels in 13 activities. The latest addition is the Touch and Drag activity, which helps students work on movement in one of four specific directions.

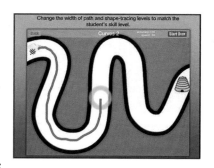

iREVIEW

Ready to Print will take the learner through incremental steps (13 activities) to becoming proficient at writing. *Ready to Print* offers plenty of entertaining practice with a game-type feel. As a matter of fact, *Ready to Print* is so absorbing that I can use it to help regulate and calm students to help them focus and get ready to learn. *Ready to Print* is easy to use, with prompts and sound effects that can be turned on/off and tracking for multiple users. *Ready to Print* is perfect for all beginning writers to master the fine motor and visual perceptual skills needed to form letters and eventually write for themselves.

TOUCH AND WRITE

Kids love learning to write, especially when they can use shaving cream, paint, and jello! *Touch and Write* recreates

TOUCH AND WRITE STORYBOOK: 3 BEARS

On each page of the story, children master the story vocabulary using our the fun and effective teaching strategy used in classrooms every day. Touch and Write uses a letter style similar to those most commonly taught in schools, so it prepares children for a real classroom.

engaging *Touch and Write* reading and writing activities. By the end of the story, children will have mastered almost 200 important vocabulary words and learned the phonics pronunciations of each word's letters!

by FIZZBRAIN LLC
$2.99

FROM THE DEVELOPER

We started FizzBrain in order to develop quality iPad/iPhone applications for all children based on best teaching practices. Our *Touch and Write* series has received numerous commendations and awards. While many of our apps are designed for all children, we also have a special interest in developing apps for children with autism spectrum issues. This is based on our many years of close personal experience with children on the spectrum. Prepare your child to become a strong reader and writer the *Touch and Write* way!

iREVIEW

My students love the *Touch and Write* series! It is full of visual, auditory, and kinesthetic input that stimulates their sensory system. On the one hand, it is a favorite app to learn pre-literacy skills such as letter sounds, letter formation, spelling, and words. On the other hand, *Touch and Write* provides terrific reinforcement. *Touch and Write* is packed with kid-friendly, motivating features such as writing with whipped cream, cool sound effects, music, graphics, and an array of luscious paper textures that keeps their attention and focus on task. My favorite feature is the ability to customize a word list based on individual needs and what the students actually want to practice. The *Touch and Write* app series comes pre-loaded with two high-frequency word lists, two alphabet word lists, numbers zero through nine, and upper case and lower case alphabet lists so that students can practice the most common occurring words. Lastly, the target area for writing the letter does not have rigid boundaries, allowing for a bit of user error as well as stops and starts. This decreases frustration and abandonment of task. As one of my colleagues put it, "I wish I could write my reports in chocolate frosting."

You will also love the entire *Touch and Write* series—*Cursive, Phonics, Shapes, Australian, Brazilian, Hebrew,* and *Turkish.* See the YouTube video for more details and demo. https://www.youtube.com/watch?v=A3J9omQadwk

WRITE MY NAME *by NCSOFT*

www.iactionbook.com/?lang=en

$3.99

FROM THE DEVELOPER

Write My Name is a fun way for children to practice writing letters, words, names, and phrases. *Write My Name* supports children ages four through six to learn how to write their name, trace upper-case and lowercase letters, and write over 100 familiar sight/Dolch words. *Write My Name* meets some of the basic reading and writing Common Core State Standards for kindergarten such as the introduction and mastery of print and word recognition concepts.

iREVIEW

Write My Name not only provides endless practice for fine motor control, but is a fantastic literacy app with common sight/Dolch words and the ability to create individualized name tags. Vibrant artwork, calming music, animations, and a reward system keep interest high and encourage your students to keep progressing through all the targeted words. Students who have name writing as one of their goals will especially benefit from the *Write My Name* learning application as it makes this task accessible and achievable to children with fine motor delays and sensory processing issues.

 View the demo at http://www.iactionbook.com/?slide=write-my-name&lang=en

Practice fine motor manipulation and control

DEXTERIA - FINE MOTOR SKILL DEVELOPMENT

Dexteria is a set of therapeutic hand exercises (not games) to improve fine motor skills and handwriting readiness in children and adults. Dexteria's unique hand and finger activities take full advantage of the multi-touch interface to help build strength, control, and dexterity.

DEXTERIA JR. - FINE MOTOR SKILL DEVELOPMENT FOR TODDLERS & PRESCHOOLER

Dexteria Jr. is a set of hand and finger exercises to develop fine motor skills and handwriting readiness. The activities are specially designed for kids ages two through six. New characters, sprite animations, music, and sound effects all add up to a fun and engaging experience for toddlers and preschool-aged children.

by BinaryLabs, Inc.

www.dexteria.net

$3.99

FROM THE DEVELOPER

Our award-winning apps are a great way to ensure that kids are ready for school and life success. Facilitating the development of fine motor skills, math concepts, correct letter formation, and spatial reasoning, our apps are instructionally sound, easy to use, and fun to play.

iREVIEW

Less expensive than a workbook, lasts forever, and has students asking to play *Dexteria*. *Dexteria* apps are great for enhancing your pre-writing, letter formations, and literacy skills. Automatic tracking makes report writing and goal setting a snap for numerous users. Each app contains a set of exercises designed to improve fine motor skills, build strength, and improve coordination, and, of course, dexterity.

 See the demo on the developer's website—http://www.dexteria.net/#prettyPhoto/1/

Chapter 22: Bilateral Coordination

Bilateral coordination is the use of both sides of the body together to perform a task efficiently and is necessary for writing, cutting, typing, and most academic and vocational activities. Bilateral coordination can be facilitated by any activity that utilizes both the right and left arms working together to complete a task. Nobody said this couldn't be fun. Note: Temple Run, Scoops, Tilt Maze, Pop Flux, and most games capture data by keeping score and building on acquired skills and levels. Remember, terms like high score, levels, or total scoops are not norms-based and will need to be converted into percentages and prompt levels.

MEMOVES *by Thinking Moves*
www.thinkingmoves.com
$9.99

Perform finger puzzles correctly to the beat of the music and watch as the screen comes alive. Based on the award-winning *MeMoves* DVD, the *MeMoves* app can provide instant calm and focus anywhere. For ages three through 103. The *MeMoves* app is an extension of the award-winning *MeMoves* DVD, which is being used in schools, homes, and therapy centers to calm, focus, and align children with autism and related disorders.

iREVIEW

This app is simple, unique, and tranquil. Help your students with sensory integration needs, ASD, depression, and anxiety to relax, calm down, and focus attention. *MeMoves* also allows teachers, therapists, and parents to refocus and re-energize. Thirty different finger puzzles are combined with soothing music and 2D/3D graphics to accomplish a centered state of being. *MeMoves* is also wonderful for increasing short attention spans and preparing busy brains to begin challenging tasks. *MeMoves* is one of the sharpest tools in the toolbox for bilateral coordination and pre-writing activities.

POP FLUX *by Nullspace Garage, LLC*
www.popfluxgame.com
FREE

Jab, poke, or head-butt bubbles as you bob and weave to avoid danger—all without touching the screen! *Pop Flux* is a motion-sensing augmented reality game that puts you on the screen and in the action. Using cutting-edge computer vision techniques, *Pop Flux* utilizes the front camera on your iPhone or iPad to detect your position and motion precisely and smoothly. Interact with both friendly and dangerous virtual objects as you pass through 30 diverse, increasingly difficult levels.

iREVIEW

Pop Flux is by far the most novel app I have discovered! Simply stand your iPad up, center yourself on the screen and begin to pinch, poke, pop, clap, bob, and weave to avoid the bubbles, bombs, and array of virtual objects that seemingly fall from the sky. As one user puts it, "it's like virtual Fruit Ninja." The user sits a couple feet from the iPad and never touches the screen. *Pop Flux* is the coolest way ever to focus on goals such as proprioception, bilateral coordination, visual special perception, and just about any upper-body coordination task.

TEMPLE RUN *by Imangi Studios, LLC*
www.imangistudios.com
FREE

FROM THE DEVELOPER

Test your reflexes as you race down ancient temple walls and along sheer cliffs. Swipe to turn, jump, and slide to avoid obstacles, collect coins, and buy power ups, and see how far you can run!

iREVIEW

You knew *Temple Run* would be in this book. This is one of the most exciting mobile games ever! Running, jumping, sliding, tilting, collecting coins, and dodging angry apes with swipe and tilt controls that are intuitive and realistic. *Temple Run* is so alluring that all I have to do is flash a picture of the icon or play the beginning audio, and students will complete any task to take a turn at this endless running game. To collect coins that are at the sides of the trail, the player tilts the iDevice left or right. This is the most challenging part of the game for students who have difficulty getting the left and right hand to work together. However, after some practice, students master and refine the subtle tilts required to collect coins/tokens. The strong appeal of *Temple Run* can be harnessed and leveraged to accomplish many goals, including academic, therapeutic, leisure, and chores as well as iPad maintenance/care. There are four _Temple Run_ games to keep user interest piqued.

DOODLE JUMP _by Lima Sky_
www.limasky.com
$0.99

cool new space achievements!

FROM THE DEVELOPER

In _Doodle Jump_, the user guides Doodle the Doodler using some of the most subtle and accurate tilt controls in existence on a springy journey up, up, up on a sheet of graph paper, picking up jet packs, avoiding black holes, and blasting baddies with nose balls along the way.

iREVIEW

Doodle Jump is one of the most popular apps in America. Your students can practice bilateral coordination while guiding their Doodle in an upward journey into the unknown. _Doodle Jump_ is easy to play; simply tilt your device left or right, and tap the screen to shoot. When your student gets good at jumping, add distracters such as walking, talking, using only one hand, or playing at different angles.

 I've heard that Doodle Jump is addicting. You can try a free version of _Doodle Jump_ to see if this is the right choice for you.

SCOOPS - ICE CREAM FUN FOR EVERYONE
by NimbleBit
http://nimblebit.com
FREE

FROM THE DEVELOPER

Over a million people are screaming for ice cream! Stack your ice cream cone high into the sky by tilting the phone left and right, catching as many scoops as you can while avoiding the vegetables (veggies ARE great apart from ice cream!). The higher you go, the faster they fall, and the more wobbly your tower! Stack similar colors together for extra points.

iREVIEW

This challenging and entertaining app is also beneficial. *Scoops–Ice Cream Fun for Everyone* not only facilitates grins, but also bilateral coordination, muscle grading, turn-taking, and friendly competition. Compare your scores with the world. *Scoops* has something for everyone, with plenty of opportunities to teach language, categories, and basic concepts. Play *Scoops Classic* and *SkyBurger* free, with six more fun theme options available via in-app purchase.

 Scoops is available for iPhone only on the iTunes Store.

 **TILT MAZE** *by Exact Magic Software, LLC*
www.exactmagic.com/products/tilt-maze
$0.99

FROM THE DEVELOPER

Tilt Maze is a fast and easy-to-play maze game. Just tilt your iPhone or iPod touch to move your marble through the labyrinth to the exit. Try your hand at 20 different, colorful mazes that will test your balance and timing. The game even remembers your best time for each maze so you can keep trying to improve your performance.

iREVIEW

Tilt Maze has 20 colorful mazes that will challenge your bilateral coordination, balance, muscle grading, and visual perception. When a student gets good at moving the marble through the labyrinth, try playing while walking, standing on one leg, with one eye closed, or with one hand to sharpen skills further.

 Have a go at the free version of *Tilt Maze* before you buy.

CRASH BANDICOOT NITRO KART 3D
by Activision Publishing, Inc.
www.activision.com
$2.99

FROM THE DEVELOPER

The richest 3D kart racing experience! Speed your way through 12 thrilling tracks and multiple environments! Race and battle against zany opponents and turn them to dust with eight devastating weapons. Tilt and twist your iPhone for truly "nitro" driving sensations.

iREVIEW

Crash Bandicoot Nitro Kart 3D is highly motivating and is good for bilateral coordination and wrist strength. As students get good at driving *Crash Bandicoot*, the occupational therapist may have them walk down the hall and play the game to improve multitasking. Options on *Nitro Kart* include sound, vibration, language, accelerometer, and visual effects. Recommended for students who like a challenge. I suggest that students review the tutorial prior to starting a game.

 This app is stimulating for both sight and sound.

Chapter 23: Motor Planning

Motor planning is the ability of the brain to organize and carry out a sequence of unfamiliar actions. Motor planning with iTherapy targets eye-hand coordination, grading, timing, finger isolation, and sequencing of the upper extremities (hands and arms). It has been my experience that individuals are so highly motivated to use iDevices that they will not give up or get frustrated on failed attempts or require additional reinforcement to participate in motor planning activities. Every activity that an individual does with an iDevice can be considered motor planning. Be that as it may, the following are some apps that offer concentrated motor planning power.

SHELBY'S QUEST
by Doodle Therapy Apps
www.doodletherapyapps.com
$4.99

FROM THE DEVELOPER

Shelby's Quest, designed by an occupational therapist, aims to instill inspiration and enjoyment in education among children. This app, which is a therapy tool specially made for occupational therapists, teachers, and parents, gives the child a fun way to practice fine motor and visual perceptual skills while allowing the ability to store and track their progress. *Shelby's Quest* guides the child along a journey, assisting Shelby the Dog as she helps her forest animal friends overcome their challenges. Set in the beautiful Pacific Northwest, students will guide Skip the Salmon upstream to help him find his family, assist Samantha the Squirrel as she collects acorns and help Maurice the Moose find his way home.

iREVIEW

Shelby's Quest is an occupational therapy tool that parents can use at home. Choose from three adventures that target pre-writing skills with game-like challenges. Track multiple student progress, across three levels of difficulty, for fine motor, visual perception, pinching, finger isolation, tracking, and sorting. Children enjoy helping the animals overcome their challenges with Shelby (the dog), all the while honing their own motor skills.

CHALK WALK *by Mrs. Judd's Games, LLC*
www.mrsjuddsgames.com
$0.99

FROM THE DEVELOPER

Introduce your kids to the first app to help children develop the pincer grip needed for school. Many children are coming into school unable to properly hold a pencil. As time spent drawing on paper or coloring with crayons is swapped for screen time, key fine motor skills remain underdeveloped. But screen time can also solve this problem and prepare kids for the pencil-and-paper tasks they encounter in school. Mrs. Judd's Games' new app, *Chalk Walk*, is designed to fill the gap: young hands get needed exercise as they use a thumb-and-finger pincer grip to play this fun, innovative, teacher-designed game.

iREVIEW

How clever—your student has to use two fingers, the thumb-finger pincer grip, on the iPad to activate the drawing feature. Although *Chalk Walk* was designed to focus on the pincer grasp, the developers included many activities for literacy, attention, and school readiness. *Chalk Walk* looks like you are writing on the sidewalk while following a prompt that ultimately completes a word puzzle. When you have put all the pieces of the puzzle together you can watch a video of your steps. A free play section is also included and highly recommended by the developer to encourage scribbling—or creating paths of their own in a divergent fashion.

SNAPTYPE FOR OCCUPATIONAL THERAPY

by Ben Slavin

http://about.me/amberlynngifford

FREE

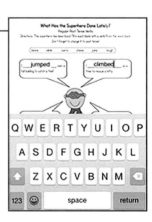

FROM THE DEVELOPER

Take a picture of your school worksheet and add text. *SnapType* is an Occupational Therapy app that helps students who have difficulty writing. Students can take pictures of their worksheets in class and use the iPad keyboard to type in the answers.

iREVIEW

What a great idea! No special equipment, no converting PDFs, no more complicated process of transforming classroom worksheets into typed documents and back. *SnapType* has made the whole process easy-peasy lemon squeezy! Simply take a snapshot (portrait only) of the worksheet, tap once and a yellow box will appear, tap twice for the keyboard in order to fill in the answer, resize to fit the answer area, and you are done. Take a screen shot of the completed work and email it off to your teacher from your Camera Roll. To take a screenshot, press the "Home" and "Sleep/Wake" buttons simultaneously. All screenshots save automatically to the Camera Roll. This app is excellent for students with dysgraphia or anyone who has challenges writing in small spaces.

 To create a new page, the user will need to close the app and restart.

 **CUT THE BUTTONS HD** *by Open Name Ltd.*
http://cutthebuttons.com/en/CutTheButtons
$1.99

FROM THE DEVELOPER

A snip here, a cut there; avoid the bolts and please beware! Now make a trim, it's time to start, make sure to keep your scissors sharp! Pick up the scissors with two fingers. Be careful—don't cut yourself. Cut off the game launch button by moving the scissor blades just like you would with real scissors. If you happen to be a left-handed player, you can configure the direction of the scissors within the settings menu. The scissors are highly maneuverable. You can use them to control the direction at which the buttons fall after being cut. You can also move the cup with the hand that is not controlling the scissors.

iREVIEW

Cut the Buttons is visually stunning and sensory rich! Hear the scissors cutting through the fabric, see the buttons fall and feel the burn in your muscles as you *Cut the Buttons*, collect points, and earn new scissors. *Cut the Buttons* is a fabulous occupational therapy tool for sensory and motor control. *Cut the Buttons* is highly recommended for everyone working on improving strength and fine motor control.

ANTS SMASHER *by SDIIMT*

www.sdiimt.com

FREE

FROM THE DEVELOPER

The game features ants you would love smashing with amazing sound effects. There is a spider friend who helps you kill more ants with her web. Get the golden ant if you can to get most points. Do not let the ants run away, or they will take your points.

iREVIEW

Yes, *Ants Smasher* is GROSS. But consider all the fun you will have developing finger isolation, pointing skills, tracking, and hand-eye coordination. *Ants Smasher* is free to try. If your child is having fine motor success, then consider the in-app purchase of a "Kids Mode."

SLIDE 2 UNLOCK *by RJ Cooper & Associates, Inc.*

www.rjcooper.com

$4.99

FROM THE DEVELOPER

Slide 2 Unlock is a great iPad teaching aid for people who need help practicing and/or understanding how to unlock their iPad.

iREVIEW

Unlocking your iPad is an essential step in accessing all the "magical" qualities of your device. *Slide 2 Unlock* breaks up the process of unlocking your device into five steps (games). Each step takes the user closer to the goal. *Slide 2 Unlock* can be used in portrait and landscape. The two final steps/games allow the user to choose the background currently on the lock screen to support generalization. I find that I can usually skip the first two steps;

however, I am glad they are there if needed. Recommended for individuals who need support mastering the swipe motion for unlocking and navigating through apps on their devices.

KNOTS *by Josh Snyder*
http://twitter.com/treelinelabs
$1.99

FROM THE DEVELOPER

Tie your fingers in knots with this classic iPhone game. When a spot appears, touch and hold until it disappears, and keep extra fingers at the ready! You can also get your fingers intertwined in two-player mode.

iREVIEW

Knots is Twister for your fingers. Play alone or with a friend. Playing this game will increase finger isolation, eye-hand coordination, social interaction, and friendly competition. Simply place a finger on a dot when it appears and remove it when the dot disappears (illustrated by rings around the dot). There is a bit of a learning curve with *Knots*; the user will need a few trials before understanding the game rules. See the "How to Play" section embedded in the app. *Knots* has been used successfully by students with Asperger's syndrome to encourage social interaction and strengthen finger dexterity.

 There is also an ad free supported version of *Knots*; this premium version will be forever ad free.

DOODLE BUDDY – PAINT, DRAW, SCRIBBLE, SKETCH
by Pinger, Inc.
www.pinger.com/content/home.html
FREE

FROM THE DEVELOPER

Doodle Buddy is the most fun you can have with your finger! Finger-paint with your favorite color and drop in playful stamps. Connect with a friend to draw together over the Internet.

iREVIEW

Doodle Buddy is the app that broke the ice with many of my students. Once they discovered that they could magically draw and stamp with their finger, they were hooked on the devices. Occupational therapists use *Doodle Buddy* for such things as eye-hand coordination, motor control, and finger isolation. I have never had to give any instructions with this app. Students at all levels seem to intrinsically know how to change colors, find stamps, and adjust the line size. In addition, I use *Doodle Buddy* in place of a white board. No dry erase marker or eraser needed; simply shake to erase and begin again. Easy, motivating, therapeutic, and free!

GARAGEBAND *by Apple*
www.apple.com/ios/garageband
FREE

FROM THE DEVELOPER

GarageBand turns your iPad, iPhone, and iPod touch into a collection of Touch Instruments in a full-featured recording studio, so you can make music anywhere you go. Use Multi-Touch gestures to play a piano, organ, guitar, and drums. Each instrument option sounds and plays like its counterpart, but lets you do things you could never do on a real instrument. Enjoy Smart Instruments that make you sound like a pro—even if you've never played a note before.

iREVIEW

How can I get my child to practice fine motor skills for hours without getting bored? Try *GarageBand*; it's a fabulous, super entertaining way to practice fine motor skills! Tap, strum, drag, sing, and record your very own song. *GarageBand* has an endless list of features, such as multiple instruments, special effects, smart keys, Wi-Fi/Bluetooth contestability to play with up to three friends, professionally recorded looks, and recording and sharing that will inspire not just fine motor skills, but also creativity and pride in accomplishment. Who knows—*GarageBand* may inspire your child to pick up a real instrument!

FISH FINGERS! 3D INTERACTIVE AQUARIUM
by Useless Creations Pty Ltd.
www.uselessiPhonestuff.com
$0.99

FROM THE DEVELOPER

Interact with your fish! Touch the screen and watch the fish follow your finger. Double tap the screen to feed them; they'll grow slowly if you do! Use any image you like as the background to your aquarium! Simply select

any image from your photo library and it'll look like your iPhone is full of water and 3D fish! Tilt your iPhone, watch the water move! Just like that time you tried to pick up your real aquarium and all the fish fell out, but without the mess!

iREVIEW

Fish Fingers! lets you practice motor control and relax at the same time. The very clever occupational therapist puts shapes and letters in the background and has the students move the fish along the shapes/letters to practice formation. The fish do not move quickly—rather, calmly. Therefore, Fish Fingers! is a lesson in controlled, purposeful movement and patience.

Chapter 24: Activities of Daily Living (ADLs)

Learning how to perform activities of daily living (ADLs) like cooking, feeding, toileting, and self-care is a crucial part of an individual's education and self-worth and how the world views him or her. ADLs are an important focus of intervention, especially those surrounding hygiene and feeding. Temple Grandin wrote of an employer who told her that her armpits stank and gave her a can of Arid deodorant – even brilliance cannot overcome body odor, unwashed hair, or food-stained clothing. Many talented developers have created effective ADL apps that cover everything from cooking to grooming and hygiene. Let's take a look!

MORE PIZZA! *by Maverick Software LLC*
www.mavericksw.com/Home.html
$0.99

FROM THE DEVELOPER

Turn your iPod touch or iPhone into a pizzeria! Choose your crust, pour on the sauce, add loads of cheese, and complete it with all the toppings you want. Then bake it right there in your virtual oven, where it will come out piping hot and ready to slice. Once you've made your pizza masterpiece, you can email the whole pie or just a slice to your friends, save a picture to your photos library, or serve it up on a plate and take virtual bites out of it!

iREVIEW

More Pizza! is an occupational therapist's dream. This app involves motor control, eye-hand coordination, muscle grading, and ADLs all in one fun program. This highly motivational app enables the user to choose the plate, crust, and toppings and then to cook, cut, and finally eat it. The directions are provided upon the first use. Speech therapists use *More Pizza!* to devote attention to labeling, following directions, verbal sequencing, and having fun (social skills). I have also used *More Pizza!* successfully in teaching vocational skills. Students can take orders from their peers, write them down, make the pizza according to order, and serve it. Pizza can even be served remotely to family and friends via email. This is an enjoyable, effective, highly recommended app for all ability levels.

 If you like *More Pizza!* you might also enjoy additional "More" apps from Maverick Software:

MORE GRILLIN' **MORE CUPCAKES!** **MORE SOUP!** **MORE SALAD!**

EACH $0.99

Each of the apps listed above takes the user from set-up to cooking and eating the desired food. Each food choice has virtually limitless combinations and customization choices. The educational benefits are also boundless. The "More" series of apps promotes increased vocabulary, muscle control, direction following, sequencing, ADL, vocational, leisure activities, and generalization skills. Enjoy!

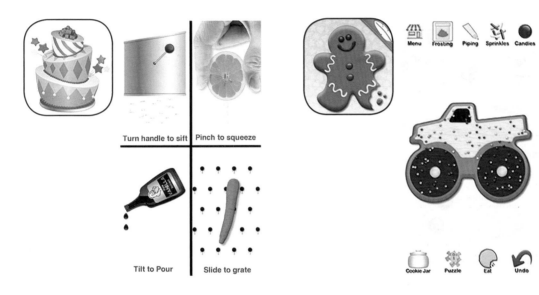

CAKE DOODLE

Need a cake in a hurry for that special occasion? Love to decorate cakes, but hate the dirty pans, messy counters, and hot kitchen? Cake Doodle is the answer!

by Shoe The Goose
www.shoethegoose.com
$0.99

COOKIE DOODLE

If you enjoy making cookies but hate the mess, this is the app for you. We provide the dough, a rolling pin, cookie cutters, and your choice of frostings, sprinkles, and candies, all in one easy-to-use package.

FROM THE DEVELOPER

Crack the eggs, shake the salt, pour in the liquids, and toss in the dry ingredients. Blend the batter and bake your cake in our super-fast-baking oven. No need to wait for the cake to cool before icing and decorating it. Eat the cake/cookie yourself when you're done or save it to your photo album. Surprise your friends with a customized cake/cookie e-mailed to them on their special day.

iREVIEW

Both *Cake Doodle* and *Cookie Doodle* provide a wealth of educational and recreational opportunities. The Doodle apps promote following directions, motor control, grading, Activities of Daily Living (ADLs), vocabulary use, sequencing, and creativity, just to name a few important skills. The user moves through the process of mixing the batter from a recipe, then baking, and finally decorating, making individual choices all along the way. After you have completed your culinary masterpiece, you can email it to your mom, dad, grandma, or best friend with a message. Best of all, there is no mess or dirty dishes in the sink. Don't forget to eat your delicious creations!

Nutrition Facts:

Calories 0

Total Fat .... 0 g

Cholesterol .... 0 mg

Total Carbohydrates .... 0 g

Protein .... 0 g

SHOE TYING 1 - ACTIVITY APP *by Accelerations Educational Software*

http://aesapps.com/activity-app/shoetying1

$4.99

FROM THE DEVELOPER

Teach your child to tie shoes in a snap with this video modeling practical app! This app combines systematic teaching and video modeling into a practical teaching environment simple enough for those not highly trained in these methods. This is an educational

power tool that anyone can use! This app takes the frustration out of teaching shoe tying for both the parent and the child. The app breaks down the task of shoe tying into individual video steps that the student can master one by one, thereby building confidence and cooperation. The app teaches both the skills and associated language with the various steps of shoe tying. The teacher can easily control the presentations to the student while eventually decreasing the level of assistance until the student is independent in this task. The teacher can easily replay individual steps and sequences in video or image formats.

iREVIEW

Teaching an individual to tie their shoes is a very important life skill. Not only does it build pride in accomplishment and help children's shoes stay on their feet, but more importantly, shoe tying develops complex fine motor skills that lead to success with other cognitive and/or daily living skills. *Shoe Tying* is meant for everyone who is learning, re-learning, or struggling with the complicated daily living task of tying their shoes.

 The *Shoe Tying 1* app comes with an integrated help system including a Teaching Guide, Using App instructions, and a page on why and how video modeling works. The integrated help system is supplied through web-based resources to make teaching and learning shoe tying an easy and enjoyable experience!

 **SEE ME GO POTTY ENGLISH**
by AvaKid Productions
www.avakid.com
$0.99

FROM THE DEVELOPER

A unique, distinctively useful, and exceptionally fun potty trainer. Fifteen actionable potty training tips included: This app includes concrete advice about preparation, behavioral reinforcement, behavioral shaping, when to continue vs. take a break, and more. Teaching with positive reinforcement and play: The Go Potty scene ends with your child's avatar happily celebrating a successful "I did it!" potty experience. In contrast, the Accident Scene ends with your child's avatar being disappointed with an "uh-oh."

iREVIEW

Using the potty is one of the most important and challenging self-care tasks we can teach our children. The key to success is showing your child what to do, but if you have ever been responsible for creating visual supports for potty training, you know how daunting and sensitive this task can be. *See Me Go Potty* really works! This app offers no complicated settings or features; the app presents an animated child avatar you can customize to look like your child and walks you through the entire routine, from "Go potty please," to "I did it!" Auditory prompts are paired with written cues via a simple voice-over narrative for step-by-step instructions that your child will instantly memorize. Yes, there is actual pee pee, poo poo, and wiping represented; however, it is very tactfully done. This app is recommended for anyone and everyone who has the goal of independence in ADLs.

 See the demo video on the developer's website, www.avakid.com/products.html.

 ## TOCA HOUSE *by Toca Boca AB*
http://tocaboca.com/
$0.99

FROM THE DEVELOPER

Welcome to *Toca House*! By the makers of *Toca Doctor*, *Toca House* enables your child to help the five app friends complete fun chores around a cozy house. Your child can virtually do the dishes, do the ironing, sweep, or plant flowers in the garden. This app is loads of fun, offering 19 different mini-games!

iREVIEW

Toca House offers 19 mini-games (chores) to play around the house. Your child will partake in cleaning, washing, delivering mail, personal hygiene, and more familiar household duties in a fun, no-rules, no-stress environment. Now they can clean their own digital house with kid-friendly controls, animations, music, and five adorable characters. Through these games, your child will learn that even housework can be fun.

 Visit the developer's website for a demo of *Toca House* and a description of other digital toys that may pique your interest: http://tocaboca.com/.

LIFE SKILLS SAMPLER HD **FREE**	**DRESS HD** **$1.99**
This sampler includes 80 of the most common words or signs in the Functional Life Skills System. The program builds familiarity with such words or signs as first aid kit, information, hospital, library, school bus stop, don't walk, bread, cashier, and receipt.	This program provides instruction about how to dress appropriately. This app covers topics such as how to get ready for the day, how to tie your shoes, how to wear clean clothes, how to wash clothes, and how to dry clothes. Six categories are provided, with a total of 80 instructional videos.

by The Conover Company

www.conovercompany.com/ipod/apps

FROM THE DEVELOPER

For some, going on a shopping trip, using basic literacy skills, understanding what to do when seeing a warning sign, or transitioning from school to work are very difficult tasks. The *Functional Skills System* software provides easy-to-understand information that allows learners to develop their capability to function independently in their homes, schools, communities, and workplaces. This system increases a user's ability to make appropriate choices. Gaining functional literacy, social, life, and work skills facilitates freedom and independence for anyone who seeks to become more functionally independent in society.

iREVIEW

Finally, I can take functional skills into the home/community where they belong and practice in real time and in natural situations. Video modeling has proven to be a fast, effective training method for teaching tasks to individuals with autism and those who require visual supports for success. Students on the spectrum are often unable to absorb information or maintain attention through a one-on-one or classroom demonstration. *Life Skills Sampler* and *Dress HD* provide individuals on the spectrum with the visual support they need to practice a skill until it is mastered. And now it is easier than ever to practice at home, at school, with parents, and with educators to encourage your child's generalization and success.

DRESS ME UP
by Captive Games
http://rockislandgames.com/index.php?iPhone
$0.99

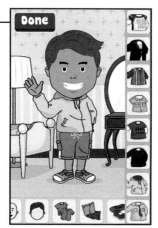

FROM THE DEVELOPER

Create a character by selecting different faces and hair styles. Then add clothes: tops, bottoms, shoes, hats, and accessories. Choose a background and you've created your own custom character. Lots of different combinations for kids to try!

iREVIEW

What should I wear today? *Dress Me Up* can help individuals make appropriate clothing choices by providing visual input. Your child can select a background (location) and then dress their personalized character to suit the setting by selecting pictures of items of clothing to add to the character. Choices are given for tops, bottoms, shoes, accessories, glasses, hair, facial expression, and skin color. The only missing feature is weather-related choices, which are important for individuals on the spectrum. In addition, *Dress Me Up* is a superb app for labeling and increasing use of descriptors (people, places, and things).

 Dress Me Up offers a free trial version of all their apps.

Part VII

General Education – Literacy

Thomas Todd is a classroom teacher for young adults with cognitive and behavioral challenges. Thomas uses both an iPhone and iPad extensively and effectively for academic and vocational goals. Thomas stated the following regarding this new assistive technology:

As a special education classroom teacher, it is my responsibility to educate my students in a way that addresses their individual needs and differences. Through the years I have had many assistive technology professionals come to my classroom and recommend expensive specialty equipment. The school purchases the equipment, and it is delivered to my classroom. More than likely, I will never see that assistive technology specialist again, and the equipment will not get used for more than a month or two.

Finally, things have changed. I purchased an iPhone several years ago and by mistake left it on my desk while I was preparing for lunchtime. When I returned to my desk, I noticed that a student had taken the iPhone and was quietly engaging in an audio book app. Since that day, I have used my iPhone and new iPad daily with my students. Most of the class did not need instructions on how to use the devices. I have successfully met or exceeded reading, writing, math, and vocational goals. Students will complete classroom tasks to have access to the devices; they can navigate successfully from apps to the web and never, ever use the iDevices inappropriately. As John Ruskin said, "Education is the leading of human souls to what is best, and making what is best out of them."

— Thomas Todd

Success Story: Rene

How Judge Judy Taught Rene Literacy

What does Judge Judy have to do with learning to read, spell and write?

Rene was especially interested in the television show *Judge Judy*. His mom reported that he is able to find *Judge Judy* in the *TV Guide* Listing. Initially Rene had no computer/iPad skills and, supposedly, no literacy skills. He was, however, able to use picture exchange as a means of communication. The following is a list of steps that took Rene to complete literacy and computer competence in about eight months. These steps are duplicable and have subsequently worked several times with other students.

1. Determine goal(s)—I want Rene to operate the computer and become literate; Rene wants to watch *Judge Judy*.

2. Show Rene that pictures and videos of Judge Judy are on the computer/iPad. Get him interested in watching short videos and seeing pictures of Judge Judy on the computer screen. Now, Rene likes and expresses interest in the computer.

3. During the next session—The computer is off, and I have a pre-made visual (task analysis) with steps to activate the computer and get to the Internet. To see Judge Judy, Rene needs to turn the computer on, and he watches as I walk through the next steps to get to the Internet, images and videos. Rene also watches at I type J-U-D-G-E J-U-D-. At this point, I ask Rene, "what's next?" and prompt him to type the "Y" and "Enter." Seemingly, magically, hundreds of pictures of Judge Judy appear. Rene can then pick a picture to print or a video to watch.

4. In the next sessions, I systematically increase Rene's participation in operating the computer, getting to the Internet, and typing J-U-D-G-E J-U-D-Y, supported by the visual task analysis and the printed words *Judge Judy*. Surprisingly, these initial steps take only a couple of weeks to master. Rene's efforts are always reinforced by a picture or short video.

5. The next step is to give Rene tasks to complete prior to having access to the Internet, such as typing his name and/or cleaning the computer. Once Rene is good at typing his name, then I give him a list of core words to type, then from words to phrases, and so on. Another task may

be to keyword search other names or concepts and print pictures of historical figures, science, or language arts-related materials. Every once in a while, a student forgets about their special interest (in Rene's case, Judge Judy) and gets interested in another subject.

6. Both goals have been met; for Rene, he has access to *Judge Judy*, and for me, Rene is doing it independently from turning on the computer/iPad to typing in keywords and printing a picture; it's a win-win.

Over the entire process, Rene's time watching *Judge Judy* videos is decreased, while time on a learning task is expanded. In about eight months, Rene was able to type and communicate basic information on a text-to-speech app while maintaining picture exchange as a means of communication.

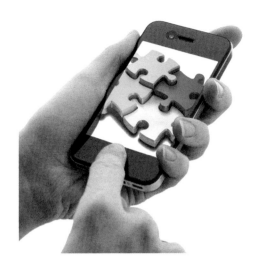

Chapter 25: Spelling

Focusing on spelling is important, because poor spelling can hamper writing and convey negative impressions. Individuals who are unable to use verbal language may express themselves via letter blocks, writing, or keyboarding. Let's make sure they can spell.

MONTESSORI CROSSWORDS *by L'Escapadou*

http://lescapadou.com/LEscapadou_-Fun_and_
Educational_applications_for_iPad_and_IPhone/
Montessori_Crosswords.html

$2.99

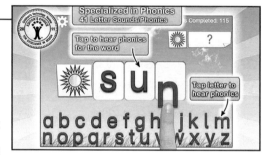

FROM THE DEVELOPER

Based on the proven Montessori learning method,
Montessori Crosswords helps kids develop their reading,
writing, and spelling skills by building words from a set
of 320 word-image-audio-phonics combinations using a
phonics-enabled movable alphabet. *Montessori Crosswords* helps kids learn and understand two fundamental concepts:

- First, the app helps kids understand that words are made up of sounds or phonemes (phonemic
  awareness). For each word, kids can touch the empty rectangles where letters must be dragged to
  complete the word and hear the sound the corresponding letter produces.
- Secondly, the app helps kids memorize the phonics associated with letters by providing a phonics-
  enabled alphabet where kids can touch each letter and hear the associated phonic.

iREVIEW

The Montessori Method is an educational approach based on the research of educator Maria Montessori
that supports the natural development of children. *Montessori Crosswords* is brilliant, as it encourages
students to explore reading, writing, spelling, and fine motor activities with compelling visual effects
and soothing audio soundtracks. There are three levels of difficulty and each level supplies the user with
a prompt, if needed. There is even a moveable alphabet that can rotate, change size, and produces the
sound of the letter when touched. There are letter case, layout, and audio choices for the user to customize their preferences. Also included is a word count; however, it cannot be reset for multiple users.

 See the demo - http://lescapadou.com/LEscapadou_-Fun_and_Educational_applications_for_
iPad_and_IPhone/Montessori_Crosswords.html

ENDLESS ALPHABET *by Originator Inc.*

www.originatorkids.com

$6.99

Interactive spelling puzzles come to life!

FROM THE DEVELOPER

Set the stage for reading success with this delightful, interactive educational app. Kids will have a blast learning their ABCs and building vocabulary with the adorable monsters in *Endless Alphabet*. Each word features an interactive puzzle game with talking letters and a short animation illustrating the definition. Before you know it, your child will be using words like gargantuan and cooperate! Note: You must be online and have ample disk space while running the app to see words beyond G!

iREVIEW

Endless Alphabet is so well done and so engaging that you will find students playing, spelling, and ultimately using the more mature words found in this app. *Endless Alphabet* comes with 50 words for your child to spell with funny interactive letters and then see the word animated by silly monster characters. Spell the word, read the word, and learn the meaning of the word through a charming animation. *Endless Alphabet* is recommended for anyone developing pre-literacy and literacy competencies.

SIGHT WORDS BY LITTLE SPELLER FREE

Sight words, also known as the Dolch List, are an integral part in learning how to read. The Dolch Word List contains 220 words that make up the most common words of the English language and are easiest learned by sight.

It is important for young readers to be able to instantly recognize these high frequency words in order to be proficient and fluent readers.

KIDS LEARNING - LITTLE SPELLER 3 LETTER WORDS $0.99

Little Speller is an exciting interactive game that helps your child rapidly learn to read, write, and spell words all with just the touch of their finger. The interface is so easy to use that even a nine-month-old baby will delight in moving their first letters around the page

PRESCHOOL GAMES - LITTLE SPELLER 4 LETTER WORDS $0.99

Heroic Support is not just what we do. It's really what makes us—well, us. It's that drive to make a difference in your life, no matter how big or small. Really, it's our way of life, because we want you to be our customer for a lifetime of fun and learning.

by GrasshopperApps.com
www.grasshopperapps.com

Flash cards be gone! *Little Speller* takes the concept of learning from pictures (flash cards) and uses the power of the iPad to turn learning into a multi-sensory, interactive game. The *Little Speller* app series has become a set of powerful tools in teaching language/literacy skills and meeting national standards in education for all of my students at every age and ability level due to extensive customization features. The graphics and audio are clear and concrete with brightly colored real pictures. Add, change, or remove pictures, graphics, and/or words to fit your individual needs and skill level. If that's not enough, the *Little Speller* app series lets the user add their own pictures, words, and letters to make the learning experience extremely personal and relevant. This is an important feature for students who may have challenges with generalization. For complete immersive language and literacy activity, have your student take pictures of meaningful people, places, and items in their environment. Then add these pictures to Little Speller so that they can learn how to read, spell, and recognize their favorite words.

 Little Speller – Three Letter Words has a free Lite version you can try.

ABC INTERACTIVE FLASH CARDS *by Alakmalak*
No developer website available
$0.99

FROM THE DEVELOPER

Parents can record their own voices and save the recording so that the next time it's played, the kid can view the flash card with a familiar voice.

- Easy to use
- Fun and interactive, with the ability to trace the alphabet letters by hand

ABC Interactive Flash Cards is a simple, minimally animated flash card app that will teach your child the letters of the alphabet along with a word that begins with that letter, but that's not the cool part. The most impressive part of *ABC Interactive Flash Cards* is the free-form tracing pad. The Tracing Pad can be a part of the screen or enlarged to fill the entire screen for practice drawing letters, writing word(s), drawing the corresponding picture, or all three. I am truly amazed at my students who seem to be averse to pencil-paper work but will willingly draw, write, and practice penmanship with the right support.

 **STARFALL ABCS** *by Starfall Education*
http://more.starfall.com/info/apps/starfall-education.php?ref=itunes&
$2.99

FROM THE DEVELOPER

Children delight as they see, hear, and interact with letters and sounds in words, sentences, and games. They learn to recognize letters and develop skills that will ensure that they become confident leaders. All children, and especially English language learners, benefit from these activities. Starfall ™ is a registered trademark. © (1/2011) Starfall Education, reproduced with permission.

iREVIEW

Finally, my favorite website (starfall.com) is available on an app. My colleagues and I use *Starfall* on a daily basis to teach not only reading skills, but also computer literacy, labeling, phonics, following directions, etc. I have not met a student who did not become instantly enchanted with *Starfall*, and now I can put it on my portable device to make *Starfall* more accessible than ever. *Starfall ABCs* (app) and starfall.com (website) are highly recommended to build literacy in all students on the desktop and on the go. An additional benefit of having the identical *Starfall ABCs* user interface on a mobile device and desktop is that students can transition from touch screen to mouse/keyboard more quickly and easily than ever before.

Check out all the amazing language-literacy apps from Starfall at http://more.starfall.com/info/apps/starfall-education.php?ref=classic&

PLAYSQUARE PRESENTS WORDWORLD'S HAPPY BIRTHDAY DOG *by PlaySquare, LLC*

http://playsquare.tv

FREE

FROM THE DEVELOPER

Did you ever wish you could jump into a TV show and be a part of the story? *PlaySquare* lets your child do just that! *PlaySquare* is not a game, your child completes activities that help propel a rich video narrative along. The characters in the story depend on your child to help them along and save the day, so kids are actively involved from start to finish. When kids are engaged, they are learning!

iREVIEW

Touchable Television is a nutritious, active, engaging new media experience that's a story and a game all in one. Touchable Television (think of interactive Blue's Clues) allows you to use your finger to draw on the screen and become part of the action. Kids are engaged from start to finish, and when kids are engaged, they are learning! Fabulous animation and loveable characters will keep your child's attention through engagement. Best of all, they don't even realize they are learning to read!

Try all the Touchable Television Appisodes.

DR. SEUSS'S ABC *by Oceanhouse Media*
www.oceanhousemedia.com/products/abc
$3.99

Aunt Annie's alligator . . . .
A . . a . . A

See **Words Highlight** with Professional Narration

FROM THE DEVELOPER

Learn your ABCs with Dr. Seuss in this interactive book app for young readers! Explore pictures, learn new vocabulary, and personalize the story with your own narration. From Aunt Annie riding an alligator to the Zizzer-Zazzer-Zuzz, learning to read is an unforgettable adventure with Dr. Seuss!

iREVIEW

You can trust Dr. Seuss to deliver quality. *Dr. Seuss's ABC* is just one of the many quality apps available from Oceanhouse Media. Each eBook features three modes of reading: read to me, read/record it myself, and auto play. As the user reads through the book, he or she can touch a picture to see a highlight of the word spoken and then attach it to the picture. *Dr. Seuss's ABC* is highly recommended for beginning readers.

Also suggested:

The Lorax · The Cat in the Hat · Green Eggs and Ham · How the Grinch Stole Christmas! · Yertle the Turtle

Listen to an audio sample of Dr. Seuss's ABC and take a look at their app demo at www.oceanhousemedia.com/products/abc/

Chapter 26: Reading

Teaching reading to individuals with disabilities can be challenging and time consuming; however, it is well worth the effort. Every student will learn at an individual pace and programming should be age-appropriate, interactive, and functional. Some students will read before they talk; however, they may not understand what they have read. It has been suggested that students with autism are "hard-wired" to read because of their strong visual skills. Therefore, just because students do not verbalize, do not assume that they cannot learn to read.

 ## Success Story: Karl

Karl is a 20-year-old male student with profound visual and sensory challenges. Karl has not been able to tolerate toileting, and attempts to encourage independence have been unsuccessful. Using Karl's two favorite stories—*Green Eggs and Ham* from Oceanhouse Media and *The Cask of Amontillado* on Audiobook Player—Karl was able to tolerate transitioning into the restroom and completed his hygiene tasks successfully. Today, Karl is independent for toileting, thanks to Dr. Seuss and Edgar Allan Poe!

PINES TO VINES - THE FOREST BIOME

Pines to Vines covers a variety of topics, including forest layers, range and climate of forest biomes, plant and animal wildlife, adaptations, benefits of forests, and forest threats. Students will learn about all major forest types, including tropical moist forests, tropical/subtropical dry forests, tropical/subtropical coniferous forests, temperate coniferous forests, temperate broadleaf forests, Mediterranean forests, riverine forests, mangroves, and boreal forests.

SEASHORES TO SEA FLOORS - THE OCEAN BIOME

Seashores to Sea Floors discusses several topics, including ocean layers, plant and animal wildlife, adaptations, benefits of oceans, and ocean threats. Students will learn about all major ocean ecosystems, including open seas, polar oceans, the deep sea, the sea floor, seamounts, hydrothermal vents, cold seeps, rocky intertidal zones, beaches, kelp forests, estuaries, and coral reefs.

BLADES - THE GRASSLAND BIOME

Blades is a state-of-the-art, elementary science book based on the grasslands biome. Developed in collaboration with the Department of Biology at Doane University and a team of educators, this standards-based, core curriculum-aligned digital science book includes both interactive enhancements and universal design accessibility features.

CRACK THE BOOKS INTERACTIVE SCIENCE BOOKS

by Mobile Education Store LLC

http://mobile-educationstore.com/itextbooks

$9.99 each

FROM THE DEVELOPER

Crack The Books is a state-of-the-art, interactive book series for upper elementary students. Developed in collaboration with top universities, scientists, educators, and specialists, *Crack the Books* is the first standard-based, core curriculum-aligned digital book series that includes both interactive enhancements and universal design accessibility features. Designed for all students, from children with special needs to students who are academically gifted, Crack the Books gives educators a powerful new teaching tool to help students of all academic skill levels meet state standards for reading comprehension.

Crack the Books™ provides the first interactive books that can be adjusted for reading level. Students can experience all of the content presented to their classmates, while reading at a level that is appropriate to their ability. Targeting third to fifth grade science and social studies core curriculum concepts, our iBooks allow for reading level adjustment from first grade to eighth grade, making it possible for all students in a classroom to access the same curriculum content regardless of their reading ability.

iREVIEW

The future is now! *Crack the Books* gives our students highly interactive text that they can adjust to their reading level. Imagine every single student studying the same core content curriculum and learning the same concepts together at the same time. With an abundance of features like five reading levels, videos, animations, assessments, text-to-speech and interactive globes, I wish *Crack the Books* was around when I was in school (I would have gotten way better grades!). *Crack the Books* is a fraction of the cost of a hardback text, will never get lost or destroyed, and is continually updated.

This is what A4cwsn had to say about Pines to Vines: "We all know that our children learn in different ways and all have their own level of abilities. This book not only provides common core content but gives each and every single student an opportunity to learn the exact same information at the level that they can manage."

 See the demo and get all the info on the developer's website http://mobile-educationstore.com/itextbooks

 **BOB BOOKS #1 - READING MAGIC HD** *by Bob Books Publications LLC*
http://bobbooks.com
$3.99

Sam had a cat.

Start your child reading with this phonics-based interactive game. The simple drag-and-drop interface can be used by even the youngest children. Your favorite *Bob Books* characters and full-color animations encourage kids along the path of learning to read. *Bob Books* were created to lead children to the moment when letters first turn into words. By slowly introducing new letter sounds, using consistency, repetition, and stories that fit short attention spans, your child will quickly find his or her own "ah-ha" moment.

iREVIEW

Your child can develop a love for reading with *Bob Books*. This app is not only a student favorite, but also a tried-and-true learn-to-read teaching method. *Bob Books* adds just the right amount of student interaction with instructions and colorful animations to keep beginning readers focused and motivated for extended periods of time. The *Bob Books* app uses the same learning methods and principles as the bestselling *Bob Books* series. The *Bob Books* app slowly introduces new letter sounds using consistency, repetition, and stories that make learning to read and spell fun for all.

Now set #two is here, with 12 new scenes and over 50 words!

 Try the free version, and you will be hooked on *Bob Books*.

 **BOOKSY: LEARN TO READ PLATFORM FOR K-2**
by Tipitap Inc.
www.tipitap.com/booksy.html
FREE

FROM THE DEVELOPER

Booksy is a learning-to-read platform for young kids. It is designed from the ground up to help young children, pre-K through 2nd grade, practice and develop their reading skills. This edition comes with two FREE books. *Booksy* is at its heart a library of age-appropriate level readers. We believe kids want to read when we give them fascinating and interesting books. That is why we partnered with experts to create books on topics kids will love. They will not only dive into reading, but they will also learn with our nonfiction series.

iREVIEW

Level readers with comprehension quizzes are available for the iPad with *Booksy*. This is a wonderful collection of attention-grabbing books that encourages students to read and interact with content that ensures comprehension. Your students can have the book read to them, read it themselves, and even record their own voices. Additionally, students can collect stars/rewards for reading while educators track the performance of up to three students.

 This free edition comes with two complete books to get you started. Additional books are available as in-app purchases. Each additional book costs only $0.99, or you can buy the entire English Pack for $4.99. What a deal!
Booksy: School Edition. Learning to Read Platform K-2 comes with 27 complete books. It may have features that a typical person won't use, but at $15.99, you can save a few dollars on books and avoid the in-app purchase process.

SIGNED STORIES *by ITV Broadcasting Limited*
www.signedstories.com/apps
FREE – (new books every month)

FROM THE DEVELOPER

READ – WATCH – LISTEN – SIGN – PLAY – LEARN

We all rely on good educational resources to learn how to read and write. But deaf children and those with special needs have been starved of what they require to

develop good literacy Parents have struggled to find quality accessible storybooks which their children can share. Teachers are all too aware of the shortage of good classroom teaching materials. We have created *Signed Stories* to fill that gap. We believe passionately in the right of every child to have access to books in whatever format suits them best. Working with some of the best international publishers, we will continue to produce a wide range of animated picture books with optional ASL, captions, and narration. It is our hope that *Signed Stories* will make a real and lasting difference in the standards of literacy by enriching the lives of all children as they find their place in the world.

iREVIEW

Brilliant, just brilliant! Finally, literacy materials that include every learner and learning style. *Signed Stories* can be used for entire class (including staff) instruction via Apple TV or individual sessions. The ASL storytellers are actually performers who bring the story to life with expression and feeling. Once a week, I have a language group with *Signed Stories* and follow up with the interactive language games that accompany each book. Everyone learns and everyone has fun, and the best part is that no one is left out!

 The first story, "The Three Billy Goats Gruff," along with a Sign Dictionary, is free to try. Additional books range from $0.99 to $5.99.

 **SENTENCE MAKER** *by GrasshopperApps.com*
www.grasshopperapps.com
$0.99

FROM THE DEVELOPER

Sentence Maker is an exciting interactive game that helps your child rapidly learn to make and complete their own sentences, all with just the touch of a finger. The interface is so easy to use that everyone will delight in moving their first words around the page.

iREVIEW

Everything is customizable! *Sentence Maker* comes with 30 categories of pre-made sentences and the ability for the user to modify each category or add their own. You can decide what phrases/sentences to focus on, word length (two through five) and, most importantly, add your own photos/images. *Sentence Maker* is a powerful tool in teaching language/literacy skills and meeting national standards in education for all of my students at every age and ability level due to extensive customization features. For complete immersion into a language and literacy activity, have your student take pictures of meaningful people, places, and items in their environment. Then add these pictures to *Little Speller* (see "Spelling," Chapter 25) so that they can learn how to read, spell, and recognize their favorite words. Next use the same pictures to customize sentences and phrases in *Sentence Maker*.

 A free version is available for you to try.

 **ENDLESS READER** *by Originator Inc.*
www.originatorkids.com
FREE

FROM THE DEVELOPER

This app introduces sight words, the most commonly used words in school, library, and children's books. Kids need to recognize these words by sight in order to

achieve reading fluency. Recognizing sight words is advantageous for beginning readers, because many of these words have unusual spelling, cannot be sounded out using phonics knowledge, and often cannot be represented using pictures. Kids will have a blast learning sight words and their context and usage with the adorable Endless monsters. Each word features an interactive word puzzle with letters that come alive and sentence puzzles with words that become what they describe. See the word "dog" as a barking dog, and see the word "up" reach for the sky! NOTE: You must be online and have sufficient disk space while running the app to get all words in the app.

iREVIEW

Enticing your child to enjoy reading has never been easier with today's technology. *Endless Reader* will not only have your child reading and spelling with high quality funny animations, but will teach the concept of the words and sentences with delightful animations that act out the target sentence(s). *Endless Reader* is highly entertaining and is designed for young learners; however, the words/sentences are not immature and can be entertaining for older students and the young at heart.

Six words free to try with additional word packs available for purchase. Even more Reader Packs will be available for purchase in the future.

STARRING YOU BOOKS BY STORYBOTS
by JibJab Media Inc.
www.storybots.com/storybooks
FREE

"Let's see," Alex said
as he picked out a book.

"This might be a good one.
I'll just take a look."

Full Library
Dozens of fun, animated books
to choose from

FROM THE DEVELOPER

The *Starring You Books* iPad app makes storytelling even more magical by making your child the star of a beautifully illustrated and animated storybook that features their face and name. Simply add a photo, and voila! Your child (or mommy, daddy, grandpa, friends, or even the family dog) is the star of the show! Once you download a book over a Wi-Fi or data connection, you're ready for a reading moment at home, in the car, on the playground, or anywhere offline. Enjoy great, educational fun wherever you are! The *Starring You Books* app is available on the iPad and comes with a free personalized book.

iREVIEW

Instill a love of reading with *Starring You Books by StoryBots*. No child can resist putting their face on the endearing animations while they read their very own personalized book. Each story is unique with gorgeous artwork, fun music, and adventures that your child will read again and again. New topical stories added each month – see the demo on the developer's website www.storybots.com/storybooks for more information and a free introduction to *Starring You Books by StoryBots*.

A *StoryBots* membership unlocks all 30+ books from our growing library and includes unlimited access to the entire collection of *StoryBots* apps for kids and parents, all for only $4.99 a month.

SHREK FOREVER AFTER KID'S BOOK HD

$2.99

CLOUDY WITH A CHANCE... KID'S BOOK HD

$0.99

MEET BISCUIT KIDS BOOK

$2.99

by iStoryTime, Inc.

www.istorytimeapp.com

The *iStoryTime* library app includes a wide selection of narrated children's storybooks from your kids favorite films, TV shows, and classic stories. All of the stories feature professional narration and vivid images. From reliving the adventures of your favorite *Zoosters* in Madagascar to following the magical little creatures in The Smurfs, woolly mammoths in *Ice Age* or *Robin Hood* in one of the great classics, the *iStoryTime* library app is perfect for learning to read, summer road trips, bedtime stories, and more!

iREVIEW

iStoryTime books are masterfully executed, with beautiful graphics and clear, articulate audio. *iStory-Time* provides the user with options to read by oneself or to be read to by others. And if turning the page (swiping) is a challenge, iStoryTime books will automatically turn the pages for you. According to the National Education Association (NEA), "Motivating children to read is an important factor in student achievement and creating lifelong successful readers. Research has shown that children who are motivated and spend more time reading do better in school." *iStoryTime* books are recommended for everyone at every ability level. iTherapy opportunities include labeling, describing, finger isolation, eye-hand coordination, sequencing, and visual integration; social pragmatic skills also will be enhanced with the use of these tools.

TOY STORY READ-ALONG *by Disney*

http://disneystories.com/customer-service

FREE

FROM THE DEVELOPER

Meet Woody, a cowboy doll that comes to life when humans aren't around. When his owner Andy receives a Buzz Lightyear space ranger for his birthday, Woody and the other toys fear they'll be replaced. Woody's plan to get rid of Buzz backfires, and he ends up lost outside the world of Andy's room, with Buzz as his only companion! The toys work together to find their way back to Andy and discover the meaning of true friendship along the way.

iREVIEW

Toy Story Read-Along is one of the best free apps I have encountered. Students can read it themselves, record their voices, or have it read to them with great audio. *Toy Story Read-Along* includes games, music, and interactive activities that keep my students engaged with excellent screen display and 3D-like animation.

 There is a similar app, *Toy Story 3* (free version), that is merely an advertisement for the higher priced *Toy Story* apps.

READING RAINBOW: READ ALONG CHILDREN'S BOOKS, KIDS VIDEOS & EDUCATIONAL GAMES

by Reading Rainbow

$2.99

FROM THE DEVELOPER

Hosted by LeVar Burton, the reimagined *Reading Rainbow* app includes an unlimited library of children's books and video field trips to ignite your child's imagination. With *Reading Rainbow* children's library, it's easy for your child to find just the right book. Kids travel to themed islands such as Animal Kingdom,

Genius Academy, Music Mountain, Awesome People, and National Geographic Kids to discover books from acclaimed authors and illustrators. Recommended "just for you" books are customized to your child's ages and interests. New books and videos are added every week, always expanding the collection.

Video Field Trips with LeVar Burton

iREVIEW

Everyone loves a good book! *Reading Rainbow* offers much more than just books—it also offers a comprehensive reading/literacy experience. LeVar Burton takes your child on exclusive video field trips to visit fascinating people and places to complement the stories they are reading. For hundreds of high-quality interactive educational/entertaining content with supportive games and video fieldtrips. It is updated frequently, (*Reading Rainbow* is an outstanding choice.)

 Free to try, download the app to explore our worlds of reading while enjoying up to five free books and a sampling of video field trips.

Chapter 27: Math

As with reading disabilities, when math difficulties are present, they can range from mild to severe. Many students have persistent trouble memorizing basic facts in all four operations (addition, subtraction, multiplication, and division), despite great efforts to do so. Providing individuals with visual supports to mathematical equations could be the answer.

KHAN ACADEMY *by Khan Academy*
www.khanacademy.org
FREE

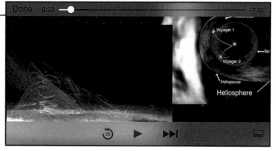

FROM THE DEVELOPER

Khan Academy allows you to learn almost anything for free. We cover a massive number of topics, including K-12 math; science topics such as biology, chemistry, and physics; and even the humanities with playlists on art history, civics, and finance. Spend an afternoon brushing up on statistics. Discover how the Krebs cycle works. Learn about the fundamentals of computer science. Prepare for the upcoming SAT, or if you're feeling particularly adventurous, learn how fire stick farming changed the landscape of Australia.

iREVIEW

Khan Academy started a revolution in education by letting learners take control of their learning! *Khan Academy* will allow you to learn what you want at your own pace and level. You can watch the over 4,200 video tutorials as many times as needed to master a concept at your learning rate. *Khan Academy* covers many topics, from math and science to history and biology; however, *Khan Academy* is best known for its excellent visual supports and lessons in math.

An iTunes review by Sydhalpenny describes how powerful the *Khan Academy* video tutorials can be for learning: "Finally, something that can actually teach me, explain to me, and help work out the problems so I understand. As a 10th grader, I give this app a five-star rating. This app has taught me more about geometry in an hour than a semester and a half of my terrible, ignorant teacher teaching this to me. Schools are so overcrowded nowadays that it's very easy to get lost and fall behind in the shuffle, teachers never have time anymore to help students individually when they need one-on-one time for help. With this app, I know I can pull through to help better my education in geometry and now even more subjects that I can review on whenever I'd like! Thank you *Khan Academy*!" Quality education that is free, forever! No ads, no subscriptions. Kahn Academy is not-for-profit because it believes in a free, world-class education for anyone, anywhere.

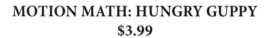

To add, you simply put two dots together

Single & double digits
Negatives & subtraction

MOTION MATH: HUNGRY GUPPY
$3.99

Your student will learn numbers and basic addition with this delightful game. It's easy to play—simply drag bubbles together to add them, then feed it to your fish. *Motion Math: Hungry Guppy* features a fish who loves to eat numbers, with 15 total levels.

MOTION MATH: HUNGRY FISH
$1.99

Feed your fish and play with numbers! Practice mental addition and subtraction with *Motion Math: Hungry Fish*, a delightful learning game that's fun for children and grownups.

Your fish is hungry for numbers. You can make delicious sums by pinching two numbers together—instant addition! Keep feeding your fish to win a level and unlock new colors and fins.

by Motion Math

http://motionmathgames.com

FROM THE DEVELOPER

In the first controlled study of an iPad learning game, kids who played *Motion Math: Fractions* for 20 minutes for five days demonstrated the following:

- Improved 15% on fractions test scores.
- Improved attitudes and confidence towards fractions by an average of 10%.

For ages five and up, *Motion Math* helps learners estimate four forms of fractions: numerator over denominator (1/2), percents (50%), decimals (.5), and pie charts. Quick and accurate perception of fractions is needed for advanced math success.

iREVIEW

Motion Math: Hungry Guppy & *Hungry Fish* are so zen like that my students use *Motion Math* apps to calm, organize, and focus their thoughts and attention. With soothing graphics and background music, children squeeze dots together and feed them to the fish. If the dot forms the correct answer, the fish eats the dot and grows bigger; if the answer is incorrect, the fish swims away. Count dots and add numbers to five with *Hungry Guppy.* With *Hungry Fish* you can add and subtract 18 levels with additional options available for subtraction and negative numbers via in-app purchase. Try all of the *Motion Math* apps and discover how educational games can foster success in school.

NEXT DOLLAR UP *by Limited Cue LLC*
www.limitedcue.com
$7.99

FROM THE DEVELOPER

Next Dollar Up is a widely utilized special education teaching strategy for those with special needs to develop independence in money management using a whole dollar amount concept. It involves looking at an item price and rounding up to the next dollar to make the purchase. Various learning styles are addressed simultaneously. Non-readers can enjoy *Next Dollar Up* as well due to the illustrative game cards and voice prompts provided. Simplicity and consistency are at the forefront of design, with the goal that the user not become lost in its functions but rather receive the maximum educational value possible.

iREVIEW

Get the practice you need with *Next Dollar Up* to feel confident making a purchase. Shopping and purchasing are often stressful situations for individuals who have challenges with money concepts. Using the *Next Dollar Up* strategy builds independence and gives parents/educators peace of mind, knowing that a person can never be overcharged by more than $0.99. *Next Dollar Up* has a simple design and clear audio. A product and price appears on the screen with a stack of ones and a voiceover that simulates a clerk asking for payment. The user slides money to the "counter" then checks their answer. Simple data tracking for 10 trials is provided on screen.

TODO TELLING TIME
by Locomotive Labs
www.limitedcue.com
$4.99

FROM THE DEVELOPER

Todo Telling Time provides playful opportunities for children in kindergarten through second grade to learn all aspects of time telling with fun, interactive mini games. With this app, children will learn to tell time to

Play time = learning time

the hour and minute, calendar concepts, digital time, and the components of a daily schedule. Todo Telling Time also addresses secondary factors necessary for mastering time telling. These include practice with ordering numbers around a clock face, counting by fives, elapsed time, and estimates of time. Each game is unique and engaging, ensuring that children continue to have fun as they learn the necessary skill of telling time..

iREVIEW

Learning to tell time is a common core standard from grades first through third. *Todo Telling Time* has six engaging multi-level games to help your child meet this standard in education. The graphics, artwork, and design are meant for younger students; however, the concepts of time can be taught to all who struggle with the passing of time, memory, and/or the notion of a schedule.

KIDCALC 7-IN-1 MATH FUN *by Steve Glinberg*
http://kidcalc.wordpress.com
$0.99

KidCalc teaches number recognition, counting, and math to preschoolers, kindergarteners, and elementary school-aged children using flash cards and puzzle games, with engaging artwork, animation, and voice-overs. *KidCalc* includes animated addition, subtraction, multiplication, and division lessons. *KidCalc* is easily configured to adjust the challenge level of counting and math puzzles. Settings vary for toddlers learning numbers, for preschoolers learning to add and subtract, and for elementary school-aged kids learning to count as high as 1,000 and to multiply and divide.

iREVIEW

KidCalc is super cute and super fun. Many of my students use this app as reinforcement. Students who have had difficulty with math concepts for years are finally motivated and making connections due to the superb visual supports *KidCalc* offers. Your child will have a blast learning to count, write, skip count, and read numbers; however, the visual calculator that adds and subtracts numbers zero through 10 with virtual objects may be the best part of *KidCalc*. *KidCalc* is easily individualized for every ability level, and fun themes make it topical for different times of the year. The developer adds holiday and seasonal themes throughout the year. Great price, great app! Even the audio is clear and articulate.

ENDLESS NUMBERS *by Originator Inc.*

http://originatorkids.com

FREE

FROM THE DEVELOPER

As a follow-up to Endless Alphabet, set the stage for early numeracy learning with *Endless Numbers*! Kids will have a blast learning number recognition, sequences,

quantity, numerical patterns, and simple addition with the adorable Endless monsters. Each number features interactive sequences and equation puzzles with numbers that come alive and a short animation that provides context and meaning to each number.

Endless Numbers is great for children learning how to count and mastering one-to-one correspondence and basic addition facts. The audio and the charming monsters reinforcement system are appealing to younger students. Students can count along with the app (verbal and graphic) as they touch each interactive number and drag it to its place. You will be surprised how much your children will learn about counting and numbers simply by playing with *Endless Numbers*.

 Try out five numbers free. The complete first number pack (1-25) is available for in-app purchase.

KNOCK KNOCK NUMBERS—JOKE TELLING AND CONVERSATIONS TOOL FOR AUTISM, ASPERGERS, DOWN SYNDROME & SPECIAL EDUCATION

by Touch Autism

http://touchautism.com

$2.99

FROM THE DEVELOPER

Get ready to laugh (and groan!) as you practice numbers and humor with 20 classic knock knock jokes. *Knock Knock Numbers* was designed by a BCBA as a fun way to teach kids how to tell knock knock jokes while working on number recognition. The app teaches 20 different jokes, and each one prompts the user to identify a number between one and 10. Settings allow the user to choose how many numbers are presented in each trial. Telling jokes is an important developmental skill that allows children to improve communication while connecting socially with others. Humor is especially important for children with autism, because studies have shown that they often exhibit delays in relating to their peers.

iREVIEW

Looking for an app to engage students with humor and fun to teach math, reading, and social skills? *Knock Knock Numbers* is perfect. Knowing and being able to tell knock-knock jokes is an essential part of growing up; furthermore, for children on the spectrum, learning how to interpret and display humor is an essential life skill that leads to making friends. Beyond learning numbers and social skills, *Knock Knock Numbers* teaches a metalinguistic approach to looking at and interpreting words/word-meanings. Metalinguistic awareness or the ability to think about words, how they are used, and their meaning is a foundational skill for pragmatic development, conversation, and further language concept acquisition.

TIME, MONEY & FRACTIONS ON-TRACK
by School Zone Publishing
www.schoolzone.com
$4.99

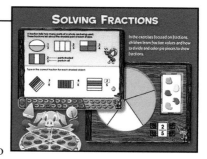

FROM THE DEVELOPER

The program's kid-friendly approach delivers solid practice that will build confidence and help children succeed in school. Exercises are presented with detailed instructions and clear examples. The section concentrating on time lets children manipulate the hands of a clock to learn about hours and minutes, while other exercises teach children to set clocks to specific times. The section dedicated to money lets children maneuver coins into a bank, an activity that teaches coin values and how to count coins. In the exercises focused on fractions, children learn fraction values and how to divide and color pie pieces to show fractions.

Performance is encouraged through audio guidance, instant grading, progress tracking, and ample positive reinforcement. In addition, each skill section has a no-stress learning area where children can explore each concept without being graded. Colorful graphics, silly sound effects, and funny animations enhance the learning experience. Plus, engaging games offer an important break between exercises. When additional practice is needed, a click of the reset button will randomize the problems for extended learning opportunities.

iREVIEW

Time, Money & Fractions On-Track offers great visual supports for students on the spectrum. General education teachers use and recommend this app. *Time, Money & Fractions On-Track* has students moving hands on a virtual clock, handling digital money, and dividing color pies, pizzas and charts to learn fractions. Games and reinforcement are incorporated into the app to provide students with motivation and keep them interested. *Time, Money & Fractions On-Track* has a general progress tracking page that lets the student monitor his or her success. This app is well worth the cost if you are targeting the core first to second grade level concepts of time, money, or fractions.

MATHMATEER™ *by Freecloud Design, Inc.*
http://dan-russell-pinson.com/contact
$0.99

FROM THE DEVELOPER

While your rocket is floating weightlessly in space, the real fun begins! Play one of the 56 different math missions. Each mission has touchable objects floating in space, including stars, coins, clocks, 3D shapes, and even pizzas! Earn a bronze, silver, or gold medal, and also try to beat your high score. Missions range in difficulty, with subjects such as even/odd numbers and square roots, so kids and their parents will enjoy hours of fun while learning math.

iREVIEW

Choose your rocket, choose your avatar, and begin your mathematical mission with *Mathmateer*! Earn medals and money to design your space machine and send it on a quest. There are 56 different math missions. Features include rocket parts, sound effects, three difficulty levels, 15 avatars, and up to five player profiles.

 Users' auditory processing skills should be adequate to follow one-step directions. There are many layers to this game, and some students should adjust sound effects and music to fit their level of tolerance. *Mathmateer* has a quick pace and may require some adult coaching to become familiar with the settings.

JUMBO CALCULATOR PLUS *by Christopher Weems*

No website available

$0.99

FROM THE DEVELOPER

Jumbo Calculator is the super simple large-buttoned calculator for everyone, ages two through 92. While sadly you can't feel the exquisite texture of its large plastic buttons (and the included solar panel doesn't actually charge your battery), *Jumbo Calculator* succeeds in accomplishing its main purposes: adding, subtracting, multiplying, and dividing. One size fits all.

iREVIEW

What you see is what you get. *Jumbo Calculator* is perfect for individuals with vision or motor difficulties. This is a straightforward, large-button calculator with voiceover support for blind and low-vision users, but it is also helpful to those with cognitive or visual processing challenges.

 A free version is available.

Chapter 28: Preschool

Students with disabilities are not always given the opportunity and time necessary to become familiar with the key words and concepts that are the building blocks of future schooling. With a trend toward more inclusive educational experiences for all children with disabilities, we should give them every opportunity to succeed and meet their goals. Children with disabilities are using preschool apps as young as three years old to get a jumpstart on their education.

Success Story: Ethan

Because many of the preschool applications use a multiple choice format, Ethan is able to show that he knows his letters, colors, and shapes (age-appropriate skills for a four-year-old), even to those who have difficulty understanding his speech. Same-age peers find it cool and love to take turns with Ethan, which presents an entirely new level of learning. He is able to be fairly independent once we get him to the game he wants to play.

Ethan mastering preschool concepts on his iPod touch

He is able to click on answers easily and is even beginning to get the hang of dragging items, which has been a major roadblock to using a computer mouse. We love that it is infinitely patient with him and that skills can be presented multiple ways to help with reinforcement and generalization. We like to use it while waiting in restaurants or at the doctor's office and in the car because it is small. The biggest problem we've run into is trying to take it away before he is finished!

INJINI: CHILD DEVELOPMENT GAME SUITE
by NCSOFT

www.injini.net

$29.99

FROM THE DEVELOPER

Injini's collection of learning games offers meaningful play to young children, especially toddlers and preschoolers with cognitive, language, and fine motor delays. The games contain an extraordinary wealth of content: 10 feature games with 90 puzzles, over 100 beautiful illustrations, eight farm-themed mini-games, and more. *Injini* is ideally suited for early intervention; it brings fun to learning and also practices children's fine motor and language skills, understanding of cause and effect, spatial awareness, memory, and visual processing.

iREVIEW

Injini was designed and tested from the bottom up for children with special needs. Each learning game features a tutorial with nine subtle levels of difficulty and a ready-set-go countdown to direct attention to each task.

    Technology in (Spl) Education puts it best with this review: "This is one of the most thought-out and comprehensive apps that we have seen." *Injini* is recommended for a stress-free, challenging way for any child to develop the preschool learning concepts of color, numbers, letters, auditory processing, fine motor control, shapes, patterns, and visual discrimination.

 Check out the demo and printable supplements, tips, and support available at www.injini.net

TOPIQ KIDS LEARNING PROGRAM POWERED BY AGNITUS *by Agnitus*

www.agnitus.com

FREE

FROM THE DEVELOPER

- One hundred plus curriculum based preschool and kindergarten skills, games, and activities

- Classic interactive, fun and educational books from Mother Goose and others

- Detailed report card of the child's performance

- Personalized learning for math, reading and writing

Fundamental Skills: 2D Shapes, colors, fruits, size comparison, visual scanning, quantities matching, ABCs matching, memory and recall, recognizing numerals, sense of quantity, counting up to 10, object-based addition, object-based subtraction, object-based multiplication.

iREVIEW

TopIQ Kids Learning Program powered by Agnitus is your doorway to a complete and comprehensive learning system mapped to Core Standards for your child. A subscription is required to start your free trial. The high-quality graphics, curriculum, interactive books, Smart report card(s), and very detailed parents' dashboard make Agnitus well worth the subscription price for teaching preschool and kindergarten level skills. Your child will never get bored with auto-adjustments for skill level and frequent updates/additions to curriculum/bookshelf.

 The initial trial is free (with subscription); additional in-app purchases are available, or you can choose a monthly auto-renew subscription.

ITOUCHILEARN WORDS FOR PRESCHOOL KIDS
$0.99

iTouchiLearn Words features an easy-to-use interface to select word activities. Your toddler, preschooler, or special education child will be treated to entertaining animations and engaging word games that teach a series of words and associated actions while making them laugh. Players receive virtual rewards for correct answers.

- Sight Words
- Reading
- Cognitive Skills
- Literacy

by Staytoooned

http://itouchilearnapps.com

ITOUCHILEARN WORDS: SPEECH & LANGUAGE SKILLS
$1.99

Engaging animations and activities teach kids about the context of words and reinforce early speech and language skills. Each activity reinforces:

- Word recognition
- Spelling-reading
- Audio
- Fine motor
- Speech-language
- Common Core state curriculum standards compliance

FROM THE DEVELOPER

With its short, colorful, and funny animations, *iTouchiLearn Words for Preschool Kids* is a must-have app for teaching early learning, literacy skills, cognitive, language, and verbal skills. Filled with frogs leaping, children dancing, monkeys swinging, fish swimming, balls bouncing, and bubbles floating, *iTouchiLearn Words* is a delightful distraction and is ideal for helping kids with early learning.

iREVIEW

iTouchiLearn Words and *Speech & Language Skills* is the first set of apps I have found that gives the user a short animated movie to teach nouns, verbs, spelling, and sight words. *iTouchiLearn* is also an excellent tool for targeting receptive language skills. I have to recommend this app because of the animated approach to teaching language concepts and vocabulary. I am so excited about this app because my students love it! iTouchiLearn apps are divided into three sections: two focus on labeling/spelling, and the third is a series of wonderful animations to teach nouns and verbs. Customization is minimal, and background music and spell word options available.

 For more early learning fun, try *iTouchiLearn Feelings, iTouchiLearn Life Skills: Morning Routines,* and *iTouchiLearn Numbers.*

 **TEACHME: TODDLER**
by 24x7digital LLC
www.24x7digital.com/
apps/TeachMe_Apps.html
$0.99

FROM THE DEVELOPER

TeachMe: Toddler is an educational iPhone/iPad/iPod touch app which teaches six different preschool appropriate subjects: letters, ABC phonics (letter sounds), numbers, shapes, colors, and counting. Parents can choose which topics they want their child to learn and even choose specific questions. Parents can review performance history for each subject to check on how their child is doing.

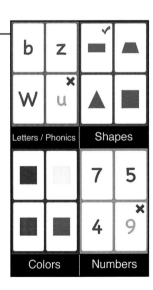

TeachMe: Toddler will teach your child letters, phonics, numbers (1-20), shapes, and colors while they earn rewards from a parent-created reward system of stickers and coins. Subjects are presented in a random order, and performance is tracked for up to 40 students. Teacher Mini guides your child through the learning process in American or British English, allowing your child to play without adult intervention.

 Be sure to try the other apps in the *TeachMe* series: *TeachMe: Kindergarten, TeachMe: 1ˢᵗ Grade, TeachMe: 2ⁿᵈ Grade,* and *TeachMe: 3ʳᵈ Grade* ($1.99 each)!

SUPER WHY! *by PBS KIDS*
http://pbskids.org/apps
$2.99

FROM THE DEVELOPER

Help your child achieve the "Power to Read" with this collection of four *SUPER WHY!* interactive literacy games. Your child can play along with each of the four main characters from the TV series—Alpha Pig, Princess Presto, Wonder Red, and of course Super Why—while practicing the alphabet, rhyming, spelling, writing, and reading. Super Duper!

iREVIEW

SUPER WHY! is super cute. If you are a beginning reader with good auditory processing skills, this is the app for you. Each character gives the user instructions on how to proceed through the game. While they are cute, they talk a lot, which may be too much for my students who have auditory processing challenges.

 There is no Settings page; the user cannot make choices regarding music, sound effects, or voices. See the demo for details at http://pbskids.org/apps/super-why-app.html

GAME FACTORY HD *by Bacciz*

http://bacciz.com

$1.99

FROM THE DEVELOPER

Use your own pictures, and you choose exactly what you want your children to learn. Load family pictures and let your child see mom and dad and grandparents in the game. *Game Factory*'s new release is a hybrid match and flash card game that allows parents to upload their own images and choose the concepts they want their kids to learn. Our app is unique because it allows you to choose the content of the app.

iREVIEW

If you are learning your ABCs, 123s, shapes, animals, a foreign language(s), or trying to reach an individual goal, this is the app for you! I recommend turning the music off; it can be distracting. *Game Factory HD* keeps track of scores but does not capture data. My favorite aspects of this app is the ability to customize to student goals and add personalization via pictures and labels.

MONKEY PRESCHOOL LUNCHBOX

by THUP Games

http://thup.com

$1.99

FROM THE DEVELOPER

Learn and have fun by helping monkeys pack lunch! *Monkey Preschool Lunchbox* is a collection of six exciting educational games for your preschooler.

Monkey Preschool Lunchbox targets a variety of concepts such as colors, matching, counting, letters, shapes, and differences with fun puzzles and activities. A student can even earn stickers. Usually, no instruction is required, and students are engaged almost immediately. Monkey Preschool Lunchbox has no settings, and the questions are randomized. Many of my students will work to earn time on *Monkey Preschool Lunchbox*. Work to work—I like it!

 Join Monkey on all his learning adventures—*WordSchool Adventure, MathSchool Sunshine, When I Grow Up, Fix-It,* and *Explorers* for an entertaining stress free learning option.

FEED ME! – PENCILBOT PRESCHOOL LEARNING CENTER

by Edutainment Resources, Inc.

www.pencilbot.com/welcome/PencilBot.html

FREE

FROM THE DEVELOPER

One-stop shopping for your preschooler's learning needs, whether learning basic knowledge and concepts for kindergarten readiness or learning a first, second, or multiple languages.

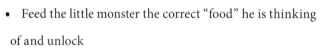

- Feed the little monster the correct "food" he is thinking of and unlock trophies for your trophy case!

- Feed the monster the wrong item, and he might get sick. But don't worry; you'll have the chance to try the question again later in the game.

iREVIEW

Feed Me! covers a plethora of language concepts from letters and numbers to opposites and rhymes. The cute purple Monster thinks of a question (letter recognition, shapes, vocabulary, spelling, math, etc.), and the user is required to feed the monster the right answer. The voiceover is a clear, articulate child's voice. Feed Me! is engaging for the students, while the educator or caregiver can focus on a specific goal(s). A benefit of *Feed Me!* is the fact that it comes in 11 languages, and settings can be personalized for up to four players. I recommend giving it a try. It is FREE and can be deleted if your child or student does not enjoy it.

 This app consists of one free sampler and 12 in-app purchases, each in a specific language. The sampler includes 20 questions in different languages to give you a taste of what the PencilBot Preschool Learning Center offers.

ALPHABET FUN *by Tapfuze*
www.tapfuze.com
$1.99

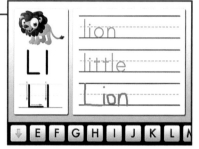

FROM THE DEVELOPER

Alphabet Fun is like having preschool right on your iPad! Filled with over 70 full-color images and large, easy-to-read text, *Alphabet Fun* provides an excellent learning platform for preschoolers. Simply scroll through the letters, colors, and numbers with the swipe of a finger. Explore how each character is written by tracing over it. Users can even practice writing entire words with ease.

iREVIEW

Give your child a jump on preschool with *Alphabet Fun*. Your child will have the opportunity to hear, write, and say their numbers, ABCs, colors, and whole words on their iDevice in five different languages. Both audio and graphics are lively and engaging for both the young and the young at heart. Recommended for anyone mastering basic preschool concepts.

 Alphabet Fun is back with even more interaction, more animals, and a beautiful new interface; check out *Alphabet Fun 2*.

Part VIII

Neurodevelopmental & Neurological Communication Disorders Dysarthria, Aphasia, Apraxia, and Dysphagia

Communication is necessary for the positive health of human beings. Poor communication may alter individuals' lives and cause them to be socially withdrawn. Whether congenital or acquired, neurological communication disorders can be devastating. Several classifications of neurological disorders exist that may cause individuals to lose their ability to understand, speak, chew, and swallow. I will focus on four of those disorders in this section. I strongly recommend using the apps in this section under the guidance of a speech-language pathologist. While none will cause any ill effects, proper and consistent use can lead to extraordinary results.

In the News:

iPad Could Be a Beneficial Device for the Disabled

By RedOrbit

When it comes to high-tech gadgets like the iPad, most people see a sleek, multi-media entertainment platform, but Professor Gregg Vanderheiden sees other potential possibilities for the Apple touch-screen device.

Vanderheiden, director of the Trace Research and Development Center at the University of Wisconsin at Madison, says the iPad could be an important tool for people with speech problems and other disabilities. "Say you have somebody who's had a stroke, for example, and they wake up and they can't communicate. Instead of buying a 5,000-dollar communications aid, you take out your iPad and download an app and—bam!—they can communicate," he told AFP.

The Trace Center helps those who are unable to speak and cannot communicate properly, and researchers from the center, including Vanderheiden, are excited about the potential the iPad is showing as a relatively low-cost communication tool.

Karen Sheehan, the executive director of the Alliance for Technology Access, a California-based group that looks for ways to expand technology to allow those with disabilities to live better qualitative lives, said there is much interest in the iPad. People with autism, spinal injuries, cerebral palsy, or ALS and stroke victims—"Anyone who's non-verbal and needs a device to speak for them"—could all possibly benefit from the iPad, said Sheehan.

There are many useful communication tools available for helping those with disabilities, "but they tend to run into the thousands of dollars, which can be prohibitive for a lot of people," said Sheehan. The iPad can be turned into a very inexpensive communication tool that does the same job as many of the more expensive medical devices.

AssistiveWare is one company that has adapted communication applications for the iPhone and iPod touch. Their *Proloquo2Go* app has been revamped to also work with the iPad and is available at Apple's App Store for less than $200.00. *Proloquo2Go* works by allowing users who have difficulty speaking to communicate using symbols to represent phrases. They can also type in what they want to say, and the words can be converted to speech using text-to-speech technology with a natural-sounding voice.

The iPad's large screen makes it more useful to a wider range of people than the iPhone and iPod touch, said Sheehan. "They've such a small area, and for someone who has limited fine motor it's hard to hit small icons. It's easier on the iPad to just click on an icon to say 'I want juice,' or 'I want to watch a movie.'"

Joanne Castellano, Director of the New Jersey-based TechConnection, which provides "assistive technology" solutions to people with disabilities, said that the iPad seems like a very useful tool, and although the touch-screen controls are part of the attraction of the gadget, it could prove to be a challenge for some people with disabilities. "The way you have to pinch some things with your thumb and your forefinger—that movement might be a problem for some people," she said. "But to turn the page of a book you just have to swipe it, so that could be very helpful."

Dan Herlihy of Connective Technology Solutions told AFP that he planned on getting the iPad to use with other tools to address the needs of people with disabilities. "And I can already think of about half a dozen things I'll run on it," he said.

Vanderheiden said the iPad is a "great platform—small, inexpensive, a lot of power, a long battery," but its greatest contribution to the needs of the disabled may be from the applications built for the device. "They offer the opportunity for just tremendous, unprecedented innovation."

RedOrbit.com is the premier Internet destinatio
for space, science, health, and technology enthusiasts
around the globe.

Chapter 29: Apraxia

"No wonder I don't talk. How am I going to talk if my lips don't move? Strange! People don't understand such a simple fact!" Insightful quote from author Tito Mukhopadhyay in *How Can I Talk if My Lips Don't Move?*

The official definition and symptomology as provided by A.D.A.M. Medical Encyclopedia, Apraxia of speech, also known as verbal apraxia, dyspraxia, childhood apraxia of speech, or acquired apraxia, is a disorder of the brain and nervous system in which a person is unable to perform tasks or movements when asked, even though:

1. The request or command is understood
2. They are willing to perform the task
3. The muscles needed to perform the task work properly
4. The task may have already been learned

A person with apraxia is unable to put together the correct muscle movements. At times, a completely different word or action is used than the one the person intended to speak or make. The person is often aware of the mistake. Symptoms of apraxia of speech include the following:

- Speech sounds and words may be distorted, repeated, or left out. It is difficult to put words together in the correct order.
- Struggling to pronounce the right word.
- Longer words are more difficult to use, either at all or from one time or another.
- Short everyday phrases or sayings (such as "How are you?") can often still be used without a problem.
- The person often can write better than he or she can speak.

Ido Kedar, in his book Ido in Autismland, gives a powerful insider's view of apraxia and the frustration that comes with the inability to express your thoughts:

> It's hard to speak because apraxia is like a bad phone connection. I know my thoughts are getting lost on the way to my mouth. I think of an idea. I try to say it and the wrong thing comes out. For example, I might really want to get a chicken dish for dinner in a restaurant, but if someone asks me if I want beef my mouth is often messing it up by saying 'yes.' It's so frustrating because I suffer through getting the wrong meal even though I responded to a question. It's like my mouth is surprising me and I have to obey it. I get irritated by my inability to get my thoughts out. It's the most horrible aspect of my autism. It's the loneliest thing you can imagine. If I could change it, I'd be so happy. It's my hardest frustration by far, and that's saying a lot.

Individuals with apraxia of speech communicate in a variety of ways, such as keyboard, text-to-speech, AAC, writing, sign language, gestures, or a combination of techniques. This chapter focuses on improving speech production and/or articulation for individuals with apraxia but will also benefit all learning the complex synchronized movements of speech.

In the Spotlight:

Exciting New iPad Technology for Non-Verbal Individuals with Autism

According to recent statistics, autism is the fastest-growing developmental disability in the U.S. today. Autism affects one in 88 children and one in 54 boys. About 40% of children with autism do not talk at all. Another 25%-30% of children with autism have some words at 12-18 months of age and then lose them. Others may speak, but not until later in childhood. In 20 years, there has been a 600% increase in the number of cases of autism. About a third to a half of those individuals will not develop enough natural speech to meet their daily communication needs.

Thanks to the development of recent technology like the iPad/iPod touch, a groundbreaking and exciting therapeutic technique to teach non-verbal students to use spoken language has emerged. *VAST Autism 1 – Core, VAST Pre-Speech* and *VAST Songs* (apps available from iTunes) combines best practices, video modeling, music therapy, and literacy with auditory cues to provide unprecedented support for the development of vocabulary, word combinations, and communication. This means that students simply watch a video of a syllable, word, phrase, exercise, functional activity, or a song being produced, see the visual representation, and hear it audibly. It's like watching a close-up movie of someone talking, singing, or performing oral motor activities with subtitles. The VAST technique is also extremely effective in providing specialized therapy to help individuals with motor planning disorders, non-fluent aphasia, apraxia, deaf and hard of hearing, speak for themselves.

Speech has always been a challenge for individuals on the spectrum. Therapies for non-verbal students may include teaching sign language, gestures, picture exchange, and/or voice output devices. To teach verbalizations, therapists attempt to have students repeat sounds or words from their model. The idea is that a student watches the therapist articulate the target word, sound, and movements and then attempts to reproduce those movements or sound(s). This technique does not usually work well due to the challenges that students on the spectrum have with making eye contact or looking at a person's face. It is difficult to see how the articulators move when the ability to look at the face is fleeting. Technology, the iPad and iPod, and the VAST technique, have made it possible to effectively demonstrate how sounds, words, movements, and word combinations are produced without the challenges of face-to-face interactions. Students with autism will intently watch VAST videos on their devices without the distraction of personal interaction.

> When Jake first saw that mouth covering the iPad screen, he looked up and gave me a sweet and silly giggle, but then he instantly zeroed in on those lips and the words almost magically popped out. Now a month and a half later, he is still enjoying these apps. He has mastered the words and phrases and now he is working on the sentences and songs.
>
> —Moving Forward in the World of Apraxia Jake's Journey to be a Little Man
> http://jakes-journey-apraxia.com/tag/vast-autism-1-core-app/

The VAST Autism 1 – Core — Videos are organized into a hierarchy of five categories, beginning with syllables and ending with sentences. Each video gives a spoken target utterance that is preceded by the written word(s). Each word, phrase, and sentence is concrete and has meaning that can be generalized and practiced throughout the day.

Providing the written word(s) will prevent a student from labeling a picture of a frog jumping as "go," a person lying on a mat as "break time," or a swing as "whee."

Furthermore, there is significant research that suggests that pairing picture symbols with words may actually increase confusion, especially when they represent abstract concepts, have multiple meanings, or serve more than one grammatical function. The ability to recognize the written target word(s) will increase functional communication and enhance the acquisition of reading, writing, and spoken language.

The progression of VAST-Autism Videos is as follows: Syllable Repetition

1. Single Syllable Words
2. Multi-Syllable Words
3. Phrases
4. Sentences

> I absolutely love using this new app with my students with autism. It is without a doubt the most effective oral language app I have used to date with this particular group of students. They love the way the video focuses just on the speaker's mouth, and they will get right up close to it as they attempt to say the words and phrases along with it. I am just thrilled with the impact it has already had on their speech development. It is clear that a lot of research went into this, because the effect it has on these students is just amazing.
>
> —Dina Derrick, Speech Pathologist on using VAST Autism – Core

VAST Pre-Speech— Children with apraxia of speech have difficulty planning speech movements of the tongue, lips, palate, and jaw (articulators), thus hindering their development of verbal speech. Some children on the spectrum may have challenges with everyday activities such as blowing their nose, spitting out toothpaste, or pocketing food.

This app utilizes the highly effective concept of video modeling and auditory cues to promote awareness of oral structures, coordination, strength, tone, chewing, the swallowing of food and saliva, and speech clarity, eventually working towards students' gaining the ability to speak for themselves. In clinical trials, the VAST videos have been highly effective in increasing a child's ability to attend to a communication partner's mouth in the natural environment.

The VAST Videos are organized into five categories:

1. Pre-Exercises

2. Oral Motor

3. Exercises

4. Making Sounds

5. Functional

VAST Songs— Singing has been used as an accepted treatment technique in speech therapy for many years. It's also well known that music stimulates several different areas of the brain. Multiple research studies have shown that stimulating different areas of the brain results in improved speech production. Singing in unison with a visual model has also been demonstrated to have a positive effect on speech production when using familiar songs.

VAST Songs supplement the accepted use of singing in speech therapy by providing extra cueing, simultaneously hearing the song while following the oral movements. The application was designed to accommodate and then challenge individuals with speech production or fluency problems.

All VAST videos can be played in full-length or separated playlists; this allows the therapist to choose the individual target(s) that best fit their students' needs. We are in the process of expanding upon this offering through future applications and via the SpeakinMotion web-based platform.

Ongoing clinical trials indicate that students are highly interested in VAST videos and will almost immediately attempt lip movements or touch their lips in response to the models. After a few short weeks, many students who were essentially non-verbal began word approximations and word attempts more readily. Perhaps the best and most unexpected therapeutic improvements have been the students' ability to generalize skills. Students actually begin attending to the speaker's oral motor movements during daily communication and continue learning speech in a more traditional, naturalistic manner.

The VAST-Autism app is more than AWESOME. My students showed immediate results. To my surprise, after the FIRST trial, they started to vocalize some sounds. You will see amazing results, especially with students who do not respond to traditional speech therapy.

—Harumi Kato, MS, CCC-SLP

The VAST Autism App Series has also been extraordinarily effective with older (18-22) non-verbal students with autism. In two individual cases, students were attempting word approximations and speaking several one-syllable words after one session of watching the VAST videos. One of those students was diagnosed with severe sensory neural hearing loss and autism. He was able to produce four words by the end of his first session.

A word about video modeling: A significant amount of research has shown video modeling to be rapid and highly effective not only in teaching new behaviors, but also in generalizing and maintaining these behaviors as well. Video modeling involves the individual or child observing a videotape of a model engaging in a target behavior and subsequently imitating that behavior.

VAST PRE-SPEECH	**VAST AUTISM 1 – CORE**	**VASTTX KEY WORDS**
$12.99	$4.99	$12.99

This app utilizes the highly effective concept of video modeling and auditory cues to promote awareness of oral structures, coordination, strength, tone, chewing, the swallowing of food and saliva, and speech clarity, eventually working towards students' gaining the ability to speak for themselves. In clinical trials, the VAST videos have been highly effective in increasing a child's ability to attend to a communication partner's mouth in the natural environment.

VAST-Autism combines the highly effective concept of video modeling with written words and auditory cues to help individuals acquire relevant words, phrases, and sentences so that they can speak for themselves. For children and individuals with strong visual skills, this can be a key to developing speech.

VAST-Autism provides unprecedented support for spoken language, combining evidence-based best practices and technology to deliver remarkable results.

Therapy approaches for apraxia of speech emphasize producing a sound using an auditory model and, most importantly, a visual model, followed by practicing the sound in word and phrase contexts. The VAST videos in this app allow users to see the movement while hearing the sound by itself, then in a key word, and finally in a phrase. It takes many repetitions of a sound in order to gain voluntary control. The design of the Key Words app allows users to do just that: hear it, see it, and practice it over and over again.

by SpeakinMotion

www.speakinmotion.com/support

---

iREVIEW

Speech has always been a challenge for individuals on the spectrum. Therapies for non-verbal students may include teaching sign language, gestures, picture exchange, and/or voice output devices. To teach verbalizations, therapists attempt to have students repeat sounds or words from their model and/or a picture. The idea is that a student watches the therapist articulate the target word, sound, and movements and then attempts to reproduces those movements or sound(s). This technique does not usually work well due to the challenges students on the spectrum have with making eye contact or looking at a person's face. It is difficult to see how the articulators move when the ability to look at the face is fleeting.

 The developers at VAST offer a custom recording service to personalize your unique messages and videos. Get the details and watch demos at www.speakinmotion.com/solutions/recording-service

 **ORAL-PERIPHERAL EXAMINATION**
by Glenn Bennett
http://speechies.com/exam
$7.99

This app will help give clinicians valuable information regarding deficits in a client's oral structure or function that may result in a speech disorder. A variety of areas will be assessed, including orofacial cleft, missing teeth, decreased tongue mobility, decreased lip mobility, lack of velar closure, and ankyloglossia. This oral peripheral examination will provide insight regarding what type of articulation errors may occur and how treatment should be addressed.

iREVIEW

Speech therapy just got easier: *Oral-Peripheral Examination* walks you through an oral exam with silly kid pictures performing the task to encourage participation. It is designed to access children with a wide range of disorders but may be used by older individuals also.

APRAXIA PICTURE SOUND CARDS APSC
by Foundations Developmental House, LLC
www.speech-ez.com
$179.99 (home version)
$299.99 (pro version)

FROM THE DEVELOPER

This is the very first app specifically created for the unique needs of children with CAS. This app includes over 775 colorful and engaging picture cards, 45 phonogram cards, and 10 number cards as well as the Speech-EZ® Hand Cues in video format. This app provides you the ability to customize your therapy session by creating specific stimulus sets based on the child's performance and ability level. The *Apraxia Picture Sound Cards* app provides you with convenience, organization, and session-by-session data collection for a single user. You are able to track and store your child's session data, allowing you to easily retrieve and review your child's measurable progress. This parent version enables you to store data and track progress for a single user.

Move your child, teen, or adult client in incremental steps to precise articulation and intelligible speech. The picture cards are beautifully clear with a white background that does not distract. Therapists can use *Apraxia Picture Sound Cards (Pro)* as a complete resource for many individuals on their caseload; likewise, parents can feel confident using the home version with their loved one. The many great features include the ability to customize stimulus sets to fit individual needs and the ability to select words to practice movement sequences by place of articulation and individual motor planning abilities.

 Want more apps to support the speech-language and learning development of the child with CAS? Check out these other great apps.

SPEECH SOUNDS ON CUE FOR iPAD (US ENGLISH)

$23.99

This application shows how to produce speech sounds and words and encourages speech, even

SPEECH SOUNDS FOR KIDS - US EDITION

$24.99

Animated stories, videos of a child's mouth saying the sound, and hand sound cues are all in people with severe speech difficulties. This easy-to-use iPad application contains over 500 videos, sound clips, and color photos designed to help adults and children to produce the consonant speech sounds in isolation, in words, and in sentences. The app now includes recording, playback, rhyming words, and randomization.

provided to help the child learn each sound. The child can record the sound or word and listen to how they went, and these recordings can be saved to monitor progress.

Speech Sound for Kids is an iPad app for promoting phonemic awareness, auditory discrimination, and speech sound production using a multi-sensory approach.

BY MULITMEDIA SPEECH PATHOLOGY
www.mmsp.com.au/speech-sounds-for-kids

FROM THE DEVELOPER

Phonemic awareness (speech sound awareness) has a causal relationship with reading and spelling development. When children become aware of individual sounds in words, they can begin to "map" them on to letters. Articulatory awareness is the knowledge of the articulation required for each sound. Studies show that individuals with dyslexia have weak articulatory awareness, and training in this domain can increase performance on literacy tasks. This software is especially helpful to those who need to hear and see a sound made; for example, patients with motor speech difficulty due to speech apraxia (verbal or oral apraxia affecting speech). Provides multi-media full-motion video cues for independent speech practice. Cues are for individual phonemes (sounds) as well as full words.

iREVIEW

If you want multi-sensory targeted speech production practice for apraxia, articulation, and phonology, *Speech Sounds* is the app for you. The video modeling component is super beneficial for students on the spectrum, as it provides a visual model for each speech sound/word targeted. *Speech Sounds* also provides images, auditory, graphic prompts, and the ability to self-monitor via recordings of the student/client.

 Get the free trial version and check out the developer's website for demo videos and supplemental materials.

SMALLTALK PHONEMES

SMALLTALK CONSONANT BLENDS

by Lingraphica

www.aphasia.com

FREE

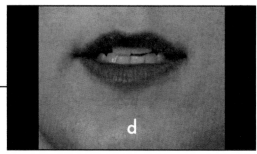

FROM THE DEVELOPER

SmallTalk Phonemes and *SmallTalk Consonant Blends*

provide a series of speech-exercise videos, each illustrating the tongue and lip movements necessary to produce a single phoneme and single consonant blend. With this app, people with apraxia, aphasia, and/ or dysarthria resulting from stroke or head injury can easily practice the specific phonemes they need and repeat them as often as they like.

iREVIEW

SmallTalk Phonemes and *SmallTalk Consonant Blends* are tools that every speech therapist should have access to. Video modeling provides an effective method for teaching new skills, particularly if an individual avoids face-to-face interactions and can readily process visual information. The *SmallTalk* articulation series is highly recommended for individuals of all ages who have difficulty producing single phonemes or consonant blends. The videos can be arranged and/or hidden as necessary.

SPEECH THERAPY FOR APRAXIA - NACD HOME SPEECH THERAPIST

by Blue Whale

https://www.facebook.com/
SpeechTherapyIPadApp

$4.99

(Progress tracking available via in-app purchase.)

FROM THE DEVELOPER

Developed by the National Association for Child Development team, including a certified speech-language pathologist, the Apraxia app provides choices of different phonemes to target and moves through a progression of levels that challenge motor planning for speech. Working at the syllable level, it begins at the production of single syllables and progresses through increasingly difficult production sequences all the way to the production of sequences of random syllables.

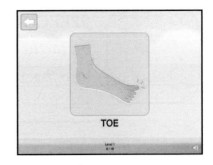

iREVIEW

Speech Therapy for Apraxia offers a great collection of eight consonant groups (19 sounds) with eight levels of difficulty. Speech Therapy for Apraxia is a highly organized program that takes the user through increasingly more difficult levels that build motor planning for speech production. This app is appropriate for adults and children in the clinic, home, and/or school to gain/re-gain oral motor control for intelligible speech.

 Check out the entire collection of *Speech Therapy for Apraxia Apps* to find the best fit for you.

SPEECH FLIPBOOK - ARTICULATION & APRAXIA
by Tactus Therapy Solutions Ltd.
http://tactustherapy.com/apps/speechflipbook
FREE

FROM THE DEVELOPER

This app includes 16 sounds and 40 words with the option to upgrade to all 2300+ recordings of words in natural speech and 125 phonemes and clusters! The full version includes all vowels and consonants of Standard American English as well as over 250 sets of homophones. SLPs can generate a word list on demand, focusing on all words that begin or end with a given sound or words that fit a particular phonological structure (e.g. alveolar-vowel-alveolar). SLPs can use whichever therapy technique is indicated (cycles, minimal or maximal contrasts, metaphon, complexity, phonological awareness, traditional drill, etc.) to treat speech sound disorders and use this app to generate the appropriate word lists!

iREVIEW

Speech FlipBook has so many uses that it should be on every therapist's iDevice. Settings are adaptable to fit your needs, such as, uppercase and lowercase phonetic alphabet, real words, non-words, and vowel and consonant placement with self-monitoring via recording capabilities. Enabling speech free of distracting sounds and images, *Speech FlipBook* is simply suitable for many speech-language goals for those addressing literacy, apraxia, phonology, articulation, minimal pairs, dysarthria, accent reduction, and auditory rehabilitation.

Additional instructions and videos on how to use the app for various purposes are available on the developer's website: http://tactustherapy.com/apps/speechflipbook

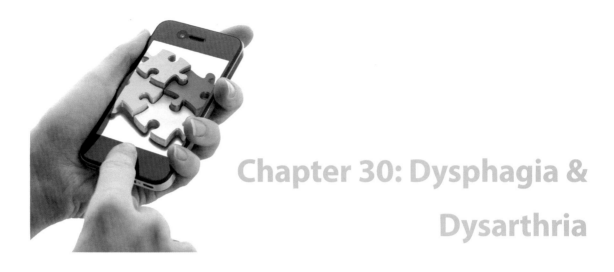

Chapter 30: Dysphagia & Dysarthria

Oral Phase Dysphagia

In the Spotlight

Dysphagia and Autism

By Diane Bahr, MS, CCC-SLP

Speech-Language Pathologist and Feeding Specialist,

Author of *Nobody Ever Told Me (or My Mother) That! Everything from Bottles and Breathing to Healthy Speech Development*

www.agesandstages.net

Dysphagia is a term that is often used in reference to those who have difficulty swallowing. However, there are actually three types of dysphagia. Oral dysphagia is a problem with the management and manipulation of foods and liquids within the mouth itself. Pharyngeal dysphagia is a problem with the swallowing of food and liquid in the throat area, and esophageal dysphagia is a problem with the passage of food or liquid through the esophagus toward the stomach.

Digestion begins in the mouth where food and fluid are taken into the oral cavity. Food needs to be manipulated properly within the mouth and mixed with saliva containing enzymes crucial for digestion and metabolism of nutrients. Proper food management within the mouth means that solid foods are placed by the tongue onto the molars for adequate chewing (e.g., 15-20 chews per bite of food or until food is properly broken down) and collected from the molars and other areas of the mouth by the tongue prior to the swallow. Dynamic cheek and lip movements are also part of good food and liquid management. The lips and cheeks are particularly active during cup and straw drinking.

Individuals with autism often have mild oral dysphagia, which is overlooked because they seem to be functionally managing food and liquid within the mouth. However, many individuals on the autism spectrum have not developed mature food and liquid management skills. Food that is not properly chewed or liquid that is "gulped down" may not be digested or metabolized well. This can contribute to gastrointestinal issues (e.g., reflux, abdominal discomfort, leaky gut, constipation, and diarrhea).

Additionally, many individuals with autism have sensory processing issues and resulting oral dyspraxia. Individuals with sensory processing issues have difficulty adequately receiving and integrating information from the many senses in the body. Oral dyspraxia is a problem with the learning of movement sequences (often called motor plans) used in specific tasks such as eating, drinking, and oral hygiene routines. Adequate sensory processing is needed for good motor planning or learning. Therefore, the process of learning the intricate motor sequences used in eating, drinking, and oral hygiene routines (with their many sensory demands) can be overwhelming for individuals with autism.

Drooling is another concern seen in some individuals with autism. This problem may involve the oral (i.e., mouth), nasal, and pharyngeal (i.e., throat) areas. To prevent drooling, a person needs to maintain a closed-mouth posture while breathing through the nose, feel saliva accumulating within the mouth, and swallow when excessive saliva is sensed within the mouth (approximately every 30 seconds throughout the day for many individuals).

People on the autism spectrum tend to have more oral management problems than pharyngeal swallowing issues. However, they may exhibit coughing or choking because they have not adequately chewed their food or have lost control of the food or liquid during the swallow. Additionally, they may not swallow frequently enough to prevent saliva from pooling in the mouth (resulting in drooling) or to keep stomach acid from coming back into the esophagus (resulting in reflux). Swallowing throughout the day helps to keep esophageal movement (i.e., peristalsis) heading toward the stomach. Individuals with autism may also have esophageal motility issues, since many seem to have a mild amount of low or low-normal muscle tone in their bodies.

An increasing number of applications accessed on electronic devices (apps) are becoming available for those who need assistance with oral and pharyngeal dysphagia. When used properly, these apps can be a great adjunct to hands-on treatment. While many are geared toward adult treatment, they may be used to teach parents, family members, care providers, and staff about the treatment needed for a child, an adolescent, or an adult on the spectrum who may not be able to use the apps themselves.

Some apps contain exercises and activities to help individuals become generally aware of mouth and throat structures and how they move. These apps may be a useful starting point for those who have poor awareness or overall difficulty with movement in the mouth and throat areas. However, the sequences of movement used in eating, drinking, and oral hygiene tasks are specific to those processes. Therefore, exercises and activities that do not involve the manipulation of food or liquid may improve the overall condition of the mechanism but are not likely to improve eating and drinking. The same is probably true for oral hygiene.

Apps that contain video modeling may be particularly beneficial when teaching individuals to explore the sensory properties of new foods, take appropriate bites of food, chew foods thoroughly, lateralize the tongue for adequate food manipulation, clear the mouth of food, drink using an appropriate pace, swallow approximately every 30 seconds, participate in oral hygiene routines, etc. People with autism tend to respond well to videos of the tasks they are learning, as this seems to relieve the pressure they often feel during hands-on treatment. Video modeling may, therefore, help prepare individuals for hands-on treatment needed to refine eating, drinking, oral hygiene, and other skills.

While currently available apps for dysphagia are a good beginning, additional apps are required to address the specific needs of individuals with dysphagia, particularly children. As new apps are developed, it is important to remember that oral exercise and general awareness activities may be used to improve the overall awareness and condition of the mechanism. Yet, actual eating, drinking, oral hygiene, and swallowing activities are needed to improve these processes. Apps do not replace, but can be a great addition to, hands-on treatment during which individuals on the autism spectrum learn to manage foods and liquids properly as well as learn to resolve drooling,

VAST PRE-SPEECH *by SpeakinMotion*
www.speakinmotion.com/support
$12.99

FROM THE DEVELOPER

Children with apraxia of speech have difficulty planning speech movements of the tongue, lips, palate, and jaw (articulators), thus hindering their development of verbal speech. Some children on the spectrum may have challenges with everyday activities such as blowing their nose, spitting out toothpaste, or pocketing food. *VAST Pre-Speech* utilizes the highly effective concept of video modeling and auditory cues to promote awareness of oral structures, coordination, strength, tone, chewing, the swallowing of food and saliva, and speech clarity, eventually working towards students' gaining the ability to speak for themselves. In clinical trials, the VAST videos have been highly effective in increasing a child's ability to attend to a communication partner's mouth in a natural environment.

iREVIEW

Traditional Oral Motor Therapy will charge students to watch a therapist perform oral motor exercises and then repeat the movement (usually around X10). This technique does not usually work well due to the challenges students on the spectrum have with making eye contact or looking at a person's face. It is difficult to see how the articulators move when the ability to look at the face is fleeting. The videos in *VAST Pre-Speech* make it possible to effectively demonstrate pre-speech and functional oral motor movements without the challenges of face-to-face interactions; students with autism may intently watch these videos, free from the distraction of personal interaction.

This iTunes review from mammakbare says it all: We absolutely LOVE this app!! We practice a little every day some days more than others. My nephew's face lights up seeing the other kids doing the variety of activities. This is a great app to help realize sensory and actions. I have been trying to get him to blow kisses for a year now, and with no prior interest in it he shocked me by blowing me a surprise kiss out of the blue!!! I am so happy I discovered you. There are no words to describe my gratitude for what you are doing and offering people like us!! You are our angels and an extended part of our team, thank you, thank you, thank you.

SWALLOW PROMPT *by Garry Brady*
www.speechtools.co/swallow-prompt.html
$2.99

FROM THE DEVELOPER

Swallow Prompt has been designed to help people who have difficulty in managing their saliva (drooling), such as those with neurological conditions such as Stroke, Parkinson's Disease, and Multiple Sclerosis who have reduced sensation. Swallow Prompt can be set to either vibrate (not supported on iPad) or beep (a wired or bluetooth headset is recommended) at a set interval. This prompts people to swallow prior to saliva spilling from their lips.

 Although our apps may be purchased by individuals, we strongly advise people to use the apps in consultation with a qualified speech and language therapist for overall communication or swallowing support and management.

iREVIEW

"Drooling is another concern seen in some individuals with autism. This problem may involve the oral (i.e., mouth), nasal, and pharyngeal (i.e., throat) areas. To prevent drooling, a person needs to maintain a closed mouth posture while breathing through the nose, feel saliva accumulating within the mouth, and swallow when excessive saliva is sensed within the mouth (approximately every 30 seconds throughout the day for many individuals)," according to Diane Bahr, author of *Nobody Ever Told Me (or My Mother) That! Everything from Bottles and Breathing to Healthy Speech Development*. *Swallow Prompt* is very straightforward and easy to use. Set the time interval, then choose beep or buzz, and you are ready to go.

 Remember that children on the spectrum may not know what a swallow is or how to initiate a swallow. Therefore, before using *Swallow Prompt,* teach your student the concept of a swallow and make sure they can follow through.

SMALLTALK ORAL MOTOR EXERCISES *by Lingraphica*
www.aphasia.com
FREE

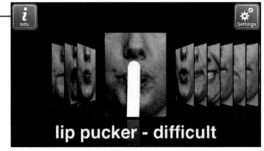

lip pucker - difficult

FROM THE DEVELOPER

Designed for people with weak mouth, tongue, and lip muscles and/or poor oral coordination, *SmallTalk Oral Motor Exercises* contains videos illustrating cheek, tongue, palate, lip, and jaw exercises that help strengthen the oral musculature. *SmallTalk Oral Motor Exercises* is easy to use and provides focused, effective rehabilitation. Because each exercise comes as an individual video, you can focus on just the exercises you need and repeat them as many times as you like.

iREVIEW

Fantastic! *SmallTalk Oral Motor Exercises* is just the best tool a speech pathologist could ask for. *Small-Talk* costs less than flash cards and provides the instructions and motivation needed for independent practice throughout the day. Videos and instructions are clear and precise, with no distractions. My secret joy is that I will not have to do oral motor exercises while counting and demonstrating again. All 50 exercises are easy to access with a swipe of the finger. Exercises can be repeated again and again for focused rehabilitation.

 Seek the advice of a physician and speech pathologist prior to starting any treatments. Oral motor exercises can compound certain medical conditions.

Dysphagia – Pharyngeal Phase

Dysphagia is the only disorder in which a speech-language pathologist can affect an individual's physical health. People with dysphagia have difficulty swallowing, which makes it difficult to take in enough calories and fluids for nourishment. Dysphagia can lead to aspiration of food or liquids and ultimately pneumonia. A qualified speech pathologist can design an exercise program and provide compensatory techniques that can significantly reduce the risk of choking and aspiration.

DYSPHAGIA *by Northern Speech Services, Inc.*
www.northernspeech.com/applications/default.php
$9.99

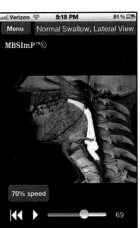

FROM THE DEVELOPER

The custom-designed video animations accurately depict normal swallow physiology and provide clear examples of varying physiologic impairments of the swallow. Video controls allow for slow motion, pause, and frame-by-frame forward and reverse. Animations are of adult physiology and include:

• Normal Swallow, Lateral View

• Normal Swallow, AP View

- Example of Penetration with Aspiration

- Impairment of Bolus Transport

- Impairment of Initiation of Pharyngeal Swallow

- Impairment of Anterior Hyoid Excursion

- Impairment of Laryngeal Vestibular Closure

- Impairment of Pharyngeal Contraction

- Impairment of PES Opening

- Impairment of Tongue Base Retraction

Therapists who work with clients that have dysphagia and students learning about dysphagia will definitely want to access the app *Dysphagia* to supplement their practice or studies. The anatomy and physiology of a swallow is one of the most challenging concepts to relay to clients. Now we can show our clients how the swallow mechanism works and explain graphically why we have to thicken water and puree meals. It even helps to boost client follow through with exercises, diet modifications, and compensatory strategies when they can see an impaired swallow in slow motion.

SMALLTALK DYSPHAGIA *by Lingraphica*
www.aphasia.com
FREE

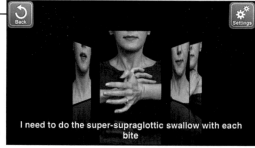

I need to do the super-supraglottic swallow with each bite

FROM THE DEVELOPER

SmallTalk dysphagia contains 50 phrases covering eating equipment, meal assistance, diet, liquids, medications, and compensatory treatment techniques. It also contains four demonstration videos of treatment techniques commonly used for swallowing. This app lets you take along the words and phrases you need to communicate your swallowing needs.

iREVIEW

It has been years since I worked in a hospital setting. We would scribble notes and tape them on the headboards hoping the overworked staff would follow through. And now, there is an app for that. *Small-Talk dysphagia* has every compensatory technique available, with short, easy-to-follow demonstration videos, clear icons, and good audio (male or female). If only I could select, print, and post or file the most important techniques, equipment, and supports to fit individual needs. Icons and videos can be rearranged and deleted as necessary. This app is highly recommended for individuals with dysphagia and their caregivers.

Chapter 31: Aphasia

Aphasia is a disorder that results from damage to the parts of the brain that contain language. Aphasia causes problems with any or all of the following: speaking, listening, reading, and writing (ASHA), and can range from mild to profound. Some individuals may have challenges understanding the words and speech of others. Some may have difficulty expressing their thoughts and ideas, while others struggle with both understanding and expressing language. Social pragmatic skills, reading, and writing are also areas of concern for individuals with aphasia.

Aphasia can be acquired; stroke, head injury, dementia, or aphasia can be developmental and begin during childhood. Developmental aphasia is defined as the failure to develop or have difficulty in using language and speech.

The speech activities presented in the following apps are used by trained speech pathologists who tailor therapy programs for the individual needs of the child/client, but they can also work very well as home programs. Now they can be put in your pocket, purse, or pack, and used any time!

VASTTX - THERAPY SAMPLES *by SpeakinMotion*

www.speakinmotion.com/support

$9.99

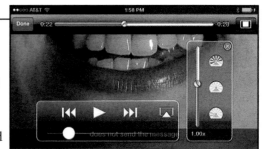

FROM THE DEVELOPER

The *VAST*™ videos involve receiving simultaneous visual and auditory input of precise oral movements, from professionally trained models, which have been recorded at a rate, rhythm, and precision level that allows individuals with significant Broca's type aphasia or apraxia of speech to simultaneously produce oral movements for connected speech. Treatment for acquired apraxia can be very difficult. The *VASTtx* series of apps provides speech language pathologists some innovative tools to use in therapy that are supported by decades of clinical experience. Speech professionals may incorporate these apps into their clients' lesson plans, offering additional practice and support outside the clinic. The app also contains an instructional guide with recommendations for using this material as part of a speech therapy program.

iREVIEW

VASTtx is an introductory app that allows the user to follow along with mouth movements on a pre-recorded video. SpeakinMotion was developed to support individuals with acquired apraxia and/or aphasia; however, it is just what I need for my students with apraxia, motor speech, and hearing-based challenges. *VASTtx* app gives the user a robust introductory set of videos for building speech and functional communication. These programs have produced extremely positive results, allowing individuals to speak full sentences, with a more natural rhythm than they would otherwise be capable of achieving. Furthermore, individuals with no prior experience or training have succeeded with this approach.

 The developers at VAST offer a Custom Recording Service to personalize your unique message and videos. Get the details and watch demos at the developer's address: www.speakinmotion.com/solutions/recording-service

LANGUAGE THERAPPY
$59.99

Four apps in one! Comprehension, Naming, Writing, & Reading *TherAppy* apps are now together in one comprehensive speech therapy toolkit. The same core functional vocabulary organized by category runs across these two receptive and two expressive apps. Built-in cues, hierarchies, languages, and customization options make these apps versatile for assessment, therapy, home practice, and telepractice.

CONVERSATION THERAPPY
$24.99

Conversation TherAppy gets people talking! Now you can use this professional speech therapy app to target higher-level expressive language, pragmatic, problem-solving, speech & cognitive-communication goals for older children, teens, and adults! With over 300 real photographs and 10 questions each, this app gives you 3000+ questions. Combine that with user profiles, group play, and customization, and you get an incredibly useful tool for therapy!

SPACED RETRIEVAL THERAPPY
$3.99

Spaced Retrieval is a scientifically proven method of improving memory of names, facts, and routines for all people, including those with memory impairments (Alzheimer's disease and other neurological conditions). This expanded interval timer will help clinicians, family members, and students to keep track of the intervals and performance as they practice up to three memory targets.

by Tactus Therapy Solutions Ltd.
http://tactustherapy.com

FROM THE DEVELOPER

Tactus Therapy Solutions specializes in apps for adult rehab, bringing evidence-based therapy to the touch screen with respectful and intuitive design. Our apps feature automated scoring, email reports, full-color photos, functional vocabulary, self-cueing, and simple navigation. See for yourself—with Lite versions available for nearly all of our apps, you are encouraged to try before you buy. We're sure you're going to love what you see and want more.

iREVIEW

This is your rehab solution! All Tactus Therapy Solution apps are an excellent choice for adults, teens, and even children to support their language goals. The user is presented with a clear, realistic photo and a clear task or target goal. There are built-in cue hierarchies, custom vocabulary selection, help and timing features that can be modified and controlled to fit individual needs. Tactus Therapy Solutions apps are originally designed for adults who are rebuilding speech and cognitive skills; however, they work very well for students with special needs who may not want/need auditory and/or visual distractions.

 Tactus Therapy Solutions offers a free version of most apps. Visit the developer's website for additional information and great resources to see all the great apps offered by Tactus: http://tactustherapy.com

THE NAMING TEST *by Brainmetric*
www.brainmetric.com
$19.99

FROM THE DEVELOPER

The Naming Test takes a novel approach to the conventional assessment of naming ability. It consists of 65 color photographic images illustrating objects or scenes that have common names. The test presentation also includes 20 sounds that have common names. If the subject cannot immediately name the stimulus, then the test allows you to present cues in hierarchical fashion. For example, one trial first shows the photograph of a dog. If the subject cannot name the picture, then the examiner clicks on a button that plays the sound of the dog barking. The next cue level is semantic: the examiner clicks on a button that displays the phrase, "This is a type of animal." The phonemic cue consists of the beginning sound element of the name: do. This is played as a standard digitized speech sound. In contrast to paper-and-pencil tests of this type, the examiner does not recite the phonemic cue. Finally, if the subject still cannot name the picture, the subject is shown a list of multiple choices and asked to choose the name.

iREVIEW

The Naming Test is a super simple expressive naming test that cues the user in a uniform, hierarchical fashion and records prompt level and correct/incorrect answers. *The Naming Test* can be given to evaluate expressive word knowledge or as a tool to measure progress.

TOKENTEST *by WhiteAnt Occasional Publishing*
www.brainmapping.org/WhiteAnt
$2.99

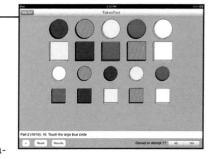

FROM THE DEVELOPER

The TokenTest is a classic language comprehension test originally published in 1962 for detection of non-obvious aphasia. This iPad application includes the original and over 13 variants (both long and short forms) published over the years. It also allows customization of the provided versions so clinicians and researchers can make their own based on those provided. Scoring is automatic, and results can be emailed.

iREVIEW

A digital *TokenTest* that automatically scores results—fantastic! Not only is it convenient, but I can also customize the test to fit the needs and abilities of my students/clients.

iNAME IT *by Smarty Ears*

http://smartyearsapps.com

$14.99

iName It is specifically designed to help individuals with difficulty recalling the names of common items found in the home. *iName It* provides users with a systematic way to recall functional words needed for activities of daily living. *iName It* consists of fifty nouns that are displayed within the context of the rooms where they are typically located, such as bedroom, bathroom, and kitchen. Each target word can be elicited by using one or more of the five different types of cues available: phonemic, phase completion, whole word, or semantic.

iREVIEW

There are five scenes (bedroom, kitchen, living room, bathroom, and garage) with 10 target items per scene. The user can have five cues to name the object in addition to the contextual clue. *iName It* is designed for adult aphasia rehabilitation, but due to the contextual cues, iName It works very well for students with special needs.

 See the demo on the developer's website before you buy: http://smartyearsapps.com/service/iname

 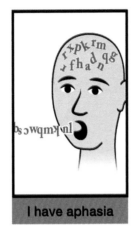

SMALLTALK APHASIA - FEMALE   **SMALLTALK APHASIA - MALE**

by Lingraphica
www.aphasia.com
FREE

FROM THE DEVELOPER

Designed for people with aphasia, an impairment in the ability to use language, *SmallTalk Aphasia* provides a vocabulary of pictures and videos that talk in a natural human voice. Take along words and phrases to use in everyday situations, such as shopping, a doctor's appointment, phone conversations, or emergencies. This app provides an easy way to make your wishes known or to practice frequently used words. *SmallTalk Aphasia* also contains mouth-position videos for practice and self-cuing, which is also great for stroke rehabilitation and recovery of speech.

iREVIEW

The *SmallTalk* app series is excellent! I have searched for video clips of the articulators for many years. *SmallTalk Aphasia* provides the user with clear audio, graphics, text, and video of common phrases. *SmallTalk Aphasia* has an additional feature of icons, which provides common phrases in written and graphic form. The *SmallTalk* series was originally meant for adults with aphasia; however, these apps work fabulously with students on the spectrum and/or students with apraxia. *SmallTalk* apps provide video modeling for speech. I would also like to note that the iPad, iPod touch, and iPhone are superb companions and time killers for individuals in the hospital. Now these same iDevices can also communicate important medical information. I highly recommended SmallTalk apps for individuals of all ages with apraxia, aphasia, dysarthria, motor speech disorders, and autism.

SMALLTALK CONVERSATIONAL PHRASES

SmallTalk Conversational Phrases contains words and phrases commonly used in conversations, such as greetings, responses, requests, and statements about well-being. This app lets you take along a set of words and phrases to use in daily conversations with friends, relatives, and people you encounter out in the world.

by Lingraphica

www.aphasia.com

FREE

SMALLTALK DAILY ACTIVITIES

Designed for people with aphasia, an impairment in the ability to use language, *SmallTalk Daily Activities* provides a vocabulary of pictures that talk in a natural human voice. This app allows you to communicate and describe your daily needs with family members and caregivers.

The *SmallTalk* family of free apps offers you extreme portability for when you want to practice your speech and more effectively communicate on the go. *SmallTalk* apps use the same icons, voices, and videos found in the Lingraphica AllTalk™, TouchTalk™, andMiniTalk™ speech-generating devices.

iREVIEW

SmallTalk Conversational Phrases & *Daily Activities* was developed to help folks who have had a stroke or head injury communicate their basic wants/needs and participate in simple conversation. My colleagues in hospitals tell me that SmallTalk apps are simple yet work incredibly well with facilitating communication with family and caregivers.

Part IX

Stuttering

According to the Stuttering Foundation, stuttering is a communication disorder in which the flow of speech is broken by repetitions, prolongations, or abnormal stoppages (no sound) of sounds and syllables. There may also be unusual facial and body movements associated with the effort to speak. Stuttering is also referred to as stammering or disfluency.

 It is strongly recommended that any app/device that focuses on disfluency be used in conjunction with a licensed speech pathologist that specializes in fluency.

Chapter 32: Disfluency

In the Spotlight

Disfluency and Autism

By Kathleen Scaler Scott, Ph.D., CCC-SLP

Assistant Professor and Board Certified Specialist in Fluency Disorders

Author of *Managing Cluttering: A Comprehensive Guidebook of Activities*

Patterns of disfluent speech have been noted in children and adults with autism since 1975. Such disfluency has been identified in those with autism with and without average intelligence. The type of disfluency included both repetitions and revisions of larger chunks of language information such as phrases and increased fragmentation of speech, such as repetitions (s-s-s-summer), prolongations (ssss-summer) or blocks (speaker cannot move forward to produce the word, sound is stopped or "stuck"; e.g., s---ummer). The latter are known as stuttering-like disfluencies and continue to be identified among individuals with all levels of autism. Other patterns of disfluency have also been noted in autism, including cluttering and word-final disfluencies (e.g., summer-er). Common among those with autism is a lack of awareness of disfluent speech and how this may impact overall communication effectiveness. The use of apps to increase awareness of disfluent moments, whether through documentation by the speech-language pathologists, family members, or clients themselves, may assist with the therapy process. Given that many with autism are drawn to technology, this method of intervention can make the support of a speech-language pathologist that much more motivating and powerful. Another difficult area among those with autism is that of carryover of learned skills to new situations. Apps can assist the client in taking therapy strategies beyond the clinic setting into everyday speaking situations.

SLP-DYSFLUENCY PLUS HD
by App-licable
www.slp-tapapps.com/slp-tapapps.com_/Welcome.html
$4.99

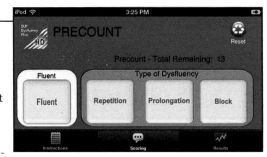

FROM THE DEVELOPER

SLP Tap Apps introduces *Dysfluency Plus HD Index Counter*, a tool designed by a speech-language pathologist for online fluency evaluation. This application not only tracks fluent vs. dysfluent words/syllables, but also categorizes dysfluencies into the three common core behaviours: repetitions, prolongations and blocks.

iREVIEW

SLP Dysfluency Plus HD is a convenient measure of fluent words, total words, and percentages. The totals are then broken down further into core behaviors of repetitions, prolongations, and blocks. This is a great way to collect and save information on student performance and response to therapy interventions.

DAF BEEP PRO *by Florian Student*
http://iqtainment.wordpress.com/about
$26.99

FROM THE DEVELOPER

DAF BEEP Pro is the first-ever implementation of a true chorus effect with up to 10 auditory feedbacks. DAF BEEP Pro implements the methods of Delayed Auditory Feedback (DAF) and Frequency Altered four crucial techniques to reduce stuttering. This will not only get you started on the right track toward full fluency, but will also help you to maintain the fluency as time goes on by reminding you of what you have learned.

iREVIEW

DAF is a powerful tool in shaping fluency. DAF therapy has two goals:

1. Increase fluent speech using the DAF technique.

2. Fade the use of the DAF support.

Studies have shown that, when combining DAF with a program designed by a trained speech therapist, individuals can increase fluency significantly.

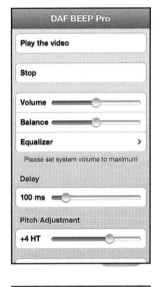

 **DAF PROFESSIONAL** *by Garry Brady*
www.speechtools.co
$9.99

FROM THE DEVELOPER

Delayed Auditory Feedback (DAF) is a well-established speech and language therapy tool which helps people to speak more slowly. However, until recently, devices have been cumbersome to carry around, difficult to adjust, very expensive, and therefore not widely used. It works by enabling someone to hear his or her own speech in an altered manner. This disruption to the normal auditory feedback loop causes the speaker to slow down. Research has shown that DAF will be of benefit to approximately a third of people who have a stammer or Parkinson's. Clinical research has not been carried out as yet on other client groups; however, DAF may well be of benefit to people with other medical speech conditions. If you find this helps your speech with a diagnosed condition, please share this in the reviews to help others see how helpful this tool can be.

 Although our apps may be purchased by individuals, we strongly advise people to use the apps in consultation with a qualified speech and language therapist for overall communication support and management.

iREVIEW

This review comes from iTunes customer TrainRiderDave: DAF Pro is elegant and amazing! After a little experimenting with the amount of delay, I have some wonderful results. The app also runs in the background, so you can keep it running while you use other apps like email and web. Thanks for this amazing tool!

Similar results have been reported by speech therapists who work with children in the school environment. *DAF Professional* works best with headsets or Bluetooth. Individuals with dysfluency will not stand out as different when using an app in conjunction with an iDevice to help remediate stuttering. I urge anyone considering the use of DAF or FAF to research the apps and obtain the advice of a licensed speech pathologist.

 **MPISTUTTER** *by Casa Futura Technologies*
www.casafuturatech.com/mpistutter
$99.99

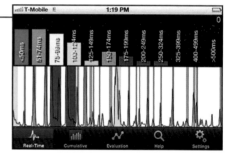

FROM THE DEVELOPER

MPiStutter is an app that supports Modifying Phonation Intervals (MPI) stuttering therapy. It analyzes the user's vocal fold activity and trains him or her to eliminate too-rapid speech elements and speak fluently at a normal speaking rate.

MPiStutter is ideal for stutterers who have learned to speak fluently in a speech clinic but are having difficulty transferring this fluency to conversations outside the speech clinic.

iREVIEW

The *MpiStutter* technique reminds me of biofeedback for dysfluency. The goal is to make the green bars tall and the red bars short; see the screenshot above. The developers suggest that *MpiStutter* can be used at home without the presence of a speech pathologist but will need a trained therapist to initiate and monitor the program.

 See the demo and read impressive research on this technique:www.casafuturatech.com/mpistutter

DISFLUENCY INDEX COUNTER

by Smarty Ears

www.smarty-ears.com

$9.99

FROM THE DEVELOPER

The easiest, cheapest, and most advanced way to track your percentage of stuttered syllables (%SS). The *Disfluency Index Counter* app allows speech and language therapists to perform a live count of the number of fluent or disfluent syllables produced. This application comes with two styles of counters: A simple and an advanced counter.

iREVIEW

Disfluency Index Counter is a straightforward app that tracks and calculates data for the user (speech pathologist). Any app that takes my data, crunches it, and then emails it to me is worth its weight in gold.

Part X

Creative Learning

by Penina Rybak, MA/CCC-SLP, TSHH, CEO Socially Speaking LLC

Ask any educator about creative learning today, and you'll usually hear explanations using the terms "multi-sensory lessons" and "imaginative teachable moments" and education that is geared to teach "outside-the-box thinking." We currently live in the iEra during which iPad App integration into best practices re: education at home and in school goes beyond conventional intervention techniques. For children with autism in particular, it is not just about using iPads to foster situation specific learning regarding IEP goals or using iOS Apps as positive reinforcements for behavior management purposes, it's about promoting overall pragmatic skills at all times. These skills include mastering language concepts, divergent thinking, problem solving, and engaging in collaboration, all of which are needed to develop crucial digital citizenship and social communication skills.

The iPad in particular, lends itself to successful instruction for children with autism in these areas. It's truly visual, easy-to-understand, and customizable user interface all make it a viable, functional option for today's educational toolbox. The iPad helps generalize learned skills that parents/professionals and students are focused on, seamlessly integrating language, literacy, fine-motor, and social skills goals into daily routines. Daily routines can be interrupted by environmental and neuro-biological factors, resulting in disorientation to person/place/time, which can then result in the following:

- Delayed or decreased retention of learned skills
- Tantrums and outbursts when things don't go as planned
- Inconsistent performance and readiness to learn

Bridging the gap between readiness to learn and actual performance is the ultimate concern of all educators and parents of children with special needs. This is why creative learning with an iPad is so crucial. Creative instruction involves "whole body learning" in which the child's muscle memory, episodic memory, and Theory of Mind all get "activated" through using the iPad. How? By providing structured, visually appealing, and predictable cognitive exposure to specific iOS apps. These apps address specific skills and their generalization in ways that traditional intervention techniques do not, including sometimes play because of the very nature of mobile technology. Such features include:

- Customizable features and sharing options which impact the degree of complexity/cues needed during the "teachable moment" and the variety and amount of review/homework needed.

- Multi-media learning using audio/video apps to record speech/activities for later discussion and springboards for future "multi-sensory lessons" and preparation.

- Time-sequenced movements, whose rhythm (especially with music and drawing/arts and crafts based apps) help children with special needs learn about the Causality Loop, which leads to better time management, better sequencing skills, and better problem solving; i.e., "outside the box thinking" overall. Another by-product is that it gives children with autism and/or special needs more natural and fun practice opportunities to develop better hand-eye coordination skills.

So when a parent or professional asks about the efficacy of iOS apps in treatment and the benefits of iPad use in today's lesson plans, you can assure them that a more child-centric, methodical, and creative learning experience can be provided using this "Swiss army knife" of tools. It can be used to both teach and prepare children with autism and special needs for changing routines, learning environments, and expectations in 21st century classrooms and communities.

 ## Success Story: Devon

Devon is a seven-year-old talkative, mildly clumsy, concrete thinker with high functioning autism (HFA) who is attending a mainstreamed first grade class with a "shadow" during group activities and recess. Devon has difficulty with reading comprehension, expressing her feelings verbally, and problem solving age appropriately, especially in social situations. Her speech therapist, who has been seeing her for two years, has good rapport with her and reports that Devon "understands what she needs to do but then freezes up." The speech therapist has reportedly tried different techniques which included a "what's wrong with this picture?" game featuring flash cards of objects/nouns, pretending to misunderstand her requests in therapy, and creating and sending home a Social Story to be read every night. Devon's parents decide to request an iPad but are unsure what to do with it. Her teacher is not sure if it's a good idea to send it to school, since Devon "frequently breaks toys without meaning to and doesn't like to share."

I patiently explain to the team at the Annual IEP Review meeting that this iPad is not a toy and is certainly not one that will be shared. It's to be considered necessary IEP equipment to help Devon learn and retain what she is learning so that she can demonstrate better carryover. I also explain that there are specific apps which will help Devon work on her fine-motor skills in more fun and more natural ways. I show that the iPad's user-interface itself will give her practice with hand-eye coordination and swiping, etc. I also demonstrate that using specific apps to allow Devon to hear and see herself "in action" will make learning problem-solving (using verbs) and all its steps a less static and abstract process. I show the team some apps I recommend for customizable and shareable creative learning and "social autopsies," such as *ArtMaker, Advanced Sequences, Stick Around,* and *Explain Everything.*

We draw up a plan to purchase these apps and teach the whole team how to use them and how they will be used in treatment. Devon really takes to the iPad and expresses happiness when using it, and she learns to verbally express displeasure when she doesn't have access to her iPad. It becomes an intrinsic motivator to behave and complete work in a timely fashion, and the special, durable casing prevents real damage when it's accidentally dropped in her zeal to perform. It also gives Devon "cool status" with her peers, who understand that it's her "helper," like glasses, and frequently engage her in conversations about it. Recording her speech and actions for more interactive, multi-media social stories and problem-solving scenarios in speech therapy slowly but surely result in carryover to class and home. Best of all, Devon is more interested in reading books on the iPad and more open to constructive criticism about it and herself in general! Her parents especially like the iPad, which also has contact, safety related, and medical (food allergies, autism alert, etc.) information listed in the Notes App for all to see when encountering Devon.

—Penina Rybak, MA/CCC-SLP, TSHH, CEO Socially Speaking LLC, is an Educational Technology

Consultant and an Autism Specialist (http://sociallyspeakingLLC.com)

Chapter 33: Creativity & Imagination

SHADOW PUPPET EDU
by Shadow Puppet Inc.
http://get-puppet.co/
FREE

FROM THE DEVELOPER

This app provides the simplest way to capture and share student work. Designed with kids in mind, students as young as five can make videos to tell stories, explain concepts, or record their progress. Common Core-aligned lesson ideas make it easy to get started!.

iREVIEW

Shadow Puppet app is super cool; Using *Shadow Puppet Edu*, you can create anything from a school project, personalized task analysis, or nifty meeting presentation to video modeling routine or flipping a classroom lesson in a matter of minutes then share over social media, email, and/or Dropbox. *Shadow Puppet Edu* is like a cross between an interactive whiteboard and an open-ended storybook with an impressive safe image search engine that includes the Library of Congress, NASA, Google, animated GIFs, and images/videos from your own Camera Roll.

 See a demo of *Shadow Puppet Edu*, examples of Puppets, examples of Shadow Puppet Edu activities that are aligned with Common Core Standards, lesson ideas, and all other possibilities this fantastic free app has to offer.

TOONTASTIC

Making cartoons with *Toontastic* is as easy as putting on a puppet show—simply press the record button, move your characters onscreen, and tell your story. *Toontastic* records your animation and voice as a cartoon video to share with friends and family on ToonTube, the app's global storytelling network for kids.

TOONTASTIC JR.
SHREK MOVIE MAKER

Toontastic Jr. Shrek inspires the creative storyteller in all children through a unique blend of imaginative play and movie-making magic. Remix and retell the classic *Shrek* movie while recording your own voice along the way! Choose from 12 classic *Shrek* scenes.

by Launchpad Toys
http://launchpadtoys.com
FREE (each)

FROM THE DEVELOPER

Launchpad Toys is building digital toys and tools that empower kids to create, learn, and share their ideas through play.

iREVIEW

If your child likes cartoons, then he/she will love *Toontastic*'s group of storytelling apps. Any school subject or language concept can be targeted while inspiring creative play creativity in this completely open-ended series of *Toontastic* apps. After the masterpiece is complete, it can be shared on ToonTube, the app's global storytelling network for kids (like YouTube for Toontastic video creations).

 Toontastic is free to all with additional in-app purchases available to those who desire enhanced special features. See the demo for Toontastic and check out ToonTube on the developer's website: www.launchpadtoys.com/toontastic/

MR. POTATO HEAD
CREATE & PLAY

MRS. POTATO HEAD
CREATE & PLAY

by Originator Inc.
www.originatorkids.com
$4.99 (each)

FROM THE DEVELOPER

Mr. Potato Head Create & Play and *Mrs. Potato Head Create & Play* feature Mr. & Mrs. Potato Head (separate apps), taters extraordinaire, in their first starring roles in mobile apps. Relive childhood memories of Mr. Potato Head and bring him to life for a new generation! Free your child's creativity with this digital version of the Mr. Potato Head toy on your iPad, iPhone, or iPod touch.

The pieces of this Potato Head will never get lost! I used a potato head in therapy for years and had to continually replace the pieces; not so with this digital version of the classic Potato Head. Build and customize your Potato Head and then go on a "spud-tacular" interactive adventure. Recommended for the young, young at heart, and the nostalgic who are building language, concepts, speech skills, attention, and creativity.

 Mr. Potato Head and *Mrs. Potato Head* are separate apps. Both apps have the same features and functionality.

 **DRAW AND TELL HD** *by Duck Duck Moose, Inc.*
www.duckduckmoose.com/support
$1.99

FROM THE DEVELOPER

Draw and Tell is an award-winning creative tool for children of all ages that encourages imagination, storytelling and open-ended play. Use the tool to draw, color, decorate with stickers, create animations, and record stories.

iREVIEW

Draw and Tell takes the creativity of the drawing app up a notch. Now you can use your iPad to craft works of art using a wide array of colors, coloring pages, free draw, patterns, specialty crayons, and/or stickers that can be animated as you tell a story. You can also add audio to your story, save it to your photo album, and then share it with the world. *Draw and Tell* gives students a means of sharing information and ideas with others at school, at home, and in the community. Self-expression is central to quality of life and essential to learning (Common Core Standard for English – Language Arts). Speech Therapists and Educators can use *Draw and Tell* to promote descriptive language, labeling, story (re)telling, concepts, generalization, and communication with caregivers. Occupational therapists can use Draw and Tell to encourage fine motor coordination, finger isolation, grasp (stylus), and the occupations of playing and learning.

Take a look at the demo video on the developer's website: www.duckduckmoose.com/educational-iphone-itouch-apps-for-kids/draw-and-tell/

BRUSHES 3

INKPAD

by Taptrix, Inc.
http://brushesapp.com
FREE (each)

FROM THE DEVELOPER

Inkpad is an open-source vector illustration app. It was designed from scratch for the iPad. It supports paths, compound paths, text, images, groups, masks, gradient fills, and an unlimited number of layers. An accelerated OpenGL-based painting engine makes painting smooth and responsive—even with huge brush sizes. *Brushes 3* also records every step in your painting. Show off your creative process by replaying your paintings directly on your device.

iREVIEW

Brushes 3 and *Inkpad* are two of the most powerful art apps available in the iTunes store. Both apps are very easy to use, yet they have advanced features that give the serious artist the tools they need to build unique works of art. Anyone who loves to draw or paint will enjoy the wide array of options, layers, and features both *Brushes 3* and *Inkpad* have to offer.

FACES iMAKE – PREMIUM!
by iMagine machine LLC
www.imaginemachine.com
$1.99

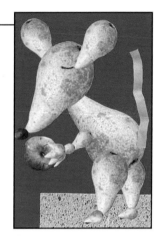

FROM THE DEVELOPER

Faces iMake is a tool for creating collages using pictures of everyday objects.
But *Faces iMake* offers much more than that! It is an extraordinary tool
for developing right-brain creative capabilities and expanding awareness.
Indeed, Daniel Pink, author of A Whole New Mind, put it very well when
he said, "It's fun and addicting if you can get it away from your kids." It has
been recognized as an intuitive tool for children with disabilities. Shannon
Des Roches Rosa, editor of The Thinking Person's Guide to Autism, wrote:
"Our kids love *Faces iMake*. Its interface is one of the best I've seen for kids with autism." It enables kids
to express themselves visually in a liberating way. An enthusiastic student will have more incentive to
articulate verbally on his/her creation.

iREVIEW

Faces iMake spurs creativity, encourages pretending, and incites a bit of the sillies. This is the most fun you
can have while labeling, describing, categorizing, and targeting fine motor skills. Show off your creations
via email or social network. *Faces iMake* comes with catchy music that you will find yourself humming all
day, or choose your own music selection from your music library.

 iMagine offers a free version of *Faces iMake*, so give it a try. Don't forget to check out the demo
video on the developer's website: www.imaginemachine.com

Chapter 34: Music & Song

Music has a natural effect on all individuals to induce positive self-expression, both verbal and non-verbal. Creative parents, caregivers, and teachers have been using music and song to teach language, concepts, encourage participation in daily activities, calm nerves, and reinforce students of all ages. Music and song are effective because they are naturally reinforcing, are immediate in time, and provide motivation for practicing non-musical skills. Most importantly, music is successful because everyone responds positively to some type of tune.

Many iDevices are made for music, and iTunes offers thousands of selections from classical and opera to "Old MacDonald" and from punk rock to pop. Students who may otherwise refuse to wear headphones or ear buds will put them on to listen to music. Here is a chance to use an iDevice as the world does—listening to music. Additionally, make some music of your own!

Success Story: Fiona

Fiona is a tiny six-year-old "whirlwind." Her first day of school was exhausting for her and the staff. She could not stop moving, climbing, and squirming. By lunchtime, she was so tired and hungry that she began crying and pulling her hair; nevertheless, she kept moving. Her teacher noticed that he may have heard her hum the tune to "Wheels on the Bus." I quickly opened the *Wheels on the Bus* app and turned the volume up. When she heard the music, she stopped crying and pulling her hair. Fiona sat next to me for the next half hour exploring the app. She was then able to eat her lunch and make it through the rest of the day. Her teacher now has *Wheels on the Bus* on his iPhone. Day saved!

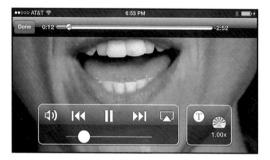

VAST SONGS 1 – INTRO   **VAST SONGS 2 - KIDS**

by SpeakinMotion
www.speakinmotion.com
$14.99 (each)

FROM THE DEVELOPER

VAST-Songs delivers an innovative set of features that integrate video modeling with music to support speech therapy. *VAST Songs 1 – Intro* provides a starter set of 12 song performances targeting music therapy for adults, while *VAST Songs 2 – Kids* provides a starter set of 10 song performances ideal for music therapy with children. Singing has been used as an accepted treatment technique in speech therapy for many years. It's also well known that music stimulates several different areas of the brain. Multiple studies have shown that stimulating different areas of the brain results in improved speech production. Singing in unison with a visual model has also been demonstrated to have a positive effect on speech production when using familiar songs.

iREVIEW

VAST-Songs supplements the accepted use of singing in speech therapy by providing extra cueing—simultaneously hearing the song while following the oral movements. The application was designed to accommodate four adjustable layers of audio supports: vocal melody, piano melody, rhythmic piano, and metronome along with three speed choices for tempo (1.0, 0.8, and 0.6). Self-monitoring is encouraged via a built-in mirror, and the user is provided with video/written tutorials. It is amazing how most students are immediately drawn to the songs and singing mouth, encouraging them to focus on the articulators without the anxiety that comes with looking at a live face.

TUNEVILLE *by Next Thing Productions, Inc.*
http://tuneville.com
FREE

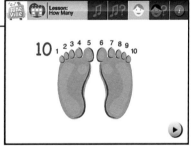

FROM THE DEVELOPER

Parents, teachers, and clinicians, whether sitting and guiding a child or allowing a child to be independently entertained, will be satisfied knowing that their child is exploring an award-winning system of learning. Music for exceptional minds; download the first lesson free and introduce students to *Tuneville*, where dynamic music, movies, and activities keep children entertained while they learn.

iREVIEW

There are four steps/tracks to each song that take the learner effortlessly from song to speech.

Track A: a learning song is presented in its entirety.

Track B: the song is repeated with key omissions.

Track C: the song topic is spoken.

Track D: the song topic is spoken with key omissions.

> "I have always researched and been fascinated by the correlation of music and language retention ... it was as if this company knew just the prescription for children struggling with language ... (they) made a tremendous difference in my students' progress and motivation in therapy. I so love the product that I tell others every opportunity I get."
>
> —Alice Warren-Brown—retired Speech Language Specialist in Dallas ISD.

For teachers and educators, *Tuneville* is an excellent app for morning circle time, with relevant lyrics that can focus your students on current classroom curriculum.

 The original lesson, "How Many," is free with additional in-app purchases available as desired for topics such as, math, vocabulary, friendship, reading, circle time, and self-care. Try the free lesson and see the developer's website for a demo: http://tuneville.com/

 **WHEELS ON THE BUS HD** *by Duck Duck Moose, Inc.*
http://duckduckmoosedesign.com
$1.99

FROM THE DEVELOPER

An award-winning tribute to a childhood classic, *Wheels on the Bus* offers a fun, interactive experience encouraging motor, language, and cognitive skills through fresh illustrations, creative interaction, and music.

iREVIEW

Wheels on the Bus is very popular with all my younger students. Take the time to make your own recording for Verse four; it's worth it. Students like the ability to change languages and instruments. *Wheels on the Bus* is also a book; the sound can be turned off, and it is a fun, interactive reading activity.

OLD MACDONALD   ITSY BITSY SPIDER

by Duck Duck Moose

http://duckduckmoosedesign.com

1.99

___

FROM THE DEVELOPER

An award-winning original tribute to childhood classics, *Old MacDonald* & *Itsy Bitsy Spider* offers children a fun, interactive, and educational experience. Follow the spider to learn about the environment and animals.

iREVIEW

This contemporary digital spin on the much-loved songs of *Old MacDonald* and *Itsy Bitsy Spider* make a highly motivating interactive learning opportunity for younger children or those who simply love the classics. Change the language or the instrument for more variety. *Old MacDonald* can actually help you learn a foreign language, as there are five languages available on this app. Both of these beloved songs can be used as a reinforcement or learning activity.

MUSIC COLOR *by SoundTouch*

https://www.facebook.com/SoundTouchInteractive

$4.99

FROM THE DEVELOPER

Entertain and teach kids about colors and have them listen to classical music at the same time! *Music Color* is full of life. It's an incredible combination of a kid-friendly interface, astonishing imagery, and classical music. Those three elements combine to produce a spectacular product that is unlike anything else seen in the app store.

iREVIEW

What a stylish way to teach color. Your student will learn that yellow is not just a square on a flash card, but will see five unique, real-life examples of yellow combined with "yellow" classical music. *Music Color* features 540 gorgeous images and 44 classical music pieces to teach and generalize the concepts of color. A matching game is included to further support the acquisition of color. Although the interface looks to be designed for younger users, the pictures and music are for anyone who is mastering the concept of colors.

 Music Color has a free Lite version for you to try.

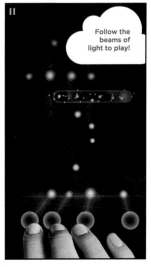

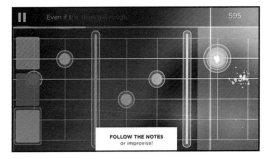

MAGIC PIANO BY SMULE

From Bruno Mars to Mozart, play the hottest songs effortlessly—no lessons needed!

GUITAR! BY SMULE

Guitar! by Smule brings you the unique experience of musical collaboration between guitarist and singer.

by Smule
http://magicpiano.smule.com
FREE

FROM THE DEVELOPER

We believe that music is much more than just listening—it's about creating, sharing, discovering, participating, and connecting with people. It is the original social network with the power to break down barriers, touch souls, and bring people together from all over the world. In 2008, we set out to create apps that enabled anyone to create, discover, love, and enjoy music. Today, 1.5% of the world's population (that's 125 million people and counting) have used Smule's apps. These individuals are creating communities, meeting new like-minded friends, and having fun making music together on Smule. So if you wake up humming, play a mean air guitar or anything in between, then Smule is for you—anyone can do it, no previous experience required.

iREVIEW

Magic Piano & Guitar! By Smule are two of my all-time favorite apps! I have prevented meltdowns with this app because it is so desirable. *Magic Piano & Guitar! By Smule* can be simple or complicated, depending on the level of the student. All modes are visually beautiful. Occupational therapists love these apps: Magic Piano & Guitar! combine sensory, motor coordination, eye-hand coordination, and finger isolation goals into one activity. Best of all, the students don't know they are working. Beautiful, therapeutic, and artistic, *Magic Piano & Guitar!* should be on everyone's iDevices.

 If you love singing, then check out *Karaoke by Smule* (requires a subscription) and all the great apps/demos on the Smule website: http://magicpiano.smule.com/. In-app purchases available for more Smule fun.

 **FINGERPIANO** *by Junpei Wada*

http://fingerpiano.net/fingerpiano/

$1.99

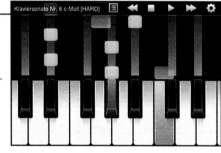

FROM THE DEVELOPER

You only need the motivation to play the music. Instead of reading the score, scrolling guides appear on the screen. Just touch the keyboard with scrolling guides, and you've mastered the game. This application provides you with over 200 famous pieces of music.

iREVIEW

Get this app! *FingerPiano* can be utilized for occupational therapy, serve as a reinforcement, build self-esteem, or to follow visual directions. A young student of mine at the single-word level uttered his first sentence to gain access to FingerPiano. Another prompt-dependent student independently uses all features of *FingerPiano*. Some students will put on performances; others will sit and play for as long as I let them. The functions are endless.

 Try the free version and visit the developer's website to see the demo videos to decide if *FingerPiano* is the right app for you.

FUN PIANO *by Gravity*

http://newtonjapan.com/

$1.99

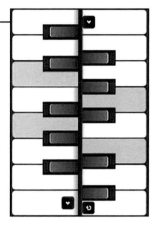

Play *Fun Piano* with your friends! Rotate the keyboard, and you can teach someone to play the piano. Enjoy!

iREVIEW

I like the *Fun Piano* app because it is interactive—I can play with a student. The student and I can take turns being the leader to create a tune. When the leader presses a key, the corresponding key (on the other side of the pad) will turn blue.

PANDORA RADIO *by Pandora Media, Inc.*

www.pandora.com

FREE

FROM THE DEVELOPER

Great music discovery is effortless and free with Pandora. Just start with the name of one of your favorite artists, songs, genres, or composers and we will do the rest. It's easy to create personalized stations that play only music you'll love. Tap into an entire world of music, including almost a century of popular recordings, new and old, well known and obscure. Create up to 100 personalized radio stations with your free account.

iREVIEW

Pandora Radio lets users create a radio station as diverse as they are. Tell *Pandora Radio* the names of your favorite songs and musicians, and then Pandora will create a radio station that will play those songs and similar songs for free!

In the Spotlight

Learning to Play a Musical Instrument is for People with Autism too!

By Dr. Stephen Shore (www.autismasperger.net)

Dr. Stephen Shore, clinical assistant professor at the Ammon school of Education at Adelphi University, outlines steps that will take your student or child from playing an instrument on the iPad to engaging in hands-on playing, reading music, and engaging in expressive arts.

Preparation

"Can you help me draw a straight line down the middle of the page?" I ask my student upon our initial meeting.

Done!

"How about three more lines, going sideways?"

Done!

Soon we have eight empty squares on what was previously a blank notebook-sized piece of paper.

A	B
C	D
E	F
G	Extra

"A!" responds my student, when I ask for the first letter of the alphabet. I then ask him to write that letter in the first box before moving on to B through G. The eighth box is filled with the word "extra."

"Excellent! Gee, could you finish writing out a line of A's on this specially prepared yellow stickie?"

Done!

"Now let's write up some B's…" We continue until we reach the letter G.

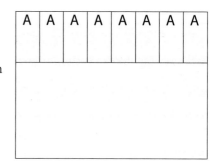

Now with a bank of letters, I'll have the child use scissors to cut the bottom part of the stickie off before cutting out each individual letter.

"Where do you think the A goes?" The child responds—often by pointing to the box with the corresponding letter on a previously prepared piece of notebook paper. Next thing we know, that paper is filled with letters. After placing all the letters in their proper location on the sheet, it is now time to explore the piano keyboard.

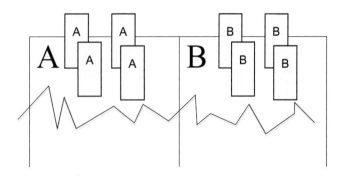

The Keyboard

"I wonder if you can guess what the 1st key on the piano is called?" Often the child responds by naming the letter A, which is correct for an 88-key piano. The note C starts off a 61-key keyboard.

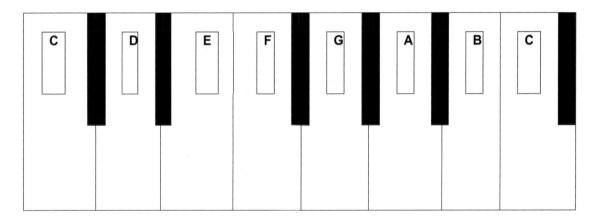

"Can you place an A on that first key?" "What comes next?" Soon the entire keyboard is filled with little stickies marking the notes. From here, we explore the keyboard, make a musical staff, and start reading music without my mentioning that is what we are doing.

Rationale

The goal is to teach the child on the autism spectrum how to play a musical instrument. I have found that children with autism tend to have very little patience for diatribes on rules, techniques, or other concepts commonly explained in the early stages of learning how to play a musical instrument. Therefore, I quickly engage the students in creating the materials used in becoming familiar with the elements of music, making the process of learning music much more meaningful to them. Very little talking or explaining is done.

Most often I start children playing either a keyboard instrument or recorder. The keyboard works well, because all the notes are laid out in a highly visible manner. Also, children with challenges in motor control can often be successful just by finding and pressing the desired key. The recorder works well for some students because it is small, relatively easy to play, and promotes good breath control. Some students will be helped by placing reinforcements on the holes to provide a better tactile sensation regarding their locations. Additionally, recorders are very portable and inexpensive (and easy to replace if lost). Finally, for those students who come in *really* wanting to learn another instrument such as tuba or trombone, I am glad to start them on those instruments as well.

The therapeutic benefits of communication, social interaction, motor control, etc., that music therapists look for when engaging a child in this expressive art are very important. However, learning how to *play* a musical instrument provides the person a real-life key to unlock the door to interacting with others as a musician, either as a soloist or a member of an ensemble. Additionally, this area of competence is especially important when there may be challenges in other areas such as communication, socialization, academics, etc. Also, music is just plain fun!

Finally, I have yet to figure out how to teach children who are not on the autism spectrum. Those with autism are so much more predictable and easier to understand!

People all over the autism spectrum can learn how to play a musical instrument. My students range from being non-verbal with significant challenges to those with Asperger's syndrome and being hyper verbal. With the advent of music education apps for the iPad and other devices such as Real Piano, Note Perfect, Ear Trainer, and Garage Band, there are more options for individuals with and without autism to learn how to play and compose music!

Part XI

Parental/Therapy Controls, Support, and Information

The iPad is a wildly useful tool for educating, communicating, and engaging in leisure activities, but did you know that it can also provide peace of mind, impart information, bridge gaps, set limits, and open doors for both the adult and child users? Let's take a look at some of the wonderful apps that make our everyday lives easier and safer.

Chapter 35: Parental Controls

Technology rocks! Technology gives our children a means of education and an endless supply of information and entertainment. However, along with this abundant source of knowledge come some safety concerns as well. As with the real world, the Internet has its share of trolls, hate groups, porn, and questionable characters. To keep our children safe from the dangers of the Internet and/or online bullying, media guidelines and precautions should be taken. *Apps for Autism* has compiled safety guidelines, precautions, and a list of apps that will help keep your child's Internet experience positive and productive.

- Set clear ground rules for Internet usage and maintain access to all passwords and accounts.
- All iDevices and computers should be used in a common area so they can be easily monitored by an adult.
- Teach your child to keep personal information private. Ensure that your child is aware of what personal information is by providing and reviewing a list of private information. Also, talk with your child and explain why some information is private and other information can be shared. Provide visuals of private vs. shareable information so your child knows the boundaries.
- As in real life, never talk to strangers!
- Also as in real life, be polite and have good manners. Use good "Netiquette."

 For comprehensive information on scams, cyber bullying, online predators, and keeping safe on the Internet, check out *No More Victims* by Dr. Jed Baker.

YouTube

We all enjoy YouTube. You can find and watch videos from virtually anywhere in the world. Sometimes we may need reminders, time limits, and content filters to keep our children on track and free from adult content. This list of apps supports parents in selecting appropriate content and time limits. Each app has unique features. Choose the right one for your family.

VIDEOMONSTER - YOUTUBE FOR KIDS
by Hans-Juergen Dorsch
http://videomonsterapp.com
$4.99

VideoMonster is the YouTube player especially for children. Your children only see videos they should see—because you've selected them.

- Search and select videos from YouTube in the Video-Chooser and store them as playlists for your children. Access to the Video Chooser is protected by a PIN.
- *VideoMonster* comes with videos. Choose one of the prepared *VideoMonster* lists and add it to your selection. Children can operate the player by themselves. It's very simple, and they don't need to be able to read.
- The built-in timer prevents kids from watching for too long.
- Videos can be watched without Internet access because *VideoMonster* stores them on the device if you want it to.
- *VideoMonster* runs on iPad, iPad mini, and iPhone. With iCloud, video lists are always up to date on all devices.

iREVIEW

You, the parent or educator, can select the YouTube videos your child can watch or choose from a pre-populated list of suggested videos, set the timer, and relax. *VideoMonster* stores the videos on the device so your child can watch anywhere or any time. *VideoMonster* can store any list of videos for many purposes to be used as resources, therefore cutting down on wasted time searching through thousands of YouTube videos.

KIDS VIDEOS AND ENTERTAINMENT – KIDEOS

by Big Purple Hippos

www.kideos.com

$2.99

FROM THE DEVELOPER

The *Kideos* iPhone app allows children to safely watch their favorite videos on the go. Kideos is simple for children to use on their own, and every video has been reviewed by a select group of parents and educators. Parents can create custom playlists for their children to enjoy. Kids will enjoy age-appropriate videos from numerous channels, including Sesame Street, Dr. Seuss, Disney, cartoon characters, cats, and many more.

iREVIEW

Just load and go! I can let my children watch videos from the Internet with no worries! *Kideos* plays all the most popular, kid-friendly, Video Advisory Council-approved online videos and games with regular updates. Videos are divided into age appropriateness, channels, and custom playlists. A search bar lets the user find special interest topics. Most videos have educational value; however, some are just plain fun. This is a highly recommended app for education, reinforcement, and filling down time. Check out "Our Story" in the "About" section of the Kideos website for the developer's heartwarming story.

KID-SAFE TUBE TV - SAFE VIDEOS FOR KIDS WITH REMOTE PARENTAL CONTROL

by Idemfactor Solutions

http://idemfactor.com/kidsafetube

$0.99

FROM THE DEVELOPER

The app filters YouTube videos based on their content to guarantee that your child is never exposed to any offensive or explicit content while browsing videos on the iPhone or iPad. Using *KidsSafe Tube* allows you to effectively regulate the content your child views by giving you the ability to bookmark

videos you consider safe for viewing and the ones you don't. You can bookmark single videos and search results and add them to your block list to protect your child from accidentally viewing any of these videos. The app also comes with a collection of pre-selected videos for children in different age groups. There are educational videos for toddlers aged one through three, preschool students aged three to five, and school-aged children aged five and above. The videos are updated weekly so there's always something new for your child to watch.

In addition to the video filtering options, the app also has a video timer which lets you set a time limit for video viewing. This encourages your child to take breaks while they're watching videos and prevents them from being sedentary for extended periods of time. You can also remotely lock the app, view your child's watching history, and add language filters to your settings. Just turn on the lockout option via your iPhone if your kids refuse to let go of the iPad, and there will be no more heartbreaking fighting.

iREVIEW

Bookmark videos, playlists, channels, and search results. Monitor with a timer, remote lock, and language filters. Parents can also keep track of what your child is viewing by watching their history or block any video that is inappropriate. Using *Kid-safe Tube TV* in passcode-protected, Parent mode will release all pre-set restrictions. Videos in parent mode are NOT filtered. Please make sure to turn on Kid Mode before handing the device to your child.

 An Internet connection is required for streaming, as this app won't work offline. For more tips, please visit our support sites and Facebook.

WEETWOO! KID VIDEOS, SAFE & EDUCATIONAL, FROM YOUTUBE & PARENT REVIEWED

by Tappister, LLC

www.weetwoo.com

$3.99

FROM THE DEVELOPER

WeetWoo supports AirPlay via AppleTV so you can see videos on your HDTV. *WeetWoo* is the award-winning, best-selling kid-safe video app, designed by parents. We've carefully reviewed and collected thousands of kid-safe videos into easy to use playlists for your child. We've got great videos to help your child learn about animals, places, people, and music. There's also a Fun Shows channel full of your favorite clips, like *Arthur, Caillou, Scooby Doo, Cory in the House, Suite Life, Spider-Man*, and many, many more. All are hosted on YouTube.com

iREVIEW

WeetWoo app supports AppleTV so your child can see their favorite video on the big screen. *WeetWoo* has thousands of YouTube videos organized into playlists.

 Make sure you have a good connection (wifi recommended)

TIMER FOR YOUTUBE.COM *by Touch Autism*

http://touchautism.com

$0.99

FROM THE DEVELOPER

Is your child too busy using YouTube™ on their device to take advantage of the many educational opportunities devices can offer? Now you can easily control how long your child has access to YouTube.com. Set a code, and only that code will open YouTube.com and will allow you to set how long the site will remain open. Once the allotted time has passed, the app will automatically shut down YouTube.com. Only entering the code again will allow YouTube.com to be re-launched.

iREVIEW

Timer for YouTube.com is a simple timer app that will allow the parent or educator to put time restrictions on how long their child can watch. *Timer for YouTube.com* does not offer controls for content.

Safe Internet Browsers

The Internet offers an endless source of entertainment, education, games and information. However, there may be content that you do not want your child to be exposed to. Safari on iPad can be completely disabled to prevent kids from accessing the Internet, but it does not have controls that allow for kid-safe browsing. Luckily there are a few great apps to help a parent or educator filter content and images. Be aware that no app or software can keep your child safe from inappropriate content with 100% accuracy. Safe browser apps can screen for keywords/phrases, block unwanted sites, and provide user data; however, they are not replacements for alert parents, therapists, or teachers.

To use any one of the excellent safe Internet browsers highlighted in this chapter, your first step is to disable Safari and set the chosen browser (*McGruff, Mobicip, MetaCert*) as the default browser.

Follow these steps:

- Go to *Settings*.
- Tap *General*.
- To enable restrictions, touch *Restrict*. You will be asked to set a passcode.
- Turn Safari off.

 While on this page you may want to consider other features to disable/allow, such as installing apps, deleting apps and/or in-app purchases.

MCGRUFF SAFEGUARD BROWSER

by Kid Friendly Software

/www.gomcgruff.com/browser/iPhone-iPad-Child-Safe-Browser.htm

FREE

FROM THE DEVELOPER

For the past five years, *McGruff SafeGuard* has helped tens of thousands of parents to keep their children and teens safe online. Now *McGruff SafeGuard* will keep your children safe when browsing on the iPad, iPhone, and iPod touch, now with multi-user login and profiles for every family member, and it sends you daily summary usage reports showing your child's activity.

- Safari-like browser for iPhone, iPad, and iPod touch

- Block sites by age and category or by website name

- Get a daily summary of your child's activity via email

- Multi-tab, bookmarks, history, reading list, and more

iREVIEW

"Take a Bite out of Crime", or in this case, inappropriate web content. Parents and/or educators can set filters based on age group and select from 60+ categories, such as porn, dating, violence, sex, and gambling. Websites can be blocked or allowed by name (URL).

 Some features require an app upgrade for SILVER or GOLD Control. The free version provides child-safe and teen-safe browsing. For descriptions of the categories and a demo of *McGruff SafeGuard*, visit: http://tinyurl.com/safeguard03

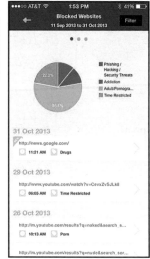

MOBICIP SAFE BROWSER WITH PARENTAL CONTROL

The optional web-based dashboard allows you to monitor browsing history remotely and set up a custom Internet filter across tablets, smartphones, and computers.

Features:

- Filter YouTube videos
- Monitor browsing remotely
- Age-based filtering
- Safari-like browser
- Categorization
- Intelligent real-time analysis
- Premium subscription for even more control of content, time limits, and inappropriate websites.

MOBICIP MONITOR FOR PARENTS & ADMINS

Mobicip Monitor is a companion app for parents and administrators using the *Mobicip* service to configure the settings and review the browsing history all conveniently from your personal iOS device!

Features:

- Review browsing activity remotely on your iDevice.
- Block/unblock websites in history.*
- Modify default filtering level.
- Review devices protected by your account.

The school filtering levels apply filtering standards used by K-12 school systems. The filter uses a combination of methods to keep your child safe, including strict safe search, categorization, and intelligent real-time content analysis.

by Mobicip.com
www.mobicip.com
FREE

FROM THE DEVELOPER

Set-up and enable *Mobicip* on your family's mobile devices and computers. Then remotely manage your settings and monitor Internet and app usage from an easy web-based monitor dashboard. Stay in touch with your family's Internet and app usage instantly from a personal iOS device (iPhone, iPod touch, iPad, or iPad mini). Receive alerts when content is blocked or allowed on the protected device. You can even override the decision instantly in the app.

iREVIEW

Protect your child or student from unwanted Internet content with *Mobicip Safe Browser with Parental Control* & *Mobicip Monitor For Parents & Admins*. A web dashboard monitors browsing history remotely. Set pre-defined filters across tablets, smartphones, and computers. Two choices of Mobicip apps give both parents and educators powerful control and monitoring of their child's/student's iDevice and/or computer for free. Upgrade to Premium and get even more control over settings, time, and inappropriate content with online management, browsing history reports, time limits, accountability mode, custom filters, and new app monitoring for up to five devices. Upgrade to Enterprise and get volume discount, delegated account management, and downloadable reports for up to 20 devices.

 Basic features of *Mobicip* are free, and advanced features are available with the Premium Enterprise upgrades. See the developer's website for details: www.mobicip.com/pricing

METACERT IPAD BROWSER WITH PARENTAL CONTROLS
by MetaCert
http://metacert.com/ios
FREE

FROM THE DEVELOPER

Perfect for families and schools looking for a safe browser that's fast, secure, reliable, and feature rich.

- Filters all major web search engines.
- Filters all major image and video search.
- Blocks 700+ million pages of pornography.
- Thousands of new pages added daily.
- Fully customizable block list—add any website.
- Offers protection of your own history with a password.

iREVIEW

You decide the limitations with multiple settings for adults and children by selectively blocking inappropriate content and websites. This app blocks 700+million pages of pornography and monitors usage by tracking date and time of visited websites.

Chapter 36: Parent/ Therapy Toolbox

The definition of "toolbox" is a box for storing or carrying tools. For the busy parent, therapist, or teacher, the iPad is that box, and the tools are apps that are used to carry out a particular function. This chapter features helpful tools to support the everyday use of the iPad and further enhances its efficacy. Like a vise-grip or crescent wrench, you will not use these apps on a daily basis, but you will be very happy you have them on your iPad when you need them.

New Third-Party Keyboards

For the first time, iOS 8 opens up the keyboard to developers. And once new keyboards are available, you'll be able to choose your favorite input method or layout system-wide. Now you can choose the perfect keyboard(s) and have it available at your fingertips. To install and enable a custom keyboard on your iDevice follow these simple steps:

1. Browse the App Store and download a keyboard that fits your needs.

2. Go to *Settings > General > Keyboard > Add New Keyboard*.

3. Choose the Third-Party Keyboard(s) you wish to use.

4. Decide if you want to allow Full Access to the developer of the keyboard.

5. To choose your favorite keyboard, tap the globe icon.

GREAT THIRD-PARTY KEYBOARDS TO CONSIDER

KEEDOGO - KEYBOARD FOR BEGINNING TYPERS
$1.99

A playful Colored theme and a more sober Gray theme as well as a QWERTY or ABC layout. Featuring lowercase letters and optional color-coded vowels, learning has never been easier. *Keedogo* can be used in any app as an alternative to the standard iOS keyboard.

KEEDOGO PLUS - KEYBOARD FOR EDUCATION
$2.99

Keedogo Plus is an iOS keyboard with word prediction designed for children and young students. The keyboard provides a simplified layout with just the essential keys so early writers can focus on developing their skills rather than being distracted by symbols and functions they don't yet need.

by AssistiveWare
www.assistiveware.com/product/keedogo

FROM THE DEVELOPER

Keedogo is designed for children and young students who just started to read, write and type. The simplified layout helps beginners to focus on learning rather than being distracted by superfluous functions like typing. Keedogo Plus adds word prediction to speed up typing and build confidence.

I put *Keedogo* on all my iPads. The color coding makes it easier for users to locate keys and the word prediction feature of Keedogo Plus increases typing fluency significantly. Third-Party Keyboards such as *Keedogo* can be easily activated and used in any app to support spelling, fluency, communication, and writing skills. Great features like; ABC / QWERTY layout, colored vowels, simplified keyboard, color/grey theme, large font, and capitalization make Keedogo essential for working with school age students.

EZ KEYS *by Panther Technology*
http://panthertechnology.com
$1.99

FROM THE DEVELOPER

Believe it or not, the six letters Q,J,V,X,K,Z make up only 2% of the keys you hit. But they take up 23% of the keyboard space. By putting these seldom-used letters on a second keyboard, every other key on your main keyboard becomes sixty-five percent bigger! You'll be amazed that you almost never miss them. And, instead, you find hitting all the other keys you need is easier. Mistakes are fewer. And typing is faster and less frustrating than ever before. Especially if you have motor issues or disabilities. *EZ Keys* also includes 49 useful phrases you can put into texting at the touch of button. And you'll also have world-class word prediction.

iREVIEW

EZ Keys gives you only the keys you use and increases the size of the keyboard making it easier to see and use. In addition, 49 commonly used phrases grouped into seven categories making phrases like, "Wanna hang together?" "That's cool!" and "I need some help." available in one or two taps. *EZ Keys* is a great option for school age students and adults who need support in spelling, word prediction, texting and communication.

FLEKSY KEYBOARD - CUSTOM COLORS, FASTER TYPING *by Fleksy, Inc.*

http://fleksy.com

$0.99

Colorful **themes**
Custom **sizes**

FROM THE DEVELOPER

Fleksy is the most fun, colorful way to type, and officially the fastest keyboard in the world. The first custom keyboard for iOS 8, *Fleksy* brings amazing accuracy, color customization and cool typing to iPhone and iPad. *Fleksy* keyboard uses next-generation autocorrect so accurate you can type without even looking, and type with record-setting speed! Type faster and save more time for the things you love.

iREVIEW

Fleksy was originally developed to be a creative, fast way to send cool messages via social media. However, it is also a great way to design a keyboard that fits your child's individual needs for visual perceptual processing challenges, light sensitivity, visual acuity, and sensory overload. Changing the color and color contrast on the keyboard may not only help the brain filter and process visual information, but also improve your child's ability to remember where the individual keys are located by color coding the keyboard. *Fleksy Keyboard* features custom colors, size, auto-correct and swiping features combined with 40 languages and 800 emoji gives the user a unique keyboarding experience. *Fleksy* boast that it is the "fastest keyboard in the world," and I would agree, but, only after a learning curve and some trial and error. This app is well worth the $0.99 and may become your favorite keyboard.

iTRANSLATE VOICE - TRANS-LATOR & DICTIONARY
$4.99

Can you imagine talking into your phone in one language and immediately hearing yourself in another language? That's exactly what *iTranslate Voice* does. Just speak into your phone and it immediately replies in one of our 42 languages.

- Instantly speak 42 languages
- Look up definitions and translations for common words and phrases simply using your voice.
- Use AirTranslate to connect devices together and easily engage in conversation with other people.
- Simply send translations via email, SMS, Twitter, or Facebook.
- Forget typing. The accuracy of our voice recognition is so amazing that you don't need your keyboard anymore.

iTRANSLATE - TRANSLATOR & DICTIONARY
FREE

iTranslate is an award-winning translation tool that helps you break down language barriers. With its state-of-the-art technology, you can speak any language in a second.

- 80+ Languages
- Voice Output and Input
- Dictionaries
- Faster Typing
- Sharing
- Favorites and History
- Romanization

 iTranslate is free to download and use. *iTranslate Premium* removes ads and unlocks voice recognition. It is available as a one-time in-app purchase.

by Sonico GmbH
www.itranslateapp.com

FROM THE DEVELOPER

iTranslate is an award-winning translation tool that helps you break down language barriers. With its state-of-the-art technology, you can speak any language in a second.

iREVIEW

iTranslate and *iTranslate Voice* are essential for communicating important information to and receiving information from non-English speaking individuals. The iTranslate apps will significantly improve communication from parent and child to therapist or teacher.

 iTranslate requires an Internet connection.

COMMON CORE STANDARDS *by MasteryConnect*
https://www.masteryconnect.com/learn-more
FREE

FROM THE DEVELOPER

View the *Common Core Standards* in one convenient free app! A great reference for students, parents, and teachers to read and understand easily the core standards. Quickly find standards by subject, grade, and subject category (domain/cluster). This app includes Math standards K-12 and Language Arts standards K-12. Math standards include both traditional and integrated pathways (as outlined in Appendix A of the common core) and synthesizes Language Arts standards with the Corresponding College and Career Readiness Standards (CCRs).

Love them or hate them, here they are, the *Common Core Standards* in Education. *Common Core Standards* is an easy, quick resource for anyone who needs to know these educational standards. *Common Core Standards* is recommended for educators, therapists, and/or parents who need handy access to this information or students who are learning/studying them for the first time.

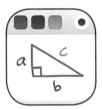

EDUCREATIONS INTERACTIVE WHITEBOARD

by Educreations, Inc.

www.educreations.com

FREE

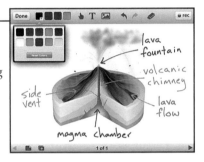

FROM THE DEVELOPER

Educreations turns your iPad into a recordable whiteboard. Creating a great video tutorial is as simple as touching, tapping, and talking. Explain a math formula, create an animated lesson, add commentary to your photos, and diagram a sports play! With voice recording; realistic digital ink, photos, and text; and simple sharing through email, Facebook, or Twitter, now you can broadcast your ideas from anywhere.

iREVIEW

Interactive whiteboards are so flexible and have so many uses that every iPad should have one. *Educreations* is incredibly robust, with tons of features like records, handwriting, drawing, text, images import and animation, creation of multiple pages, and the ability to share and embed. Once your video has been created, you can showcase it on educreations.com and share your knowledge with the world. Here are some great ideas for utilizing interactive whiteboard apps and whole-class participation.

*Modified From - Ways to use Interactive Whiteboards in the Classroom (from the Instructional Technology Department of the Wichita Public Schools).

- Keep parents and caregivers "in the loop."

- Send lessons home for homework or reinforcement.

- Save lessons to present to students who were absent.

- Use the built-in maps to teach about continents, oceans, countries, or states and capitals or just find your own home.

- Promote public speaking abilities by presenting presentations created by the student or teacher.

- Have students create e-folios including samples of their work and narration.

- Digital storytelling of and visual supports.

- Teach whole group computer or keyboarding skills.

- Brainstorm.

- Reinforce skills by using online interactive web sites.

- Use a highlighter tool to highlight nouns, verbs, adjectives, etc.

- Teach students how to navigate the Internet.

- Illustrate and write a book as a class. Use the record feature to narrate the text.

- Teach steps to a math problem.

- Teach vocabulary.

- Access the Electronic Word Wall.

- End each day by having students write one thing that they learned.

 See all the educational videos from teachers, parents, and therapists around the world at: www. educreations.com

GETTY IMAGES

Designed for creative and media professionals, the *Getty Images* app puts over 60 million powerful images at your fingertips. Access our entire collection from client meetings, the coffee shop or anywhere in between. You can search, save and share a world of creative stock photos as well as editorial and archival imagery

GETTY IMAGES STREAM

Designed for your personal use, Stream is your doorway to discovering captivating, hand-selected photos that speak to what intrigues you most. See the world through the lens of *Getty Images'* world-class photographers - from today's news told through crisp, compelling photos to historic moments in time captured forever in our image archives.

by Getty Images Inc.
www.gettyimages.com
FREE

FROM THE DEVELOPER

Getty Images is among the world's leading creators and distributors of award-winning still imagery, video, music and multi-media products, as well as other forms of premium digital content, available through its trusted house of brands, including iStock© and Thinkstock©.

If you are looking for gorgeous images to add to your visual supports, then *Getty Images* and *Getty Images Stream* may be the app(s) for you. Using *Getty Images* you can find anything from historical affairs and sports to current events and celebrities. An endless array of spectacular photos for you to use and enjoy.

FOTOFARM HD *by PaperNappkin*
www.papernappkin.com
$0.99

FROM THE DEVELOPER

FotoFarm gives kids a fun and easy way to find images from the web using Google Images. *FotoFarm* lets you quickly search, crop, and save photos for homework or projects so you can get back to being a kid!! *FotoFarm* is the ONLY image search app built for kids! Whether it's a photo of Abe Lincoln for a report or an image of Justin Bieber to use as a screensaver, *FotoFarm* makes finding photos a breeze. Plus, your parents will rest easy knowing that Foto-Farm utilizes Google SafeSearch technology to filter grown-up results from its searches.

iREVIEW

Find, crop, and save just the right images for creating a custom visual supports or any project that involves youngsters. Images are easy to search and are presented on a white background that minimizes distracting content. Feel more confident searching images with your child or student with *FotoFarm*.

 FotoFarm provides users with a free trial version. Also, please note that *FotoFarm* and other image search apps ONLY filter search WORDS—they do NOT and cannot analyze photos to determine which aren't appropriate.

i-HEAR - HEARING AID *by Idan Sheetrit*
http://idans.yolasite.com/
$4.99

FROM THE DEVELOPER

Use your iPhone as hearing aid/assistant (read disclaimer below). The first app that does it perfectly! Simply plug in a regular headset, and you are good to go! Download now and try it out!

iREVIEW

Use your earbuds or headphones as a hearing aid with *i-Hear – Hearing Aid*. This app is awesome for individuals who are hard of hearing and can also be helpful when working on auditory processing skills. The volume and filter can be easily adjusted by the individual or therapist to fit the needs of the situation. An adult, therapist, teacher, or parent should adjust volume prior to using the app with a child or person who may have difficulty with volume controls. To adjust audio volume balance between left and right channels, go to *Settings > General > Accessibility > Mono Audio*. Mono Audio—When you're using headphones, you may miss some audio if you're deaf or hard of hearing in one ear, because stereo recordings usually have distinct left- and right-channel audio tracks. iOS can help by playing both audio channels in both ears and letting you adjust the balance for greater volume in either ear, so you won't miss a single note of a concerto or word of an audiobook.

 Try the free version to see if this is the right support for your hearing needs. Both the developer and I warn that, if used inappropriately, *i-Hear – Hearing Aid* or any volume enhancing app could damage your hearing, and one should consult with a qualified health care professional before using any app or software developed to increase volume.

MAKE IT BIG *by An Trinh*
www.atrinh.com
FREE

FROM THE DEVELOPER

Type a message to *Make It Big*! The message will be enlarged to fill the entire screen. Change Font, Change Text Color, Change Background Color, Enable/Disable Shake to Flash mode.

iREVIEW

Do you need to get a message to someone across a crowded, noisy room, have poor eye sight or just need extra visual support, then Make It Big is for you. *Make It Big* does just that; this app fills the screen with your typed message. Users can customize font color, background color, and font style. If large colorful fonts are not enough to get attention, simply shake your iDevice and your screen will flash your message.

I put on my robe and wizard hat

Chapter 37: Autism Information

"Knowledge is power (*Ipsa Scientia Potestas Est*)"

—Sir Francis Bacon

Remember the words of Temple Grandin's mother, who explains that autism makes Temple "different" but not "less." When a child is diagnosed with autism or a disability, caregivers often feel a range of emotions as well as feel overwhelmed. Obtaining accurate information regarding their child's disability and the resources that are available is a first step. Doctors, healthcare professionals, educators, and support groups can all be invaluable resources in determining what combination of interventions and services are right for your child. The World Wide Web provides a virtual plethora of information for individuals with disabilities, as do the following apps.

NO MORE MELTDOWNS
by SymTrend, Inc.

https://www.symtrend.com/tw/nmm-public

$10.99

FROM THE DEVELOPER

It could happen at home, school, the grocery store, or a restaurant; meltdowns are stressful for both child and adult. However, Dr. Baker's No More Meltdown app can help! His popular book gives the tools to deal with and prevent out-of-control behavior. Now you can have those tools with you in the moment to help you prepare your child for the situations as they arise. Dr. Baker has teamed with SymTrend to create an app and a website for you to follow his four-step model:

- Manage your own feelings so you can calmly help your child.
- Learn strategies to de-escalate and soothe your child in the moment.
- Understand common triggers to challenging behaviors.
- Create plans to anticipate these triggers and prevent future problem behaviors.

iREVIEW

No More Meltdowns provides caregivers basic techniques for preventing and, if necessary, managing meltdowns. Give your child and yourself the tools needed to deal with challenging situations and the ability to analyze triggers. *No More Meltdowns* comes with a companion website that allows the user to keep an "electronic diary" that tracks, analyzes data, and identifies situations that may be a challenge to your child. *No More Meltdowns* offers the user lots of basic information on managing feelings, identifying triggers, and preventive strategies. *No More Meltdowns* can track the data of one child. For a comprehensive resource on preventing and managing meltdowns, please refer to Dr. Baker's book, *No More Meltdowns*.

AUTISM NEWS READER *by Richard de los Santos*

http://splaysoft.com/Site/Autism_News.html

$0.99

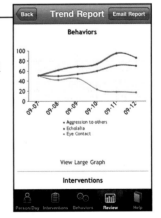

FROM THE DEVELOPER

Autism News Reader grabs the top stories from the best autism health news and information sites and delivers them to your iPhone. Keep up with autism issues and developments in one place: *Autism News Reader.*

iREVIEW

I no longer have to spend hours sorting through articles, newsletters, and emails for up-to-date, reliable information. I can easily find the latest scientific, human interest, and educational/conference information as well as instant access to websites, blogs, and discussions. This *Autism News Reader* is a huge time saver.

AUTISMTRACK
by Handhold Adaptive, LLC
www.handholdadaptive.com
$0.99

FROM THE DEVELOPER

AutismTrack™ can help parents of children with ASD answer the ongoing and ever-puzzling question: "What seems to be working, and what's not?" Daily log screens provide a snapshot of any particular day's interventions and behaviors. Users may also graph symptoms and monitor compliance over periods of time. These daily logs and trend reports may be emailed (in PDF format), so that parents and other caregivers can review useful information on their search for the unique patterns and trends experienced by individuals with autism spectrum disorders (ASD).

iREVIEW

Track your child's behaviors and analyze trends to design custom interventions that work for individual needs. *AutismTrack* monitors five behaviors and nine interventions, enabling caregivers and educators to determine which treatment options are right for each student or child. Additional interventions and behaviors can be added for enhanced customization. Parents and educators can enter data and add notes to encourage teamwork and carryover throughout the day. Once interventions, behaviors, and trends have been reviewed, the user can email the data to each member of the team or make a printout to keep for records.

AUTISM ASSESSMENT - A QUESTIONNAIRE FOR THE SIGNS AND SYMPTOMS OF AUTISM SPECTRUM DISORDERS

by Touch Autism

http://touchautism.com/app/autism-assessment

$1.99

FROM THE DEVELOPER

The test is made up of 72 questions written for the caregiver of the person (called client) in question. Each question represents part of the definition and diagnostic criteria for a diagnosis of an autism spectrum disorder. The results of the assessment can be easily e-mailed from the app. This test is for educational purposes only. It should not be used to diagnose or treat any disorder. The test is based on the definition of and diagnostic criteria for autistic disorder, which specifies that a person must display qualitative impairment in social interaction and communication and display restricted repetitive and stereotyped patterns of behavior.

iREVIEW

As the developer points out, the *Autism Assessment* app should be used for information only. This app does not diagnose! There have been false positives and negatives. If you are concerned about yourself or another, please see a specialist. When seeking a specialist, please make sure that person is familiar with autism spectrum disorder. That being said, this is a place to start if you are wondering if you should get yourself or your child screened. There are 72 yes/no questions to answer (I scored slightly autistic). *Autism Assessment* has some good resources and information regarding autism.

 Please be aware that no screening tool or assessment is 100% accurate; therefore, the results from this assessment do not ensure whether the client does or does not have an autism spectrum disorder.

iAUTISM TODDLER SCREENING TOOL
by iCrysta
http://icrysta.com
$4.99

FROM THE DEVELOPER

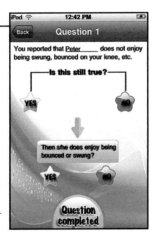

The *M-CHAT* can be administered and scored as part of a well-child checkup and also can be used by parents, specialists, or other professionals to assess risk for ASD. The primary goal of the *M-CHAT* is to maximize sensitivity, meaning that it will detect as many cases of ASD as possible. Therefore, there is a high false positive rate, meaning that not all children who score at risk for ASD will be diagnosed with ASD. To address this, there is a structured follow-up interview for use in conjunction with the *M-CHAT*. Users should be aware that, even with the follow-up questions, a significant number of the children who fail the *M-CHAT* will not be diagnosed with an ASD; however, these children may be at risk for other developmental disorders or delays, and therefore, evaluation is warranted for any child who fails the screening.

iREVIEW

iAutism Toddler Screening Tool should be used for information in conjunction with a physician. The Modified Checklist for Autism in Toddlers (*M-CHAT*) is used to access the risk of autism in toddlers between 16 and 30 months. It is also designed to bring awareness to those who use it. M-CHAT has two parts: a checklist and a follow-up interview. Please see a specialist for diagnostic purposes.

AUTISM DX / TREATMENT *by ZBobbApps.com*
http://drbrownsapps.com/?ref=aba4autism
$1.99

FROM THE DEVELOPER

Dr. Gary Brown's *Autism DX/Treatment* is a short informational applet that is designed to help you find the proper diagnosis and treatment for your child on the autism spectrum. This app contains useful and easy-to-understand information that can help both you and your child. It is filled with links to ABA-approved resources such as books and other apps, including our Discrete Trial Training (DTT) apps, and has links to other apps that we use and test every day at our clinic. This app also contains warnings for unproven treatments to watch out for.

iREVIEW

Autism DX/Treatment is a fundamental easy-to-read, well-organized resource to help parents and other caregivers find basic information on autism and treatment. Within *Autism DX/Treatment* are links to further information and programs that are proven beneficial to individuals on the spectrum.

Chapter 38: Gluten Free

A gluten-free diet simply means avoiding foods or drinks that contain gluten (wheat, barley, rye, oats, or anything made from these grains). Some suggest that individuals with autism have gastrointestinal difficulties that make it hard to digest grains properly, affecting behavior adversely. Maintaining a gluten-free diet is difficult because gluten is present in many foods and can be hidden in prepared foods. Let's take some of the workload off parents, caregivers, and individuals by providing this information at their fingertips.

FIND ME GLUTEN FREE *by Gluten Free Classes, LLC*

www.findmeglutenfree.com

FREE

FROM THE DEVELOPER

Find Me Gluten Free helps you eat a gluten-free diet. View local business ratings and reviews, gluten-free menus, get directions, and call them right from the app. Also, easily view gluten-free menus and allergen lists of chains and fast food restaurants. Find gluten-free pizza, bakeries, fast food, local businesses, and more!

iREVIEW

If having a gluten free diet is not hard enough, try sticking to a gluten free diet when traveling or on vacation. Find Me Gluten Free has taken the headache and worry out of traveling and eating out for folks who do not tolerate gluten in their diets. Once you locate a business that is gluten free, *Find Me Gluten Free* will provide you an option to call, get directions, check reviews, and share with friends or family. This app is sort of like Yelp for gluten-free individuals and businesses.

 Explore the developer's website for more reviews, information, and the latest details of living gluten free: www.findmeglutenfree.com

IS THAT GLUTEN FREE? *by Garden Bay Software*

http://isthatglutenfree.com

$7.99

FROM THE DEVELOPER

"Is that gluten free?" This question can be confusing and often overwhelming. But that's about to change!! We have done the legwork and complied tons of data to provide you with verified gluten-free product information at your fingertips! Is That Gluten Free? is designed for those with gluten sensitivities or Celiac

Disease or anyone wanting more information on gluten-free products or leading a gluten-free lifestyle.

iREVIEW

The *Is that Gluten Free?* app has compiled tons of information to answer the question, "Is that gluten free?" The "Defeat Autism Now! Protocol" recommends that every child with autism be placed on a gluten-free, casein-free diet for at least three months. Is that Gluten Free? can help caregivers and individuals with this seemingly overwhelming task of identifying food products that are truly gluten free. I know from personal experience that diet can make a difference among those with autism. Please do not try any diet without the guidance of a physician and/or nutritionist. Every person is different; not every individual on the spectrum will benefit from a gluten-free diet.

Now we can help you make gluten-free decisions while eating out! No need to search the internet for gluten free menus. We have done the legwork to provide you with verified gluten-free restaurant information at your fingertips!!

New and updated brand and product filters make it easy to find the latest new gluten-free products. This is a great way to discover your new gluten-free favorites!

ICANEAT FAST FOOD GLUTEN FREE AND ALLERGY FREE

IEATOUT GLUTEN FREE & ALLERGY FREE

by AllergyFree Passport
http://glutenfreepassport.com
$4.99 (each)

FROM THE DEVELOPER

Looking for gluten-free and allergy-free fast food in the US? Personalize this app for safe meals based on your allergen concerns. With *iCanEat Fast Food Gluten Free* and *Allergy Free*, you can easily browse menus of US restaurants by hiding foods that contain gluten, wheat, eggs, milk nuts, peanuts, soy, fish, and/or shellfish from the 4,000-item database. Avoid gluten, wheat, dairy, eggs, peanuts, nuts, soy, corn, fish, and/or shellfish anywhere. With *iEatOut Gluten Free* and *Allergy Free*, you can confidently order safe meals in Chinese, French, Indian, Italian, Mexican, steak, and Thai restaurants close to your home or around the world without being restricted to finding gluten-free menus or allergy charts.

iREVIEW

iCanEat and *iEatOut* provides individuals and caregivers easy access to invaluable dietary information for fast food menus and restaurants. Recent literature has suggested that food allergies play a role in causing or worsening autism. While this has not been proven, many parents have noted positive changes in behavior when certain foods have been removed from their child's diet.

 We all know that every individual, as well as his or her diet and possible food sensitivities, is different. Consult a physician and/or nutritionist prior to starting any diet.

Part XII

Cool Stuff

Now that we have equipped our children and students with the tools befitting of who they are, cool. Now let's take it a step further—SUPER COOL! In this chapter, I will take this information over the top with gadgets, cases, holders, and yes, even clothing. Some of the items in this chapter are beneficial, some are protective, some are crucial, and others are completely outrageous!

Chapter 39: Cool Stuff

ORIGINAL DESIGNS

This company provides wonderful creations by artists who have worked through personal challenges to create meaningful designs or opportunities to design your own T-shirt. The *QR Code iD* designs have been selected to show how cool and loved our loved ones are! Please support the artists!

IF I NEED HELP
https://www.qrcodeid.org/
FREE—Sign up and become a member.

FROM THE DEVELOPER

QR Code iD alerts people to knowing that this person needs help by displaying the phrase "IF I NEED HELP" in large red letters. People who have autism, dementia, Alzheimer's, Down's syndrome, or other cognitive or physical condition that hinders their ability to provide personal information can benefit from having a personal code. The person who finds the wanderer can scan the QR code with a smartphone or iPad or manually enter the number associated with the code into the website to obtain the contact information to reunite the person with loved ones. Also, any information that is important during an emergency for the finder to know, such as ways to sooth or medical conditions and how to deal with them, will be provided. This information can be changed in real time by logging into the site. There is a password-protected area in which documents that may be wanted for reference can be stored

iREVIEW

Wandering and personal safety are huge concerns for individuals on the spectrum or anyone who has difficulty communicating accurate information for themselves. *QR Code iD* is a successful means of communicating important information about an individual with special needs, such as whom to call, medical information, and what may keep them calm in a stressful situation.

Here is one such story from Team Lueck regarding this technology:

Amazing! I tell every parent I meet about *QR Code iD*. I was a little shocked to hear that we might be one of the first success stories. We have a large family (five children) and travel with lots of stuff. While attending an all-day sporting event for our son, we were asked to move to a different field after each game. We were in the process of setting up for the last game when we realized that our five year old was missing. My husband and I left the other children with friends and split up to find him. While frantically running across the fields towards the restroom, I got a call. A woman had seen the patch on my son's shirt, scanned it, and called me. That feeling of gratefulness and being able to breathe again was overwhelming, even more so with our kiddo being autistic and possibly not able to clearly communicate his needs. We picked him up at the sandbox with lots of hugs and tears. Thank you Erin and *QR Code iD*; you have a client for life!

 QR Code reading apps are abundant, and most are free. Here are some excellent choices.

QRUNCH IT
by tApp tApp Studios

QR READER FOR IPAD
by TapMedia Ltd

SCAN-QR CODE & BARCODE
by QR Code City ($1.99)

Wandering among children with autism is common and dangerous and puts a huge amount of stress on families. QR Code iD offers a means of identifying children or individuals who may wander or run from a safe place. Prevention of this hazardous and potentially life-threatening behavior is everyone's goal.

Apps for Autism is pleased to offer the following tips to prevent wandering:

- **Secure Your Home:** Place the door lock out of reach. We use a door lock in which a numeric code has to be entered to exit. Consider a home security alarm system, door alarms, fenced yard, stop signs on doors, and dead bolts that lock on both sides.

- **Tracking Device:** Tracking devices can be worn as "jewelry" or concealed in the clothing of your child.

- **Introduce Yourself and Family Member:** Visit your neighbors and local first responders to introduce yourself and family members who may wander. Provide them with pertinent information and a current photograph. Knowing your neighbors and first responders can save valuable time and reduce risks before an incident occurs.

- **Water Safety:** Teach your child to swim and handle themselves in water. Know where your local pools and bodies of water are located (Google Maps can help) and check there first.

- **Act Immediately:** If your child or loved one does go missing, call your local law enforcement immediately, alert neighbors, and begin searching.

- **Triggers:** Be aware of and possibly eliminate all potential triggers that may lead to wandering.

 For more information and to download the Big Red Safety Box, visit AWAARE: The Autism Wandering Awareness Alerts Response and Education Coalition: http://awaare.nationalautismassociation.org/

GRIPCASE

http://gripcase.com

$39.99 (iPad & iPad Air)

FROM THE DEVELOPER

They say necessity is the mother of invention, and so it was with Gripcase. It all began with a two year old and a shiny $600 toy. For Christmas, my wife and I bought our son, Charlie, an iPad. Like many, we saw the value in tablet technology to engage and explore learning in a fun and innovative way. However, our two year old had other plans. We learned very quickly that this new technology had to conform to his native learning environment: behind the sofa, under his train table, up and down the stairs, in and out of the car.

A designer at heart, I began drafting up a case that would fit the needs of my family. My design criteria were simple:

1. It would need to protect the tablet from the terrors Charlie could inflict.

2. It would honor the minimalist nature of the iPad and showcase its beauty.

3. It would be built with child-friendly materials, and 4. It would empower and inspire my son to explore his world.

iREVIEW

I love this super-durable, handsome case! I have used my Gripcase for over two years and had not one casualty. It is dropped countless times, tossed, sat on, and chewed on a daily basis. Despite its unique look and indestructible quality, the best feature by far is the control it offers me, the therapist. Gripcase has handles on every side; I do not have to let go in uncertain or challenging situations. Additional accessories include a stand for desktop work and an adjustable carrying strap for the person on the go (sold separately).

 $19.99 $12.00

iBALLZ
www.iballz.info
$24.95

The iBallz shock absorbing bumper case has reinvented tablet protection. Dropped from any angle, its patented design adds virtually zero weight and enables your tablet to bounce, not break, while remaining safely elevated above floors or sticky surfaces.

BIG GRIPS
http://biggrips.com/index.html
$34.95 (iPad) $24.95 (iPad Mini)

Big Grips Frame is the iPad case made for kids. It's big, squishy, easy to grab, comfortable to hold, and very grip-able.

- Non-toxic
- BPA, lead and latex-free
- Phthalate and PVC free

- Resistant to oils, chemicals, stains, mold, and germs
- Durable and lightweight
- Easy to clean

ARMORBOX KIDO SERIES LIGHTWEIGHT CONVERTIBLE STAND CASE

www.i-blason.com/ipad-air-cases-for-kids.html

$29.99

The ArmorBox Kido Series Lightweight Convertible Stand Case utilizes impact-resistant PCB construction, along with lightweight building materials and a choice of many different colors which give your child's iPad flash and character when they are using it. The case uses impact-resistant materials on the edge and double impact-resistant materials on the corners to absorb impact from drops and other unnatural impacts that would normally hurt the inner workings of the device.

iGUY

www.speckproducts.com

$39.95 (iPad) $29.99 (iPad Mini)

Meet iGuy, the free-standing foam case for the new iPad 4, iPad 3, iPad 2 and iPad original. Every bit as protective as he is a blast to use, iGuy iPad 4 cases are the perfect iPad accessory for kids and grown-ups alike. He's lightweight and easy to hold, and he can stand on his own two feet, even while holding up your iPad. He may look like he's all about fun, but his soft, squishy body disguises tough EVA foam protection. iGuy iPad 3 covers will help you feel more secure as you hand your iPad over to your baby or small child!

iREVIEW

There are a plethora of great iPad cases available for your child or student. Each one has unique qualities and/or characteristics that will fit your lifestyle and appeal to your child. Involve your child in choosing an iPad case, carrying case, and color. I have listed prices for the cases only; however, each case has accompanying accessories that are sold separately (see the manufacturers' websites for details). For even more help in choosing a just-right case, see the Feature Matching Table For iPad Cases.

Case	Droppable	Spill Proof (indirect spills)	Carrying Case	Stand	Notes

Lois Jean Brady

www.iTherapyLLC.com

itherapyllc@gmail.com

What's The Best Case for My Child

Choosing the right case to protect your iPad and let your child express their individuality is, in some ways, just as important as choosing the right applications. Individuals with autism are using iPads in many different environments and for purposes that are as individual at they are. Below is a feature matching chart that will help you decide what case is right for you. The Feature Matching Table will help you narrow the field from the hundreds of available choices by determining what features are important to your child's needs.

Droppable

When considering cases for students with autism or any youngster, it is a good idea to make sure it offers protection from drops and bumps. Cases should be able to absorb the shock of a drop as high as a desk as well as the occasional toss.

Spill Proof (indirect spills)

Some cases offer protection from spills by elevating your pad off the surface of a table or desk. By raising your iPad off the surface an area is created between the surface and the iPad. This buffer allows spills to simply run off without making contact with the iPad; however, there is no protection from direct spills on the iPad itself. For added protection from liquid spills during messy activities such as lunchtime, place your iPad into a Ziploc plastic bag. There are several waterproof cases available as well, but they are not recommended for everyday use.

Carrying Case

Individuals with autism often use their iPads as a means of communication and need to have it with them throughout their day. A carrying case can make the transportation of an iPad from place to place easy and stylish. Custom-made carrying cases can provide extra protection from knocks and falls when traveling from place to place in your busy day.

Stand

When the iPad is meant to be used on a student's desktop or table, then a sturdy stand is an important feature to consider. Stands that let the user adjust the angle and move back and forth from landscape to portrait quickly and securely are highly desirable in the classroom environment.

There are hundreds of cases available for the iPad. I chose five to highlight that have kept my iPads safe and allowed my students accessibility; however, they are not the only cases appropriate for use for students with autism. Use the Feature Matching Table to determine which iPad case is right for your child or student.

iADAPTER – IPAD PROTECTIVE AMPLIFIED CASE
www.amdi.net/index.php?route=common/home
$198.00 (iPad Mini) $265.00 (iPad & iPad Air)

FROM THE DEVELOPER

The iAdapter™ is an iPad-protective amplified case designed for the Special Needs community. It is fully compatible with the iPad®, iPad Air, and iPad® Mini with Retina Display (versions 3 & 4). We have strengthened the case and now offer two colors, black and gray. Our case is made from high-impact ABS plastic that is designed to help protect your iPad from everyday wear and tear!

iREVIEW

Wow! iAdapter offers the user all the great features we have been asking for: durability, speakers, a threaded mount, and a way to block curious fingers from pressing that pesky little "home" button. Please visit the website for more information and additional accessories. With iAdapter, the iPad is now just as durable as any other device on the market. iAdapter is an excellent choice for individuals who will have their iPad permanently mounted on a chair, table, desk, or bedside.

LIFEPROOF

www.lifeproof.com/en/?path=TopNav

$129.99 (iPad) $119.99 (iPad Mini) $59.99 (Lifejacket)

FROM THE DEVELOPER

Introducing heavy-duty protection for your tablet. *LifeProof* for iPad safeguards your tablet from drops, dirt, splashes, and submersion, all in a case so unbelievably slim and light, it seems to be barely there With your iPad protected from day-to-day dangers, you can do more, in more ways and places, than you ever imagined—classrooms, boardrooms, job sites, transportation, outdoors—the sky's the limit!

iREVIEW

Lifeproof is heavy-duty protection against everything, even spills (liquid). One case is waterproof, dirt proof, snow proof, and shock proof, while allowing complete access to all functions. *Lifeproof* cases are highly recommended for individuals who may drop, bump, and/or submerge their iDevice or have others in their environment who may do the same.

Waterproof your iDevice

ZIPLOC BAGS and ZIPLOC FREEZER BAGS

iREVIEW

Waterproof and spill-proof your wonderful iDevices with a simple plastic bag. You can put your iDevices into a Ziploc plastic bag and still use the touch screen. I use the Ziplocs during snacks and mealtime to prevent damage from sticky, wet spills. The plastic bags work excellently in this capacity. Use the Ziplocs anytime the environment may be clammy, damp, or soggy such as rainy days, in the shower room, or cooking dinner.

 Obviously the plastic bag has its limits. Do not take into the swimming pool or submerge it underwater, or your iDevice could drown. *Note: For a little extra protection, use freezer bags.

CAPACITIVE STYLUS *by BoxWave*

www.boxwave.com

$12.95 (mini stylus) $15.00 (universal stylus)

The durable rubber tip and smooth glide feel of the Capacitive Stylus will have you rethinking using your finger as your touch screen tool of choice. The included 3.5 mm headphone jack adapters continue to make transportation and storage options limitless.

TOUCH SCREEN STYLUS *by suck uk*

www.gripcase.com

$11.99

Draw more accurately on your phone or tablet. There are two types of touch screens, capacitive and resistive; the Touch Stylus works with both. Ideal for children, educational apps, and games.

CHOPSTAKES *by Ipevo*

www.ipevo.com

$34.00 / pair

For fine control and multi-touch versatility, Chopstakes Styli help you get the most out of your iPad apps. The Chopstakes instruments are held in both hands and act in tandem for the type of precision you've been looking for—whether it's drawing, typing, gaming, Garage Band music creating, and much more.

TXTRNG;) *by txtRng;)*

www.txtrng.com

$19.99

An innovative, modern "On-Hand" stylus ring designed as a FUNctional, ergonomic accessory that is fabricated from high-grade silicone to fit on the thumbs or index fingers, and enable accurate texting, Internet navigation, drawing, gaming, and typing on touch screens.

Are you unable to access your touch screen with the pads of your fingers or are you mastering the use of a writing utensil? Try a stylus. Styluses or Styli come in a wealth or sizes, shapes, colors, weights, and styles. As always, when choosing a stylus, consider your child's strengths, interests, and abilities as well as the goal of using a stylus. For example, if your child is working on the tripod grasp, the mini stylus will work well; if your child struggles with fine motor control, a larger chunkier stylus may be the answer. For expert advice on choosing the right stylus for your needs, consult an occupational therapist.

iVISOR AG - ANTI-GLARE *by Moshi*
www.moshi.com
$29.99

FROM THE DEVELOPER

iVisor AG for iPad is an advanced, anti-reflective screen protector specifically designed to protect your iPad's touchscreen while reducing smudges. Unlike other screen protectors that require a tedious installation process, iVisor's proprietary

design allows for a flawless, bubble-free installation in seconds; it's the easiest screen protector to install on the market today. iVisor's multilayer construction is engineered to offer excellent scratch and smudge resistance while retaining optimal touch sensitivity. iVisor AG is equipped with a unique polymer adhesive that allows it to be washed and reapplied repeatedly.

iREVIEW

Visual processing disorders affect how the brain interprets visual input and can occur with or without a visual impairment. Children with visual perceptual processing disorder may have the following traits –

- **Look at you or objects from the side of their eyes, side-viewing.**
- **Staring at spinning objects or light.**
- **Flick their finger(s) or objects close to their eyes.**
- **Cascade material such as sand, water, or dirt close to their eyes, usually on the side of their head.**
- **Occasional/frequent squinting or crossing eyes.**

A child who has challenges with visual perceptual processing may be distracted by the glare and/or reflective surface of an iPad screen. To increase visual focus, lessen the effects of obnoxious glare, or prevent a headache, try an anti-reflective or anti-glare screen protector. Not only will you get reduced glare, but iVision also reduces those distracting smudges and trapped bubbles that may be taking your child's attention away from the task at hand.

iPAD MOUNTS *by RJ Cooper & Associates, Inc.*
www.rjcooper.com
Prices vary according to needs

FROM THE DEVELOPER

Hi! I'm RJ Cooper and I make special software and hardware products for persons with special needs.

iREVIEW

For iDevice mounts, clamps, stands, and bumper cases, this is your place. RJ offers two sizes of "arms" that are positional and secure. Both arms include clamps that can attach to tables, desks, and bedrails. See RJ's website for more information, prices, and pictures. iPad Mounts are also great for lightweight AAC devices and netbooks!

RAM MOUNTS *by RAM*
www.rammount.com
Prices vary according to needs

FROM THE DEVELOPER

When something is designed to travel with you no matter where you go, you need mounting solutions that are up to the task. RAM has you covered with a full complement of holders for the most popular iPhone, iPad, and iPhone models. With an assortment of docking, locking, weather-resistant, and spring-loaded holders, we guarantee the perfect mounting solution for your mobile environment.

iREVIEW

Mount anything, anywhere, with RAM! RAM is your one-stop solution for any and all your mounting, docking, locking, and secure equipment needs.

 See the developer's website for demo videos and all the great mounting solutions: www.rammount.com

ETRE TOUCHY GLOVES

FIVEPOINT GLOVES

HAND-STICHED LEATHER

www.etretouchy.com

Etre Touchy Gloves: £20 GBP (That's about $33.98 USD or €25.28 EUR.)

FIVEPOINT Gloves: £22.50 GBP (That's about $38.22 USD or €28.44 EUR.)

Hand-stitched Leather: £125 GBP (That's about $212.35 USD or €158 EUR.)

FROM THE DEVELOPER

Etre Touchy Gloves are a stylish way of keeping your hands warm while using your mobile phone, smartphone, iPod, iPad, camera, and other electronic devices. They're different from other pairs of gloves. Here's why:

While normal pairs of gloves keep your hands warm and dry, they don't work with modern touchscreen devices like the iPhone, iPad, or iPod touch, as these devices respond only to skin-on-screen contact. These gloves' bulkiness also leads to fat-fingering misery when using the tiny keypads of other mobile devices. Thanks to their special contactwoven® fingertips, they do what other gloves don't: They let you use touchscreens without having to take them off.

How nice these are! Etre Touchy Gloves come in a selection of great stylish colours or elegant leather. Imagine keeping your hands warm and cozy while operating your device in the cold winter months. Etre Touchy Gloves are 100% pure wool; launder with care. Wash in cold water and air dry.

 Etre Touchy is located in London; however, it will ship anywhere. You can also purchase Etre Touchy Gloves on Amazon.com.

iPOTTY

by CTA Digital
www.ctadigital.com
$37.99 (available at Target)

Potty training can be a challenge for even the most patient parents, and one of the biggest hurdles is gaining the child's interest and then keeping their attention long enough to properly potty train. This potty training seat features a special stand to securely hold the iPad and safely entertain kids while they play with apps. The adjustable stand can be rotated 360° to switch between horizontal and vertical views and also includes a removable touchscreen cover to guard against messy accidents and smudges.

iCARTA 2

by Atech Flash Technology
www.atechflash.com
$59.99

- **Play music from your iPod, iPhone, iPad, or other mobile devices via Bluetooth®.**
- **Control your music from your mobile device.s**
- **2 compact speakers deliver optimum sound.**
- **Modern styling to match most bath interiors.**
- **Power/pairing button with audio feedback.**
- **Volume up/down buttons with audio feedback.**
- **LED for power and pairing status.**
- **Play up to 20 hours of playtime with 4 x AA batteries.**
- **Stream your music from up to 10 meters.**

Don't laugh—iCarta Stereo Dock for iPod with Bath Tissue Holder & iPotty are invaluable tools when it comes to encouraging daily hygiene routines, especially toileting. Plenty of parents have bought an iDevice just for the purpose of potty training. it is highly motivating and can provide visual and audio supports as well as reinforcement.

UNIVERSAL GAME WHEEL
$24.99

PARABOLIC SOUND SPHERE
$39.99

by Allsop
www.clingo.com

FROM THE DEVELOPER

It's pretty simple, really; Clingo products hold your phone. It doesn't matter if it is a BlackBerry, iPhone, Droid, or Samsung. Whether in your car, at the office, at home, or wherever, Clingo holds it … Any phone, Anywhere.

iREVIEW

I found Clingo last year at MacWorld. The vendor gave it to me for a free trial. I was a little skeptical, at first, about the gel pad. My students not only love the gaming/sporty look of the Universal Game Wheel, but they also can actually hold an iPod touch or iPhone with ease. As for the gel pad, it still sticks! One year and many, many hands later, the gel pad has never released my iPod touch, and the students have never dropped the Game Wheel. I have cleaned it twice, following manufacturer's directions, with no problems. The Parabolic Sound Sphere is also a great product that enhances the audio without speakers.

Again, my students have had no problems holding the Sphere. Take a look at all Clingo products to find the one that fits your needs.

 Clingo products work with the smaller iDevices such as iPhone and iPod touch.

PROPER

www.studioproper.com.au

$49.99

iPAD HEADREST MOUNT

www.boxwave.com

$26.95

The X Lock™ Headrest Mount stays well out of the way. The last thing you want is an overbearing claw to hold your iPad in place. The sleek, X Lock™ Headrest Mount is crafted in Aircraft grade aluminum and looks beautiful whilst ensuring that it integrates perfectly with your car interior.

The Headrest Mount has been designed for simple installation into all vehicles. You won't need to remove your headrest, and our newly designed mount means it now fits all cars, regardless of headrest pin size.

BoxWave's Headrest Mount is not just a case, but an all-in-one mounting solution that gives your car passengers hands-free viewing of your iDevice.

The Headrest Mount safely tucks your iDevice and locks it in place with a buttoned flap. Inside, it is layered with soft velvet to prevent scuffs, while giving you access to all of the control buttons. The mounting straps are fully adjustable, making the Headrest Mount capable of fitting any car!

iREVIEW

iPad Headrest Mount(s) offers on-the-go communication, education, and entertainment for those in the back seat. Just slip your iPad into the Headrest Mount, and you will not have to worry about spills, drops, or crushing your iPad with packages. Your iPad is accessible and safe on the road. Headrest Mounts come in many styles to fit your car and needs. X Lock Headrest Mount and BoxWave's Headrest Mount are two of the most popular and versatile systems for keeping your iPad safe and accessible on the road.

TYPILLOW *by Accessory Workshop*
www.buytypad.com
$34.95

___

FROM THE DEVELOPER

Experience the softer side of iPad® with the Typillow. This super-soft microsuede pillow holds your iPad securely in place while you lounge. On the couch, in your favorite chair, in bed, wherever! Special microbead filling adjusts to enhance form and memory for a contoured fit every time! Measures: 17 x 17"

iREVIEW

For those individuals who are bedbound, are chair bound, or have orthopedic challenges, TyPillow is a handy solution for making your iPad more obtainable. Just give TyPillow a turn for an adjustable viewing angle that gives the user the choice of landscape or portrait modes. TyPillow is 17 x 17 inches and comes in black. Pink TyPillow is 16 x 13 inches. TyPillow for iPad Mini measures 14 x 11 inches.

iPAD SUIT *by MOHAN's Custom Tailors*
www.mohantailors.com
Customer Pricing

___

iREVIEW

An upscale Manhattan tailor has designed a one-of-a-kind suit jacket with an iPad pocket. MOHAN's Custom Tailors, founded in the '70s before men needed gadget pockets, said the "somewhat gimmicky-looking iPad suit is the result of customer requests." This one falls into the "REALLY?" category.

Part XIII

Choosing an App(s)

In the News:

Apps Support Evidence-Based Practice (EBP)

By Jessica Solari, M.A. CCC-SLP (http://consonantlyspeaking.com)

When using any tool in therapy, it is important to use evidence-based practice (EBP). According to the American Speech-Language Hearing Association (ASHA), "the goal of EBP is the integration of:

    a. Clinical expertise/expert opinion

    b. External scientific evidence, and

    c. Client/patient/caregiver perspectives to provide high-quality services reflecting the interests, values, needs, and choices of the individuals we serve" (ASHA, 2004).

There are four steps to using evidence-based practice:

    Step 1: Framing the Clinical Question: PICO

    Step 2: Finding the Evidence

    Step 3: Assessing the Evidence

    Step 4: Making the Decision

When framing the clinical question, use the acronym PICO, which stands for Population, Intervention, Comparison, and Outcome. For example, if one is looking for a language application for a story re-tell application for a client, one might frame the question as "are school-aged children ages six through eight with language delays consistently able to correctly re-tell one-event narratives with story grammar in sequential order with the use of a graphic organizer than without?" Next, one would find evidence associated with the question asked by using looking in a research article database, ASHA's research compendium (http://www.asha.org/research/), or a research journal. Next, it is important to assess the quality of the evidence. One way to do this is to look at ASHA's systematic reviews online. Another way is to use what you know about validity, population, statistics, how data was collected, and time frame. Finally, after finding evidence that meets what one needs for his or her client, it is important to find an application that supports the evidence-based practice from the research study. Some applications may be more appropriate in terms of a client's age, cognitive level, needs, and interests than others, so it is important to compare applications and try different ones out to find the perfect fit. For a pre-made PICO template for selecting and justifying applications, visit Wakefield Consultant Services' website to make your search a bit easier.

If one is lucky, an application developer or other researcher will have already found the evidence to look over and justify the way to use the application appropriately for the client to make progress. For example, the author of this book has a grid of iPad applications that can support evidence-based practice (see table below). However, if evidence for the application's use is not found, that does not mean the application cannot be used in therapy. One can use the application in conjunction with another researched therapy technique or adapt it to appropriate use. Finally, keep in mind that some applications are great for reinforcement of a skill, developing rapport, or for a short break between activities and that one can use his or her own data to show that an application is improving a client's skills.

EBP & Autism Spectrum Disorders

According to The National Professional Development Center (NPDC), many interventions for autism exist, but only some have been shown to be effective through scientific research. Interventions that researchers have shown to be effective are called evidence-based practices. The Center has identified 24 evidence-based practices.

The National Autism Center (NAC) has identified 11 established treatments. Established Treatments are those for which several well-controlled studies have shown the intervention to produce beneficial effects.

Below is a list of 22 EBP with corresponding app suggestions for both speech language pathology and autism spectrum disorders. There are over a million apps on the market today and hundreds more are added every week; the apps represented in the table are only examples of what is available. Every student will have individual needs, preferences, and characteristics. It is up to the educator/therapist to choose the best fit for each student. The table is meant for informational purposes only to illustrate how apps support evidence-based practice and for use as you determine appropriate.

Evidence-Based Practice	Supporting App
Technology-aided instruction and intervention (TAII) – Instruction or intervention in which technology is the central feature supporting the acquisition of a goal for the learner.	*Martha's Dog Party* *First Phrases* *Little Speller* *Crack the Books* *Language Builder*
Functional Communication Training – A systematic practice to replace inappropriate behavior or subtle communicative acts with more appropriate and effective communicative behaviors or skills.	*InnerVoice* *aacorn AAC* *Proloquo2Go*
Discrete Trial Training (DTT) – Each trial or teaching opportunity has a definite beginning and end; thus the descriptor discrete trial. Within DTT, the use of antecedents and consequences is carefully planned and implemented. Data collection is an important part of DTT.	*Dr. Brown's Apps (colors, words, shapes, etc.)* *SR – Naming* *TherAppy Apps* *First Words*
Naturalistic Intervention – These practices are designed to encourage specific target behaviors based on insights into the learner's interests and to provide responses that build more elaborate learner behaviors that are naturally reinforcing and appropriate to the interaction.	*Toca Boca* *My Play Home* *More Pizza, More Salad, etc.* *Cake Doodle, Cookie Doodle* *"Talkers" (Furry Friend, Smurf, Tom, etc.)* *The Surprise – You're The Storyteller*
Parent Mediated Instruction and Intervention - This involves parents directly using individualized intervention practices with their child to increase positive learning opportunities and acquisition of important skills.	*Most iPad apps are appropriate for parents to implement at home and in the community.*
Picture Exchange Communication – Learners are taught to give a picture of a desired item to a communicative partner in exchange for the item.	*InnerVoice* *Aacorn AAC* *My Choice Board* *ComApp*
Pivotal Response Training – PRT builds on learner initiative and interests and is particularly effective for developing communication, language, play, and social behaviors.	*Toca Boca Hair, Kitchen, Store, etc.* *Tuneville* *Wheels on the Bus* *Jib Jab Jr.*

Evidence-Based Practice	Supporting App
Functional Behavior Assessment - A systematic set of strategies that are used to determine the underlying function or purpose of a behavior so that an effective intervention plan can be developed.	*SLP Scoring Plus* *Data Tracker Pro* *Autism Tracker* *Behavior Tracker Pro* *Socially Speaking*
Self-Management – Helps learners with autism spectrum disorders (ASD) learn to independently regulate their own behaviors and act appropriately in a variety of home, school, and community-based situations.	*VAST – Autism (mirror feature)* *Self-Regulation Training Board* *Social Scale* *Sosh* *Small Talk Pain Scale*
Social Narratives/Scripting – Interventions that describe social situations in some detail by highlighting relevant cues and offering examples of appropriate response. They can be verbal and/or written descriptions about a specific skill or situation that serves as a model for the learner. Scripts are usually practiced repeatedly before the skill is used in the actual situation.	*FlummoxVision* *Model Me Going Places* *Functional Skills System* *I Create... Social Skills Stories* *Pictello* *Strip Designer (fun social narrative)*
Social Skills Groups – Used to teach individuals with autism spectrum disorders (ASD) ways to appropriately interact with typically developing peers.	*FlummoxVision* *Socially Speaking* *Quizzler Dating & Quizzler Family* *Social Skill Builder* *Everyday Social Skills*
Speech Generating Device – Electronic devices that are portable in nature and can produce either synthetic or digital speech for the user. SGD may be used with graphic symbols as well as with alphabet keys.	*InnerVoice* *aacorn AAC* *Touch Chat with Word Power* *Functional Communication System*
Video Modeling/Modeling - A mode of teaching that uses video recording and display equipment to provide a visual model of the targeted behavior or skill.	*Video Scheduling* *My Video Schedule* *iMovie* *VAST Autism and Pre Speech (video modeling for speech)* *Video feature on the iPad*
Visual Supports – Any tool presented visually that supports an individual as he or she moves through the day.	*I Get It.....* *iCommunicate* *Time Timer* *First-Then Visual Schedule*
Using Social Stories to Teach Social Skills - Social stories are interventions that describe social situations in some detail by highlighting relevant cues and offering examples of appropriate response.	*I Create... Social Skills Stories* *StoryMaker for Social Stories* *Pictello* *Stories2Learn*

Evidence-Based Practice	Supporting App
Joint Attention Intervention - Joint attention often involves teaching a child to respond to the nonverbal social bids of others or to initiate joint attention interactions. Examples include pointing to objects, showing items/activities to another person, and following eye gaze.	*Draw and Tell HD* *Dinosaurs!* *Talking Ginger, Talking Rex, etc.* *ElfYourself*
Principles of Motor Learning in Treatment of Motor Speech Disorders	*VAST- Autism 1 Core* *VAST Pre-Speech* *VAST Songs*
Naturalistic Intervention - These practices are designed to encourage specific target behaviors based on insights into the learner's interests and to provide responses that build more elaborate learner behaviors that are naturally reinforcing and appropriate to the interaction.	*Shape Builder* *Talking News* *StoryBots* *Songify* *Draw and Tell* *Etc.*
Use of graphic organizers and story webs to support reading comprehension and knowledge	*Kidspiration Maps* *Poplett* *iThoughts* *Writing an Opinion*
Use of storybooks that are predictable to facilitate language	*The Monster at the End of the Book* *Mr. Brown* *Green Eggs and Ham* *Etc.*
Task Analysis - Task analysis is the process of breaking a skill into smaller, more manageable steps	*Video Scheduler* *FTVS HD – First-Then Visual Scheduler* *Choiceworks* *I Get... My Daily Schedule, Recall My Day...*
Exercise - Increase in physical exertion as a means of reducing problem behaviors or increasing appropriate behavior.	*C-Fit Yoga- Classroom Fitness* *Workout Producer* *TGFU Games PE* *Cardiograph*

www.iTherapyLLC.com

Oh, Wait! The center has just completed (2014) an expanded and updated review, which yielded a total of 27 practices, Hmmm. The newly added evidence-based practices, if applicable, are included in the above table.

According to the NPDC, a review of more than 29,000 studies identified 27 autism therapies as worthy to be called "evidence-based." This is up from 24 autism therapies that the authors identified as solidly backed by research in their first review, published in 2008.

For more information and a complete list of all EBPs (24, 11 or 27), please visit the following sites:

The National Professional Development Center (NPDC)

http://autismpdc.fpg.unc.edu/content/ebp-update

The National Autism Center (NAC) National Standards Report

www.nationalautismcenter.org/pdf/NAC%20Standards%20Report.pdf

Feature Matching Checklist

What app should I choose? This is a common question from family member(s), teachers, and therapists seeking to determine the best apps to fit with the individual needs of their child or student. Unfortunately, there is no one answer; every person is an individual with a unique interests and learning style.

There is an overwhelming flood of information in the media today. Feature matching is an effective tool to assess the usefulness of a particular app based on the characteristics of the user. By matching features available in an app with the user, their environment, and abilities prior to purchasing that app, you maximize the probability of a good fit. This allows you to conserve your time and money and increases the effectiveness of your iPad as a learning tool.

Download The Quick Feature Matching Checklt at http://proactivespeech.files.wordpress.com/2014/01/quick_feature_checklist_updated_12_2013_blog.pdf

By using the newly updated Feature Matching Checklist, you can effactually wade through the plethora of choices to find the most suitable app(s) for your child's needs.

Animations / Actions

Apps that contain animations or incorporate videos are becoming very popular for teaching language concepts, verbs, social skills, tasks, etc. They not only let the student see a model of the activity but are

Quick Feature Matching Checklist

Category	Feature								Notes
	Price								
Data/tracking	Allows Note Taking								
	Saves Your Profile								
	Multiple Profiles								
Voice Output	Record Your own Voice								
	Prerecorded Human voice								
	Synthesized High Quality								
Displays	Icon/Caricature Based								
	Real Image Based								
Customization	In-app Picture Taking								
	In-app Web Search								
	Difficulty Level								
	Animations & Actions								
	Photo Personalization								
Sensory	Visual On/Off								
	Sound On/Off								
Self/Monitor	Record Play/Back								
	Mirror Feature								
	Scoring								
Share/email	Student Work								
	Social Network								
	Data/Graphs								
Motor Skill	Drag								
	Pinch								
	Touch								
	Swipe								
Prompt	Visual Prompting								
	Remote Prompting								
	Auditory Prompting								

ITherapy
Productive Essence Therapies

©iTherapy LLC

www.iTherapyLLC.com

also engaging, eliciting increased focus and attention. Apps such as InnerVoice AAC, Noodle Words, WordToob, VAST Pre-Speech, and First Phrases harness the power of action and go beyond flash cards to teach communication and important life skills.

Photo Personalization

The ability to personalize an app by adding a photo of yourself or your favorite character increases the "fun factor" and buy-in of any educational material. StoryBots, InnerVoice AAC, Toca Boca, and others are taking the iPad to a whole new level for learning and communication. Look for photo personalization if you want to tap into the power of edutainment (educate + entertain). Research indicates that, when communication is fun, people communicate more.

Remote Prompting

Remote prompting is a new approach to teaching communicative independence, using iDevices (iPad, iPhone, and iPod touch). This technique allows learners to receive a prompt on their iDevice that guides them to the correct response. With InnerVoice AAC, prompts are sent via wi-fi or bluetooth from the educator's device to the user's iPad to ensure that the child will perform the correct skill and reduce the probability of errors and frustration. Remote prompting reduces confusing verbal explanations that interfere with the communicative intent or message.

Data / Tracking

If you are an educator or therapist, then data/tracking student progress is not only important but also a huge time-saving option. Many educational apps allow the user to collect and save data for a single or multiple students as well as take notes. Check data tracking features prior to buying to help increase your efficiency. Parents can also monitor progress on goals at home.

Voice Output

The proper fit for voice output can support the acquisition of both language and speech. Research has shown that students on the spectrum prefer synthesized voice output over the human voice. Also, students with auditory processing challenges may respond better to high-quality synthesized voices.

However, not all students have the same preferences or respond to voice output in the same manner. It is highly desirable feature to have a choice of both synthesized and digitized voice for those apps that have an auditory output component.

Customization

The ability to add personalized pictures and content to any app is highly motivating for the student on the spectrum. Having the convenience of customization features within the app can save time and allow the user to create individual lessons/communication boards on the fly.

Adjustable difficulty levels reduce frustration when a task to too challenging and allows a student to move up levels as they master concepts.

Display

Does your student recognize icons or symbols or are real pictures preferred? Some apps give the user a choice of real pictures or choose from a library of icons/symbols.

Sensory

Sounds and visuals can be motivating or distracting to a child trying to complete a task. Having the choice to turn them on/off without leaving the app is a feature that makes using the iPad a seamless educational tool.

Self-Monitoring

Whether you are self-monitoring or being monitored by a parent/educator, the ability to track progress can facilitate success.

Share / Email

Being able to share students' work and accomplishments with others is my favorite feature. Parents may want to share a memory book with family, therapists may want to share student progress with other educators and individuals may want to share thoughts/ideas with friends via social networking.

Motor Skills

Know what fine motor skills an app requires prior to purchase. What are your child's/student's motor abilities? Do they have the ability to interact with a particular app, are they working on motor skills within the app, or do they enjoy lots of tactile interactions?

Price

The price category is for reference only. Price should not be a feature to consider when determining if an app is a good fit for a child or student. Educational materials usually have a high cost. The introduction of the iPad and apps has significantly reduced the price of communicating and learning. A pack of flash cards, board game, or workbook can cost from $9.99 to $89.99. I am happy to pay $0.99 to $49.99 for materials that are continually updated, re-useable, never break, don't rip or require lamination, are easy to carry, and are highly motivational for all of my students.

AAC EVALUATION GENIE
by Hump Software
http://humpsoftware.com
$11.99

FROM THE DEVELOPER

AAC Evaluation Genie is an informal diagnostic tool that is intended to assist speech-language pathologists and others to identify skill areas that relate specifically to the language representation methods commonly found on augmentative communication systems. The purpose of *AAC Evaluation Genie* is not to identify a particular speech-generating device, but rather build a framework for selecting an appropriate augmentative communication device for ongoing evaluation and/or device trial.

iREVIEW

Yes, there is an app that helps you determine the best AAC app. By evaluating a child's strengths, challenges, and current abilities and then making comparisons to features on AAC apps, we can make informed choices and have a better chance at success. There are 14 subtests that can be administered with screening options available for each subtest. *AAC Evaluation Genie* is a systematic way to gain information on how to set up a communication system for your child, such as how many cells per page, whether I can use category pages, whether my child is ready for word prediction, and whether I should use pictures, icons, or words. The data is crunched and presented in an easy-to-decipher format that can be printed or emailed. The *AAC Evaluation Genie* provides us invaluable information about an unfamiliar AAC user; however, given the strong visual skills and literal interpretations of language that individuals on the spectrum have, some of the icons may be questionable.

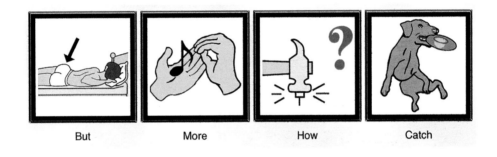

But   More   How   Catch

Conclusion

"The iPad might be the difference between communication with the outside world and being locked in a closed state."

—Dr. Stephen Shore

Bear in mind that there are over 1 million apps available, with more being added to the list every day. I have made an attempt to provide you with an excellent list of potentially invaluable apps to support individuals with disabilities in their daily lives; however, there are jillions more. It is my sincere hope that I have provided enough information for you to use your iDevices to their fullest capacities and individualize your app selection to fit your personal needs. Remember, even though technology is moving forward at a rapid pace, your iDevice will last for years. The apps, movies, and music you put on your iDevices today will continually be updated—usually for free—and remain relevant. If not, simply change the content as your needs and goals change. I have the first iPad that Apple put on the market. The iPad is still working; however, I have changed its content several times. Your iDevice will last a long time.

If this book has assisted you with communication, educational, social, leisure activities, and aspirations, I'd love to hear from you. Contact me at www.itherapyllc@gmail.com and/or catch me on Facebook: https://www.facebook.com/lois.j.brady

Giving Something Back: The iDevice Recycle Program

Portable, socially cool devices like the iPad, iPod touch, and iPhone are vital for communication, education, social, and leisure skills. They are also inexpensive and fun to use. However, not every individual who could benefit from an iDevice has access to one. I am so excited about the possibilities of this seemingly boundless technology that I would like to see every individual who could benefit from an iDevice (educators, individuals, parents, and caregivers) have access to one. To that end, I am asking for donations of working iDevices. I will furnish the iDevices with apps and offer them to individuals who would not otherwise have access to these wonderful Apple creations.

Let's put an iPad, iPod touch, or iPhone into the hands of every individual who would benefit from them!

Please send your iDevices to:

Apps for Autism

649 Main Street #229

Martinez CA 94553

How to Get an iPad for Your Child (Grants, Fundraisers, and More!)

Over the past two years, iPads have proven to be an essential tool in augmenting communication, language, literacy, and life skills for students with autism. Unfortunately, not everyone who could benefit from an iPad has access to this wonderful device. Thank goodness there are many incredible people, groups, and foundations that are making resources available for everyone to enjoy the benefits of having their own iPad.

The following is a list of websites that offer opportunities to acquire iPads, along with tips on how to win grants and submit applications. Lastly, an additional list of alternative means of procuring an iPad for your child or student on the spectrum is provided.

Websites

- Autism Speaks: www.autismspeaks.org/family-services/resource-library/family-grant-opportunities
- Autism Cares: www.autismcares.org/site/c.mqLOIYOBKlF/b.4844551/k.9606/Technology_Grant.htm
- ACT Today: www.act-today.org/act-today-grant-program.php
- HollyRod Foundation: www.hollyrod.org/
- Babies with iPads: http://babieswithipads.blogspot.com/p/babies-with-ipads-grant-application.html
- iTaalk: www.itaalk.org/#!grantapplication/c19r1
- Conover Company: www.conovercompany.com/grants/
- Danny's Wish: www.letschatautism.com/ipads-for-autism-application/

- First Hand Foundation: https://applications.cerner.com/firsthand/FirstHand_1a.aspx?id=28729
- Gia Nicole Angel Foundation: www.giafoundation.com/extensions
- Small Steps in Speech: www.smallstepsinspeech.org/events/event/application-deadline/
- Zane's Foundation: http://zanesfoundation.org/site/?page_id=23
- iHelp for Special Needs: www.ihelpforspecialneeds.com/iHelpWelcome/Need_An_iPad_App.html

Tips For Filling Out an Application

1. Read and understand the guidelines before starting your application. Follow the guidelines carefully, including deadlines and attachments to ensure that your application does not end up in the "round" file.

2. Be very specific in describing your needs and goals. Remember to answer the five (wh) questions; who, what, when, where, and why you need an iPad.

3. Make sure all questions are answered, boxes are filled out, and spelling and grammar are checked. If possible have another set of eyes read your application for completeness and double check for errors.

4. Don't get discouraged if you do not receive the grant. Keep trying! Remember that there are thousands of people trying to get grants, and even the most well written applications do not always get funding. Send a thank you note and try again.

5. If you do get the grant, send a thank you note with photos of the iPad in action and share how the iPad has helped your child or student.

What Else Can I Do to Get an iPad?

1. Website Fundraisers – The following websites will let you set up accounts so that family and friends can send love and donate funds to your specific campaign.
   - PayPal for Personal Fundraising
   - Fundrazr
   - Give Forward
   - The Puzzling Piece
   - GoFundMe

2. School District – Try contacting your local school district's technology department. Most districts have iPad programs in place. If yours does not, then inquire about an evaluation for your student.

3. Happy Holiday – Ask friends and families to forgo the usual presents and give Apple/iTune gift cards for birthday, Christmas, holiday favors, etc. This adds up quickly, and most students will have enough funds for an iPad and apps within four to six months.

4. Local Community Groups – Inquire about donations from local businesses, community, or charity groups. Many local groups will help with community fundraising by having a pancake breakfast or rummage sale.

5. Credit Card Points – Many credit cards give points for dollar(s) spent. Points can be redeemed for an iPad or cash to purchase an iPad. Check with your credit card company to see if they double points on certain purchases (gas and groceries).

Keep Updated on All the Latest, Greatest Information

There has been a tremendous explosion of technology, which has become a crucial element in the lives of individuals with disabilities. This problem, however, is finding an effortless, dependable way to keep up with the ebb and flow of the latest technology.

So how do you do it? How do you keep up with technology and still have time in the day for your job, your family, and yourself? Below are five practical resources that will keep you updated with the latest trends, news, apps, developers, and updates without having to spend countless hours searching the Internet or combing through articles and blogs.

- iTherapy: www.iTherapyLLC.com iTherapy has a great companion newspaper for *Apps for Autism.*—A place where readers can come to learn about iTherapy, download app updates, get the latest information on new apps and the best accessories, and join an online community to support and learn about the best that technology has to offer individuals with disabilities.

- *Apps for Autism* Facebook Page: https://www.facebook.com/AppsForAutism?ref_type=bookmark. From time to time, developers will offer their apps for FREE. The *Apps for Autism* Facebook page will list today's FREE apps as well as keep you up to date on the latest app-related information and blogs.

- Autism Brainstorm Google+ Hangout: *Apps for Autism* Google+ Hangout hosted by Autism

Brainstorm's Kathleen Tehrani happens every 4th Sunday at 6:00 (Pacific Standard Time).—https://plus.google.com/u/0/s/autism%20brainstorm%20apps%20for%20autism. We discuss how to get the most out of technology at home and school. Look for special guests, researchers, therapists, educators, and developers to answer your questions live online or watch all the *Apps for Autism* Google+ Hangouts archived at http://autismbrainstorm.org .

- Lauren S. Enders, MA, CCC-SLP "Pinterest"—www.pinterest.com/lasenders—Lauren's Pinterest boards have all you every wanted to know about Augmentative Alternative Communication and Assistive Technology. She has assembled an amazing clearinghouse of the latest information.

- Squidalicious: www.squidalicious.com/ The Adventures of Leo and his Potty-Mouthed Mom. On this information-filled website, you will find an abundance of material on parenting, autism, iPads, and Geekery. Shannon Des Roches Rosa will keep you updated with the latest news and blogs about what's important in the world of autism.

The Final Word

Disruption, DynaVox, and the iPad

By Russ Ewell (http://digitalscribbler.com)

DynaVox was recently purchased by Tobii for 18 million dollars. Naturally Tobii trumpets this as an excellent partnership for the future. Those of us who have witnessed and participated in the revolutionary impact of mobile technology on the disability community wonder if there is more to this story. Did the disruptive effect of iOS and Android devices lead to the bankruptcy and sale of DynaVox?

The truth is difficult to know since this purchase is not on the radar of mainstream business analysts, but that fact alone is revealing. If the mainstream investment community ignores the sale of DynaVox, what does this tell us about the industry, especially when their new competitors are household names?

Mobile technology and the in-the-garage development of apps for those with disabilities has brought Apple, Google, and Samsung into competition with DynaVox and Tobii. Individuals with disabilities limited to a few companies willing to meet their needs suddenly have significant choices. For the first time, those with disabilities are purchasing the same cutting edge technologies coveted by the general public. They are benefiting from the purchasing power of the majority, which creates ever decreasing prices combined with constantly improving features.

Additionally, a slow but steady population of software developers for mobile devices are creating software designed for those with disabilities. These tools are being used by parents, siblings, and caretakers of all types. In many cases, these amateurs are being coached by professional therapist, allowing families to deliver at home care in support of therapeutic sessions, increasing progress and the possibility of significant breakthroughs.

This is what disruption looks and feels like, which is why not only DynaVox but Tobii and all similar business models are at risk. How likely are we to see Tobii and other assistive technology companies disrupted? This is unlikely in the near term since Tobii in particular has a diverse portfolio of products and is technologically savvy. Even more significant is the state of the insurance industry, which at this point is more likely to reimburse for purchases of legacy products from DynaVox than an iPad from Apple. Despite these facts my long term bet is on a complete disruption of this industry.

There are five questions whose answers will determine the veracity of my prediction. I believe each one will be answered in favor of complete disruption of the status quo

1. Can parents and caretakers use their purchasing power to convince educators, therapists, and companies to serve them rather than sell products?

2. Will increasing numbers of therapist partner with engineers to create their own versions of assistive technologies?

3. Will the public school system embrace BYOD for special education encouraging insurance companies to reimburse for iPad's etc.?

4. Might Apple, Google, or Samsung develop product features rendering legacy assistive technologies obsolete (eye-tracking etc.)?

5. Could a new generation of teachers and therapist more comfortable with iPads than DynaVox make one through four happen quickly?

Resources, References, and Research

Since new apps are emerging daily and research studies, blogs, articles, and websites are also being developed to help us choose and use technology in ways that are relevant, meaningful, and evidence based; I have listed further resources, references, and research to support using iDevices for individuals with special needs.

Ambrose, N. G. and Yairi, E., 1999, Normative disfluency data for early childhood stuttering. *Journal of Speech, Language, and Hearing Research*, 42, 895–909.

American Academy of Pediatrics Council on Communications and Media. (2010). Policy Statement - Media Education. *Pediatrics*, 126(5), 1-6. Doi: 10.1542/peds.2010-1636.

Apple Education. (2006). iPod helps special-needs students make the grade. "Profiles in Success: Louisa-Muscatine Elementary School. Apple Computer. 15 Nov. 2006.

ASHA. (2011). *Applications (apps) for speech-language pathology practice*. Retrieved from www.asha.org/SLP/schools/Applications-for-Speech-Language-Pathology-Practice

Bavelier, D., Green, C. S., & Dye, M. W. G. (2010). Children, wired: For better and for worse. *Neuron*, 67(5), 692-701.

Brabazon, T. (2006). *Socrates with earphones: The ipodification of education*. Centre for Critical and Cultural Studies, The University of Queensland. Retrieved June 20, 2006, from www.uta.edu/huma/agger/fastcapitalism/2_1/brabazon.html

Chiong, C., & Shuler, C. (2010). Learning: There's an app for that? Investigations of children's usage and learning with mobile devices and apps. New York: The Joan Ganz Cooney Center at Sesame Workshop

Department of Education and Early Childhood. *iPads in Special Education from the Development*. www.ipadsforeducation.vic.edu.au/userfiles/files/DEECD%20iPad%20support%20booklet%20for%20special%20education.pdf.

Fernandes, B. (2010). Apps to revolutionize your therapy. *Advance Magazine*, 20, 15.

Green, J. L. (2011). *The ultimate guide to assistive technology in special education: resources for education, intervention, and rehabilitation*. Waco, Tex.: Prufrock Press.

Horst, H., Herr-Stephenson, B., & Robinson, L. (2010). Media ecologies. In M. Ito, S. Baumer, M. Bittanti, D. Boyd, R. Cody, B. Herr, H. A. Horst, P. G. Lange, D. Mahendran, K. Martinez, C. J. Pascoe, D. Perkel, L. Robinson, C. Sims & L. Tripp (Eds.), *Hanging out, messing around, geeking out: Living and learning with new media*. Cambridge: MIT Press.

Kelly, B., Phipps, L., & Swift, E. (2004) Developing a holistic approach for e-learning accessibility. *Canadian Journal of Learning and Technology*, 30(3). Retrieved

October 13, 2006, from, http://www.academia.edu/1387005/Developing_A_Holistic_Approach_For_E-Learning_Accessibilty.

MacDuff, G. S., Krantz, P. J., and McClannahan, L. E. (1993). Teaching children with autism to use photographic activity schedules: Maintenance and generalization of complex response chains. *Journal of Applied Behavior Analysis*, 26, 89-97.

Plowman, L., McPake, J., & Stephens, C. (2008). Just picking it up? Young children learning with technology at home. *Cambridge Journal of Education*, Vol. 38, No. 3 September 2008, 303–319

Purcell, K., Entner, R., and Henderson, N. (2010). *The rise of apps culture*. Washington, DC: Pew Research Center's Internet and American Life Project. Downloaded September 16, 2010, from http://pewinternet.org/Reports/2010/The-Rise-of-Apps-Culture.aspx

Scaler Scott, K., Tetnowski, J. A., Flaitz, J., & Yaruss, J. S. (2014). Preliminary study of disfluency in school-age children with Autism. *International Journal of Language and Communication Disorders*, 49(1), 75-89.

Scott, K. S., Grossman, H. L., Abendroth, K. J., Tetnowski, J. A., & Damico, J. S. (2007). Asperger Syndrome and Attention Deficit Disorder: Clinical disfluency analysis. In J. Au-Yeung & M. M. Leahy

(Eds.). Research, treatment, and self-help in fluency disorders: New Horizons. *Proceedings of the Fifth World Congress on Fluency Disorders* (pp. 273-278). Dublin, Ireland: International Fluency Association.

Sherer, M., Pierce, K. L., Paredes, S., Kisacky, K. L, Ingersoll, B., & Schreibman, L. (2001). Enhancing conversation skills in children with autism via video technology: Which is better, "self" or "other" as a model? Behavior *Modification*, 25, DOI: 10.1177/0145445501251008

Shuler, C. (2007). *D is for digital: An analysis of the children's interactive media environment with a focus on mass marketed products that promote learning.* New York, NY: The Joan Ganz Cooney Center at Sesame Workshop.

Shuler, C. (2009a). *iLearn: A content analysis of the iTunes App Store's Education Section.* New York, NY: The Joan Ganz Cooney Center at Sesame Workshop.

Shuler, C. (2009b). *Pockets of potential: Using mobile technologies to promote children's learning.* New York, NY: The Joan Ganz Cooney Center at Sesame Workshop.

Simmons, J. Q. and Baltaxe, C., 1975, Language patterns of adolescent autistics. *Journal of Autism and Childhood Schizophrenia*,5(4), 333–351.

Tanenhaus, J. (February/March 2011). Diskoveries: Apple iPad and Apps for Special Needs. *Closing the Gap*, 29(6), 7-13.

Thai, A. M., Lowenstein, D., Ching, D., & Rejeski, D. (2009). Game changer: Investing in digital play to advance children's learning and health. New York: The Joan Ganz Cooney Center at Sesame Workshop.

Warschauer, M., & Matuchniak, T. (2010). New technology and digital worlds: Analyzing evidence of equity in access, use, and outcomes. *Review of Research in Education*, 34(179), 179-225.

Yairi, E. and Ambrose, N., 1992, A longitudinal study of stuttering in children: a preliminary report. *Journal of Speech and Hearing Research*, 35, 755–760.

Index

A

S